APPLIED SPORT
BUSINESS ANALYTICS

Christopher Atwater, PhD
Troy University, Troy, Alabama

Robert E. Baker, EdD
George Mason University, Fairfax, Virginia

Ted Kwartler, MBA
Harvard Extension School
DataRobot, Vice President
Boston, Massachusetts

HUMAN KINETICS

Library of Congress Cataloging-in-Publication Data

Names: Atwater, Christopher, 1974- author. | Baker, Robert E., 1957-
  author. | Kwartler, Ted, 1978- author.
Title: Applied sport business analytics / Christopher Atwater, Robert E.
  Baker, Ted Kwartler.
Description: Champaign, IL : Human Kinetics, Inc., 2023. | Includes
  bibliographical references and index.
Identifiers: LCCN 2021042229 (print) | LCCN 2021042230 (ebook) | ISBN
  9781492598534 (paperback) | ISBN 9781492598541 (epub) | ISBN
  9781492598558 (pdf)
Subjects: LCSH: Sports administration--Mathematical models. | Sports
  administration--Statistical methods.
Classification: LCC GV716 .A79 2023 (print) | LCC GV716 (ebook) | DDC
  796.06/9--dc23
LC record available at https://lccn.loc.gov/2021042229
LC ebook record available at https://lccn.loc.gov/2021042230

ISBN: 978-1-4925-9853-4 (print)

Acquisitions Editor: Andrew L. Tyler; **Developmental Editor:** Judy Park; **Managing Editor:** Anne E. Mrozek; **Copyeditor:** Chernow Editorial Services, Inc.; **Indexer:** Andrea J. Hepner; **Permissions Manager:** Dalene Reeder; **Graphic Designer:** Sean Roosevelt; **Cover Designer:** Keri Evans; **Cover Design Specialist:** Susan Rothermel Allen; **Photograph (cover):** Adam Davy - PA Images via Getty Images; **Photographs (interior):** © Human Kinetics, unless otherwise noted.; **Vector images in design:** pp. i, viii, 16, 60, 108, 164, 196, 206 Pickup/stock.adobe.com; Abstract background in sidebars: Kamjana/stock.adobe.com; **Photo Asset Manager:** Laura Fitch; **Photo Production Manager:** Jason Allen; **Senior Art Manager:** Kelly Hendren; **Illustrations:** © Human Kinetics, unless otherwise noted.; **Printer:** Walsworth

Printed in the United States of America   10 9 8 7 6 5 4 3 2 1

The paper in this book was manufactured using responsible forestry methods.

Human Kinetics
1607 N. Market Street
Champaign, IL 61820
USA

United States and International
Website: **US.HumanKinetics.com**
Email: info@hkusa.com
Phone: 1-800-747-4457

Canada
Website: **Canada.HumanKinetics.com**
Email: info@hkcanada.com

E8084

Tell us what you think!
Human Kinetics would love to hear what we
can do to improve the customer experience.
Use this QR code to take our brief survey.

CONTENTS

PREFACE

Analytics has become integrated into the managerial fabric of the sport industry. Data-driven decisions are more commonplace, yet the capacity to fully apply sport analytics remains in its infancy. Often, managers lack the ability to ask the right questions in order to know how to use appropriate metrics to inform their decisions. Similarly, data analysts' ability to select and communicate information is lacking as well. Yet the translation of metrics into usable information is of paramount importance in informing managers, guiding decisions, and maximizing efficiency in achieving desired outcomes. Being able to understand and translate the concepts surrounding sport analytics is critical for aspiring managers and analysts in sport settings.

With a dramatically increasing amount of data available, how sport organizations and managers use that data to improve performance and efficiency is only going to grow in importance. Metrics provide evidence, offer rationale for decisions, and justify a specific course of action. Certainly, the size of the organization, the stakeholders involved, the required pace for action, the capacity to collect and analyze data, and the anticipated impact of the action will influence decisions. However, employing sport analytics yields metrics that can enhance effective decision-making in the conduct of sport, whether on the field of play or in the front office.

This book addresses the fundamental use of analytical metrics to inform sport managers. Its core framework is rooted in R and RStudio, and the authors have included the coding required to achieve the same results contained herein. Datasets are available on the HK*Propel* website for readers to use and get comfortable with the world of data science. The book is not intended to be a statistics book, nor is it intended to fully prepare data analysts. Instead, it is intended to frame sport analytics for practical use within organizations. The book is organized to present the background of sport analytics, why it is useful, selected techniques and tools employed, and the application of sport analytics in sport organizations. Framing when, where, and how analytics can inform sport managers is the key to the usefulness of data for informing decisions. In answering these questions, this book provides a translational knowledge of sport analytics to readers, whether they are aspiring sport managers, data analysts, or other practitioners.

HOW THIS BOOK IS ORGANIZED

This book is, by design, a five-chapter text (rather than a more traditional 10- or 16-chapter text) for the primary purpose of covering large and related topical areas. There is no expectation that instructors will teach these topics on a week-by-week basis. The robust chapter format allows instructors and students to actively work hands on with the topical area and content over multiple weeks throughout the semester.

Chapter 1 begins with the social, economic, and business foundations of sport analytics, tracing the history of its development and its emergence into prominence in the sport industry. Next, the focus shifts to methods commonly employed in analytical problem-solving and decision-making. Establishing a typical framework for sport analytics allows both managers and analysts to speak the same language or, at the very least, translate their analytical perceptions and needs.

Chapter 2 focuses on typical quantitative statistical analyses used in sport analytics. This is what many people first conceptualize as analytics, and it is a big component of how to analyze and make data useful. It introduces R and RStudio to the learner and explains how to begin coding. Framed within the concept of making data useful, the authors discuss descriptive, exploratory, and inferential statistical measures as well as provide an introduction to predictive analysis and forecasting.

Chapter 3 addresses the visualization of data for the purposes of revealing and communicating results of data analyses. The open-source software R is used extensively with the accompanying datasets to illustrate data plotting concepts and possibilities. Readers are provided with scripts that can be used within the context of the materials contained in the book and ancillaries, as well as with personal datasets they may be working on, thus providing great utility and transferability from the book to personal and everyday managerial applications.

Chapter 4 concentrates on the interrelationship of sport leaders and analytics through four distinct case studies. Topics covered include women's professional basketball, European football, American football, esports, and a comparative analysis of salaries and prize money in men's and women's professional sport. Both leaders and analysts can benefit from the translation of data analytics needs and measures in efforts to optimize efficiency. The chapter further explores the managerial implications and applications of sport analytics.

Cutting-edge analytic mechanisms and the use of resultant metrics are covered next. Chapter 5 is dedicated to text mining and natural language processing, with discussion of the methods, appropriate documents, and an array of uses in social media applications. Social media provides massive amounts of data; however, that data only becomes useful if properly harnessed through appropriate analysis.

INTENDED AUDIENCE

Readers can use this textbook to acquire a firm understanding of sport analytics. The development, tools, methods, and applications of data analytics in sport are condensed into one informative, translational book that is intended for both sport managers and data analysts. Sport managers interested in maximizing their organization's effectiveness will benefit from a broader and deeper knowledge of the use of sport analytics and an improved ability to both communicate their needs and translate data analyses into evidence for decision-making. Analysts who want to learn more about applying their trade in sport settings will be better able to translate data analyses into meaningful metrics employed by managers to guide their decisions.

STUDENT AND INSTRUCTOR RESOURCES

STUDENT RESOURCES

A wide variety of supplemental content is available in the free online study guide at HK*Propel*. They include six datasets for students to use as they work through the book, figure supplements, and additional content to dive further into selected topics. The figures available online are provided directly from the authors and contributors so that students can check their work, particularly the colors in the charts and graphs, which will be more accurately displayed online.

Students will also find 36 video lectures on key topics. There are exercises for each chapter and one case study included in the web ancillaries to further allow students to interact with the content. Flash cards of key terms are available as student study aids for each chapter, and gradable chapter quizzes may be assigned by the instructor and completed within HK*Propel*.

Student access codes are included with the purchase of a print book or ebook through Human Kinetics. Student access codes are also sold separately on the Human Kinetics website.

Art

Supplemental figure 4 Grand total athletic expenses and total Directors' Cup Points in the Power 5 conferences 2016-2018.

Key Terms Activity

boxplot

Click to flip

1 of 8

INSTRUCTOR RESOURCES

Instructors using this text in their courses will find a wealth of ancillary materials available in HK*Propel*, including an instructor guide and chapter quizzes. The instructor ancillaries also include convenient access to the video clips.

The instructor ancillaries are free to course adopters.

Instructor Guide

Specifically developed for instructors who have adopted *Applied Sport Business Analytics,* the instructor guide includes a sample syllabus and a guide for each chapter. Chapter guides include playlist summaries for the student YouTube videos, links to solution videos for the student assignments, and overviews of the available downloads, assignments, and forms. Answers to the student quiz questions are also provided.

Chapter Quizzes

These ready-to-use short quizzes test students' understanding of the most important concepts in each chapter. Chapter quizzes are formatted to be delivered to students through HK*Propel*.

FOUNDATIONS OF ANALYTICS FOR SPORT MANAGERS

groveb/iStockphoto/Getty Images

CHAPTER OBJECTIVES

After completing this chapter and the associated online exercises, you will be able to do the following:

- Define data analytics and sport analytics.
- Identify the growth of analytics.
- Briefly describe the sport industry context.
- Discuss the economic and business foundations of sport analytics.
- Describe a brief history of the use of analytics in sport.
- Describe data-informed decision-making.
- Describe analytics within the context of evaluation, both summative and formative.
- Understand how systems theory relates to sport analytics.
- Understand the role analytics can play in strategic planning.
- Describe some common applications of analytics by sport managers.
- Recognize the role of translation when using data to inform decision-making.

KEY TERMS

data analysis
data-driven decision-making
data-informed decision-making
data-inspired decision-making
formative evaluation
key performance indicator (KPI)

learning organizations
predictive analytics
program evaluation
Sabermetrics
SMART goals
sport analytics

strategic planning
summative evaluation
systems thinking
text mining

Data analytics begins with the identification and acquisition of data. Whether locally generated or a component of large datasets (i.e., big data), the volume of data available is rapidly increasing. More data was generated in the last two years than in the entirety of human history before that (Galov, 2021). The massive volume of data stems from expanding global use of electronic devices as data sources. And, in the next year, amassed data will amount to 44 zettabytes or 44 trillion gigabytes, 10 times the current level. According to Galov, there are 40,000 Google searches conducted every second, 300 hours of video uploaded to YouTube every minute, 100 terabytes of data on Facebook daily resulting from 31 million messages, and 2.7 million video views per minute. Smart devices produce 5 quintillion bytes of data daily. And the rate of data creation has accelerated to the point where the average human is producing 1.7 million megabytes of data per second. Yet 99.5 percent of collected data goes unused or analyzed (Galov, 2021).

The process of **data analysis** involves examining, cleansing, transforming, and modeling data for practical purposes, such as informing operational decisions. The use of statistical methodologies to analyze data yields evidence for management decision-making, which is in alignment with the concept of evidence-based management (Pfeffer and Sutton, 2006). The production and use of metrics support evidence-based, informed decision-making. For example, accessing metrics about sport fans' locations and interests can inform marketing and sponsorship strategies. About 79 percent of executives believe that the use of data is instrumental for success (Galov, 2021). Garnering useful information generated from data analysis can improve managerial actions. The practical application of data analytics is to deliver empirical evidence to support managerial decisions intended to resolve a problem or improve performance. In the world of sports, data analytics fosters scientifically guided decisions, informs improved strategic processes, and assists operational effectiveness (Xia and Gong, 2015).

Common software techniques and statistical applications used in data analytics in sports will be described in future chapters. For example, **data mining** involves the analysis of data from various sources using statistical modeling for predictive rather than purely descriptive purposes. **Predictive analytics** involves forecasting. And **text mining** involves applying statistical analyses and related techniques to extract and codify information from words. For data analytics to be useful, it follows that the dissemination of the data analyses, often in the form of visual displays, is imperative (Sherman, 2014). The graphic display of analyses on practical dashboards facilitates their usage. If data is to be useful for decision-making purposes, it is essential that the analyses are communicated appropriately by data analysts to decision-makers. Conversely, it is essential that managerial decision-makers have a working knowledge of how data can inform their decisions.

In sport organizations, managers who have a knowledge of data analytics have an advantage over those who do not. In turn, data analysts who have a working knowledge of sport operations are able to provide more useful information and potentially have a greater impact on decisions. However, throughout sport, the need to better inform both decision-makers and analysts is evident. Often, the available data is either not analyzed for useful purposes, or it is presented in such a way that does not inform decision-makers. In contrast, decision-makers may not be ready to use informative data. The ability of decision-makers to ask the right questions and understand the implications of the data analyses in informing decisions is essential. If decision-makers do not enhance their knowledge base and skill sets related to data analytics, they are not maximizing evidence-based decision-making.

This book is directed toward informing sport managers who are responsible for decisions or informing those responsible for decision-making. This information is not intended to create data analysts but to prepare sport managers to use data analysis to influence decisions. In that context, **sport analytics** is the application of data analytics in a sport setting.

Visit HK*Propel* to access the welcome video for the book.

A BRIEF HISTORY OF ANALYTICS IN SPORT

One of the things that first comes to mind when considering sport analytics is the popular phenomenon of *Moneyball*. The book by Michael Lewis (2003), and the subsequent movie directed by Bennett Miller and starring Brad Pitt, brought attention to the concept of using statistical analyses to maximize performance. In this specific case, the focus was on the application of data analytics by Billy Beane, general manager of the Oakland Athletics. While baseball was already heavily influenced by statistics since the late 19th century, Beane's use of statistical analyses to make personnel decisions yielded both increased efficiency in expenditures and increased performance in terms of wins. His team famously won 20 games in a row that culminated in first place in the American League West with a record of 103 wins to 59 losses. The documented and prominently celebrated success of analytics with the 2002 Oakland A's opened the floodgates for the steadily growing wave of interest in the application of data analytics in sports.

While the publicity associated with the mass commercial success of *Moneyball* prompted many sport executives to embrace sport analytics, these statistical analyses had been gradually accumulating support. For example, **Sabermetrics**, or objectively examining baseball through the application of statistical analyses, was popularized by Bill James in 1980. While analysts were becoming commonplace in Major League Baseball (MLB), James' employment with the Boston Red Sox contributed to the 2004 and 2007 Red Sox World Series wins, their first since 1918, breaking the famed Curse of the Bambino. The tipping point had been reached with advanced data analyses having an increased prevalence in the MLB. The resulting baseball data includes metrics that go beyond the typical box scores that have been publicly reported for over a century. While Sabermetrics applies to baseball, the similar application of analytics has been intensifying in most other sports during the late 20th and early 21st century. For example, soccer began using rudimentary analytics in the 1950s. But like many sports, it was not until the 1990s that the Premier League routinely began to employ technology-based analytical processes.

In 2021, most if not all professionalized sports were committed to the application of data analytics. The escalating desire to apply metrics in the decision-making process stimulated the development of entire departments with teams of analysts. The result

Hugh Fullerton's data-based prediction that the Chicago White Sox would defeat the Chicago Cubs in the 1906 World Series is regarded as the genesis of sport analytics.
Library of Congress, Prints & Photographs Division, LC-USZ62-53418.

has been a growing need not only for analysts but also for sport managers who have a foundational knowledge of the use of data for decision-making.

EVOLUTION OF SPORT ANALYTICS AND THE MIT SLOAN SPORTS ANALYTICS CONFERENCE

The proliferation of professional interest in sport analytics led to the development of numerous relevant events with the most auspicious being the MIT Sloan Sports Analytics Conference. The mission of the conference is "to provide a forum for industry professionals (executives and leading researchers) and students to discuss the increasing role of analytics in the global sports industry" (MIT Sloan, 2021). The conference has been successful in advancing the development of data analytics in sport and fostering innovation by bringing stakeholders together. The conference was founded in 2006 by Daryl Morey (MIT Sloan class of 2000), president of basketball operations for the Philadelphia 76ers, and Jessica Gelman (Harvard Business School class of 2002), CEO of Kraft Analytics Group. The conference draws attendees from professional sports teams in the MLB, the National Basketball Association (NBA), National Hockey League (NHL), National Football League (NFL), Major League Soccer (MLS), Premier League, and beyond. Since 2015, over 21,000 people have attended the conference, while thousands have viewed afterward (MIT Sloan, 2021). As one of the premier outlets for sport analytics, the conference attracts substantial sponsorship and media coverage from the likes of *ESPN*, *Sports Illustrated*, *The Wall Street Journal*, *Forbes*, *NBC*, and *Fox Sports*. In addition to the numerous popular conferences and a dedicated publication, the *Journal of Sports Analytics*, several college programs have emerged for sport analysts and managers familiar with sport analytics. Sport analytics is regarded as a valuable tool not only among professionals in the sport business sector but also among sport management educators and researchers. A well-developed understanding of analytics in sport is considered a current and future competitive advantage.

Whether referencing data analytics, data science, or artificial intelligence, each managerial decision is specific to the context in which it occurs; therefore, sport analytics requires contextual knowledge. Garnering a basic awareness of the sport industry is essential to developing an understanding of analytics in sport. The effective application of data collection and analyses in the sport industry requires a contextual knowledge of that industry.

Sport is $1.5 trillion economic sector (Plunkett Research, 2019). As sport has become an integral component of society, it is viewed by many to be a social institution akin to government, religion, or education, with structural power in society (Coakley, 2017; Wolf, 1990). As a microcosm of broader society, with its increasing acceptance of the generation and utilization of data, wherein sport both reflects and influences society, the sport sector has embraced the application of data analytics.

Data analytics has become integrated into the managerial fabric of the sport industry. Data-driven and data-informed decisions are more commonplace, yet the capacity to fully use sport analytics remains in its infancy. At times, the ability of managers to ask the right questions and use appropriate metrics to inform decisions is deficient. A fundamental understanding of data analytics would allow a manager to inquire about the type of data available that directly informs pending decisions. For example, a data-savvy intercollegiate athletics manager might request that data analysts provide information on the specific factors that are most influential in the Cup rating of athletic programs from the National Association of Collegiate Directors of Athletics (NACDA). Conversely, data analysts' ability to select and communicate information in a usable format might be deficient as well. For example, one who analyzes data for the sake of analysis may not provide the necessary data analyses to inform decisions. In such a circumstance, an analyst may provide a massive amount of high-level statistical analyses, but those analyses may either be based on irrelevant data or presented in an ineffectual way to a manager. The translation of metrics in a useful way is of paramount importance in informing managers, guiding decisions, and maximizing efficiency in achieving desired outcomes. The ability to understand and translate the concepts surrounding sport analytics is critical for aspiring managers and analysts in sport settings.

With a dramatically increasing amount of data available, how sport organizations and managers use that evidentiary data to improve performance and efficiency is of crucial importance to the sport industry. Metrics provide evidence, offer rationale for decisions, and justify specific courses of action. Additionally, the size of the sport organization, the stakeholders involved, the required pace for action, the capacity to collect and analyze data, and the anticipated importance and impact of the decision will influence decision-makers. Employing sport analytics yields metrics that can enhance effective decision-making in the conduct of sport, whether on the field of play or in the front office.

Sport analytics involves the fundamental use of analytical metrics to inform sport managers. The framing of sport analytics for practical use within sport organizations affords sport managers insights into the utility of data analyses. That is distinct from fully preparing analysts in data manipulation and statistical techniques. In supporting the utility of sport analytics, this book addresses the background of sport analytics, why it is useful, selected techniques and tools employed, and its applications in sport organizations.

Dr. Debi Corbatto, Deputy Athletic Director, Internal Operations and Risk Management, George Mason University

Analytics is the difference-maker for many teams. The use of data is critical in our industry to optimize performance *and* manage risk. Descriptive analytics can guide scheduling, training sessions, and recruiting efforts of the coaching staff. Forecasting analytics can guide resource allocation, return on investments, and ticketing operations. In short, every part of our athletic business is impacted by the data. Having strong support in the area of analytics will be the game-changing differentiator for the sports business!

DATA AND DECISION-MAKING

Data-driven, data-informed, and data-inspired are terms that describe the interaction between the circumstances and methods of data usage (Stewart, 2019). Being data-driven requires the precise data needed to make a decision, yielding an exact answer. Being data-informed requires an awareness of the current metrics in order to inform strategies. Being data-inspired requires predictive inference and trendspotting derived from multiple data sources.

Data-driven decision-making uses data meant to answer a very specific question. Data-driven strategies indicate that the data to determine the outcome is available. Data-driven decision-making requires the most specific type of metrics and is rigid in its data use. For example, the data to be analyzed is predetermined, along with the methodology to ensure a properly implemented plan for measurement. Generally, large sampling is required to ensure stability and replicability. Knowledge of statistical methodologies are essential (Stewart, 2019).

Data-informed decision-making strategies imply that data analyses are employed along with experiential and other factors in the decision process. Data-informed decision-making requires existing knowledge of **key performance indicators (KPIs)**. Upward and downward trajectories are observable and explainable, reflecting both the what and the why (Stewart, 2019). Data-informed analyses are used to refine and inform future strategies—for example, when addressing inevitable organizational or environmental changes (Fullan, 2008). Employing a hypothesis-driven analytics approach informs decision-makers on why a particular strategy will work. Stewart (2019) noted that, in opposition to a data-driven approach, a data-informed analysis does not form a conclusive course of action; rather, it contextualizes and informs new strategies.

Data-inspired decision-making is exploratory in nature, imposing no expectations on specific outcomes. Generally, data from multiple sources is used and commonalities across data sources are sought. Often data-inspired analytics draw on intuition and inference as opposed to concrete, statistically sound methodologies of data-driven and data-influenced analytics. Whereas data is readily used to reveal impacts of the past and project possible futures based on past trends, it is employed less frequently for the creation of innovative ideas. However, data-inspired strategies can analyze disparate metrics and be used to inspire new ideas. Data-inspired processes will not determine a conclusive action, but they can reveal concurrent trends and broader context than the aforementioned methodologies. Data-inspired metrics are not concrete and could reflect spurious interactions.

There are risks and limitations in each of these analytics approaches, yet each serves its purpose, ultimately contributing to the success of an organization.

Also contributing to organizational success, **program evaluation** is directed toward understanding the successes and failures of a program through a repetitive, systematic, organized approach to gathering and analyzing information to identify the factors that contribute to the program, the decisions that need to be made, and the actions that need to be taken based on the findings of the evaluation process (Durning and Hemmer, 2010). Evaluation involves the review, analysis, and application of data gathered. Clearly, data analytics is a tool in program evaluation, ultimately informing and guiding organizational decisions.

There are two distinct approaches to, and purposes for, evaluation: summative and formative. **Summative evaluation**, or summative assessment, focuses on the outcomes of a program or its KPIs. In sport, the final score is a summative outcome. **Formative evaluation**, or formative assessment, summarizes the participants' development at a specific time in a process of continual improvement. For example, employees who demonstrate effectiveness may be formatively evaluated and provided additional tools for ongoing development. Both summative and formative evaluations are connected to data analyses in that they are evidentiary metrics and used to determine program or participant effectiveness. The emphasis on data allows decision-makers to focus on evidence and continual improvement. The application of data analytics in the form of program evaluations and KPI assessments ensures that organizations and participants are doing what they say they are doing and determines how well they are doing it. Learning organizations are those that employ evidentiary assessments to pursue continuous improvement.

The *Moneyball* movie premiere in Oakland, California, added a glamorous touch to the analytical work of Billy Beane.
Steve Jennings/WireImage

SYSTEMS AND ANALYTICS

Learning organizations are a key concept in **systems thinking**, wherein systems comprised of inputs, throughputs, and outputs, along with feedback loops, are organized to disclose organizational effectiveness (Senge, 1990). Assessment measures inform the system. Data analysis and its application to decision-making are also central to systems thinking. The logic model of evaluation aligns with systems thinking (Chelladurai, 2014; Knowlton and Phillips, 2012; Senge, 1990). This framework defines the intended links between the program resources (or inputs), the program strategies or treatments (or throughputs), the immediate results of program activities (or outputs), and the desired program accomplishments (or goal-related outcomes). Systems are influenced by internal (proximate) and external (distal) environmental factors.

Senge (1990) noted that every system is perfectly designed to yield the results that are seen. Using the systems framework of input-throughput-output and feedback (internal and external), the concepts of systems thinking, continual improvement, and learning organizations are inextricably intertwined with data analytics as an essential tool to obtain accurate and informative results (Chelladurai, 2014; Knowlton and Phillips, 2012; Senge, 1990). While everything can be measured, measuring the right things using the right measures is foundational to establishing effective evidence with which to inform systems. The appropriate use of data analytics in the acquisition, analysis, and application of information provides the evidentiary measures necessary for informed decision-making and strategy development.

Measuring the right things using the right measures is critical in sport analytics. What metrics come to mind as measurable with this image?
Laura Young/Getty Images

Analytics and Strategic Planning

Strategy is a comprehensive, premeditated, long-term plan of action directed toward a desired outcome. It is distinct from the tactics, or actions, employed in pursuit of the strategy. Sun Tzu noted in the *Art of War* that "strategy without tactics is the slowest route to victory. Tactics without strategy is the noise before defeat" (Sawyer, 1994). While planning is an essential managerial function in any pursuit, properly applied data analysis is a critical component of the strategic planning process. **Strategic planning** is used to identify goals, strategies, and evaluation systems directed toward the organizational mission and intended outcomes. Strategic plans provide direction to organizations, help in avoiding distractions, and inform the resource needs in pursuit of identified goals. **SMART goals**, based on the mission, guide organizational objectives and direction. SMART stands for goals with the following characteristics:

- Specific
- Measurable
- Achievable, Action-oriented, Agreed-upon
- Realistic, Relevant, Result-oriented
- Time-based, Tangible, Trackable

While each organizational system is unique, the strategic planning process is based on a clearly stated mission and vision establishing a contextual framework. A SWOT (strengths, weaknesses, opportunities, threats) or SOAR (strengths, opportunities, aspirations, results) assessment is conducted to further inform the process (Stavros and Hinrichs, 2009). Internal and external stakeholders can contribute to the SWOT or SOAR assessment. These assessments guide the data analytics necessary to develop an informed strategy. The strategies based on the mission-driven SMART goals and the SWOT/SOAR assessment yield action plans, inform resource needs, and determine evaluation and assessment procedures. To close the loop in the analytics process, it is necessary to identify data sources, analysis protocols, and tools for tracking progress and providing essential feedback to inform strategies and guide managerial decision-making.

Effective strategic planning is built on the analysis of data. In establishing data analytics for strategic support, an organizational system must involve the right stakeholders. For example, individuals or units responsible for each strategy must be held accountable. Managers must have a working knowledge of the KPIs and should use them to support decisions. Managers must ask the right questions. For example, an appropriate strategic plan can address strategic questions:

- What do we do well with respect to our goals?
- What KPI outcomes do we need to improve on?
- Where do we want to be in year two, three, etc.?
- How will we proceed to get to our intended KPI outcomes?
- Who is accountable for strategic actions and outcomes?
- How will success in our KPIs be measured?
- What data is needed to inform our strategies and tactics?
- What stakeholders need to be involved?

Tactically, managers should enact procedures to assemble the right data from appropriate sources. The processes should use the appropriate tools and methodologies for collection and analysis. Again, everything is measurable if properly planned and executed. Managers are responsible for ensuring the appropriate application of data analytics to inform system strategy and decision-making. Organizational systems must direct analytics toward identified mission-driven goals and desired outcomes, or KPIs. Reflecting progress toward intended outcomes, KPIs can measure individual performance or systemic organizational performance. More and more organizational systems have a double or multiple bottom line in which two or more outcomes are intentionally sought (e.g., financial profitability and social responsibility). In this case, analysis of multiple datasets aligned to measure KPIs related to diverse outcomes is mandated. Managers must therefore be able to identify the proper KPI. While not necessarily responsible for data analysis itself, managers must understand the system they manage, the KPIs that inform strategies, and the questions that prompt data collection and analysis—and they must understand how available data analyses inform decisions in pursuit of strategic initiatives.

In short, managers are responsible to make data-driven, data-informed, or data-inspired decisions where appropriate. They are also responsible for employing appropriate data analyses and making decisions based on appropriate measures. Managers are not intended to be traditional data analysts who collect, process, and statistically analyze available datasets. Managers do, however, need to contextualize these analytical processes and analyses. While analysts collect and process data, managers must both inform data analyses and be informed by data analyses. Managers, who ultimately use the data analyses, must effectively communicate with analysts. Managers and analysts who are effective at communicating and translating data needs and analyses and how they can be used are more impactful decision-makers and therefore more employable. Therefore, the better managers understand the role of the analyst, the tools analysts employ, and the context within which they operate, making the data analytics process more systemically effective.

Analytics in the Sport Sector

The role of communication and translation is critical in sport analytics. Many organizational systems in sport have data analysts. Some even have teams of analysts. However, when push comes to shove, the divide between analysts and managerial decision-makers is often a deep chasm. This phenomenon is not limited to sport organizations. In fact, it permeates the manager–analyst relationship. Success stories are not as commonplace as one might believe, given the attention paid to those that have been shared (e.g., Moneyball). However, sport managers who achieve a level of data fluency enjoy a marketplace advantage, putting their sport organizations at a competitive advantage as well. Framing when, where, and how analytics can inform strategies and decisions

DIVERSITY IN SPORT ANALYTICS

The majority of sport analysts are white men. While the number of positions related to sport analytics has grown dramatically, the composition of the field remains lacking in diversity. The lack of diversity is very evident at the annual MIT Sloan Sports Analytics Conference (SSAC). However, there is a rising tide of hope for increased diversity. For example, MIT Sloan sponsored 10 Black undergraduate students to attend the virtual SSAC conference, and 150 sport analytics professionals participated in "Measurables Office Hours," a program designed to connect practicing professionals with interested prospects from underrepresented groups. Numerous university programs are offering professional preparation in sport analytics. Learning of the opportunities in sport analytics and gaining hands-on experience is a crucial step in diversifying the landscape.

Successful analysts who are Black are emerging in the industry and setting the stage for the future. For example, John Tobias, a statistician at ESPN, gained both exposure to analytics and experience during an internship with the Charlotte Hornets and has since begun teaching college students about sport analytics. His role in the preparation of aspiring analysts might well afford more Black students an opportunity to enter the career. An analyst for the Seattle Mariners, Spencer Weisberg understands the isolation of being a Black analyst in sport. Inspired by the book *Moneyball*, he focused his interest in math and computer science toward a career in sports, beginning with an internship with the Mariners. Also, John Drazen, former college basketball player, sees the opportunity for sport analytics to make itself more diverse through education, examples, and partnerships. As an assistant coach, he inspired student-athletes to learn and use analytics. Drazen summed up the lack of diversity, saying, "I think that not having diversity in analytics is a huge missed opportunity for empowering and inspiring our diverse American population" (Benbow, 2021).

for sport managers is the key to the usefulness of data analytics. Managers should understand current tools, methodologies, and analytical results relative to KPIs. They must ask the right questions to prompt the appropriate analyses, and they must be able to contextualize the results (i.e., KPIs) to inform a course of action. On the other hand, analysts should understand the context of the system within which, and the purpose for which, the data will be used. A broad knowledge of sport analytics, with the ability to translate the context, processes, and results for others, will enhance the performance of sport managers, data analysts, and their sport organizations alike.

Within the sport sector, there are many common applications of data analytics. Sport analytics can inform strategies and decisions on the field of play or in the boardroom. For example, general managers can use analyses of predetermined KPIs to inform draft choices or free agent acquisition. The KPIs would reflect the desired outcomes of the team, and if properly constructed and measured, they would indicate which available players are best aligned with said KPI-based characteristics. Coaches can use an analysis of specific team and player tendencies to inform game decisions, such as whether to pass or run on third down and four in the fourth quarter against a specific opponent, or whether to employ a full court press against a specific team or apply ball pressure to a specific guard. Predictive analytics can be used to inform the likelihood for success, in relation to a KPI, perhaps related to individual player performance or overall team outcomes. For example, what factors statistically correlate to a team's or a player's success? Free throw percentage, points in the paint, deflections, or screens resulting in a score? These and many other measures could inform the decision, but it is entirely dependent on predetermined team goals and style of play.

In the front office, trends and preferences can be analyzed for marketing and sponsorship purposes. Where are a team's supporters? What is being said on social media? Where (and who) are the influencers, either evangelical or detractor? The more knowledge is gleaned from data analytics, the better the organization's ability to segment. For example, targeted marketing to a distant yet enthusiastic fan base would look very different from strategies employed for an enthusiastic local fan base. If a sport organization intends to engage in a double bottom-line strategy, a ticket manager might pursue KPIs that measure a specific campaign's profitability and its social impact. For example, if a socially responsible sport organization chooses to develop a campaign to promote additional attendance while overtly supporting environmentally sound practices, analyses of specific KPIs for both attendance and environmental impacts would be necessary.

It is evident that sport analytics has grown increasingly popular, increasingly sophisticated, and increasingly effective. The application of data analytics in sport is warranted at all levels and in all domains of sport organizations, including private enterprises, government agencies, public entities, nonprofit or voluntary organizations, and commercial ventures. While each sport, each level of play, and each component of the sport industry has distinctly different purposes, needs, resources, and desired outcomes, sport analytics is a useful and relevant tool. According to Grand View Research (2021), the global sport analytics market size was valued at $885 million in 2020. It is expected to expand at an annual rate of 21.3 percent from 2021 to 2028. The managers who are prepared to engage data analytics to support strategy development and decision-making are becoming the sport leaders of the future.

EMERGING APPLICATIONS OF SPORT ANALYTICS

Sport analytics have evolved beyond professional sport leagues and franchises to other facets of sport. A plethora of data measures, including numbers, text, and video, has yielded an abundance of data ripe for analysis. Data is readily used in marketing, customer service, strategic planning, and human resources management, including the management of player personnel. For example, decisions about upcoming draft prospects or free agents, such as those portrayed in the *Moneyball* scenario, are informed by statistical analyses of relevant data. Additionally, coaches can be informed by predicative analytics that inform decisions about game strategy (Baker and Kwartler, 2015). And, if analysis of social media and other data informs sport managers that there is a dearth of promotional activity in a specific region that exhibits simultaneous intensive fan interest, specific fan engagement strategies can be implemented.

Venues, facilities, and events also use a variety data. Data analytics is used to identify key trends within facility data and afford better facility management. Data analyses can inform data-influenced decisions and strategic initiatives. Typical facility metrics influence schedules, costs, building operations, and customer service through such measures as response time, downtime, visibility, and capacity. For example, signage prices can be influenced by the number of typical views. Data can also be used to enhance fan experiences. It can be used to forecast space needs, budget requirements, and staff composition in a facility. Metrics can be compared with other facilities, or perhaps competitors, to determine benchmarks and even overall performance. Beyond the typical facility metrics, building systems can be measured for efficiency. Smart facilities can effectively use data analyses to prepare for risk and emergency management. For example, data collected throughout a facility can yield metrics that efficiently guide fans to an exit in the case of an emergency or that guide individuals with disabilities to appropriate accommodations. The increasing use of artificial intelligence (AI) and machine learning has analytical applications in smart buildings.

With fantasy sports revolving around statistical performances of athletes, it is only fitting that sport analytics are inextricably connected to the fantasy sports realm. Many of the tasks affiliated with fantasy sports are akin to player personnel management. Of course, salary caps and team dynamics are not influential factors. The selection of individuals for a team is solely based on individual performance in specific categories. There are no intangibles. Therefore, analyzing data can be crucial when building a team lineup. Chances of success are enhanced by effectively predicting future performance or tracking and testing existing team and individual performance on a per-game basis.

How can attendance trends and fan engagement analysis impact marketing decisions?
Pavel Losevsky/fotolia.com

Aside from athletic skill and luck, winning in sports involves analyzing and strategizing. Like traditional sport, the evolution of a rapidly expanding phenomenon such as esports also has a logical connection to data analytics in an attempt to enhance performance and drive monetization. A large amount of data is generated in the use of games, well beyond the simple high score. Data can reveal successful strategies and be a vehicle for improvement. As with any other sport, not only can self-improvement be enhanced by tracking performance tendencies and results, but the strategies and tactics of opponents can be evaluated and applied in future contests. In spectator-based sports, properly employed analytics also offer an avenue through which to better engage with spectators. Again, as in any spectator-sport setting, sharing real-time statistics, interesting graphics, alternate camera angles, instant replays, superimposed technologies, and virtual interactions can enhance the fan experience.

Another noticeable use for sport analytics is in media coverage of sports. As information is disseminated in sport settings by sports reporters, journalists, and broadcasters, using metrics can strengthen their communication patterns, whether in play-by-play reporting or broader public relations campaigns. The use of analytics can improve clarity in sports reporting, enhance spectator understanding, and build evidence-based assessments of sport-specific circumstances. Along with communication officers employed by teams and leagues, media outlets are embracing analytics as a foundation of their consumer communication process. And while data can be manipulated to influence desired reporting outcomes, more often than not, the use of metrics supports, clarifies, and improves overall communication, regardless of the modality of that communication. The infusion of sport analytics through digital outlets, broadcast media, or traditional publications is clearly trending upward.

Professional Highlights

Academics and Practitioners Making an Impact in Sport Analytics

- Dr. Margaret Jones is a professor and the director of the Patriot Performance Lab at George Mason University. She is a Fellow in the American College of Sports Medicine and the National Strength and Conditioning Association (NSCA). Focused on human performance and athlete health, she uses analytics such as wearable technologies to monitor athlete loads and inform coaching decisions.

- Dr. Bill Gerrard is a professor of business management at the University of Leeds. He is one of the innovators of data analytics in sport. He focuses on using an evidence-based approach to support decision-making in both individual and team sports relevant to talent identification, development, game tactics, and various aspects of team management, including valuation, financial performance, and the relationship between salaries and performance. He has worked with several elite sports teams around the world. Billy Beane wrote that Gerrard's work has "not only benefited the Oakland Athletics but the sports industry as a whole" (Gerrard, 2018).

- Billy Beane is the executive vice president of baseball operations for the Oakland Athletics. During his 23-year tenure, the A's compiled a .532 record, which is the sixth best in Major League Baseball. His teams attained seven American League West titles and 11 playoff appearances. Beane and the A's were the subject of the book *Moneyball: The Art of Winning an Unfair Game*, which also became an Oscar-nominated film starring Brad Pitt as Beane.

- Jessica Gelman is the CEO of Kraft Analytics Group (KAGR), which provides data management, advanced analytics, and strategic consulting to the sports sector. Along with Daryl Morey, Gelman cofounded and continues to cochair the MIT Sloan Sports Analytics Conference, the first and largest conference of its kind. She has a BS and MBA from Harvard, where she was a decorated student-athlete.

SUMMARY

This book is not intended to create data analysts but to prepare sport managers on how to use data analysis to influence decisions. It is intended to provide a working knowledge of analytics for sport managers who are responsible for making decisions. In that context, sport analytics is the application of data analyses in a sport setting. Data analysis involves examining, cleansing, transforming, and modeling data for practical purposes, such as informing operational decisions.

Analysts use statistical methodologies to analyze data. These analyses yield evidence to inform the sport manager's decisions. This is conceptually evidence-based management applied to sport (Pfeffer and Sutton, 2006). Sport analytics as a practice supports scientifically guided decisions, improved strategic processes, and operational effectiveness in sport organizations (Xia and Gong, 2015). Sport organizations function as systems wherein organizational resources (or inputs), such as personnel, facilities, equipment, and finances, inform the organization's strategies (or throughputs), such as procedural actions. The inputs and throughputs yield immediate organizational results (or outputs) and goal-related accomplishments (or outcomes), such as performance. Organizational systems are influenced by both internal and external environmental factors. Recognizing sport organizations as systems with identifiable input-throughput-output as well as internal and external feedback is fundamental in recognizing the impact of sport analytics. The concepts of systems thinking, continual improvement, and learning organizations are inextricably intertwined with data analytics as essential tools to obtain accurate and informative results (Chelladurai, 2014; Knowlton and Phillips, 2012; Senge, 1990).

Senge (1990) noted that every system is perfectly designed to yield the results that are seen. Effective evaluation and strategic planning is built on the proper analysis and application of data within an organizational system. While anything can be measured, measuring the correct things using the correct measures is critical if sport managers want to provide effective evidence from which to inform decisions.

Data-driven, data-informed, and data-inspired decision-making strategies often reveal data analyses that are employed along with experiential and other factors in the decision-making process. The application of data analytics using KPI assessments measures whether organizations and participants are doing what they say they are doing and determines how well they are doing it. By indicating progress toward intended outcomes, KPIs can measure individual or systemic organizational performance. It is essential that organizational systems direct their analyses toward these identified mission-driven goals and desired outcomes, or KPIs. As a result, within organizational systems, sport managers must have a working knowledge of KPIs and use these measures to support decisions.

Most sport organizations are committed to the application of data analytics. The escalating desire to apply metrics in the decision-making process has stimulated the need not only for analysts but also for sport managers who have a foundational knowledge of the use of data for decision-making. Sport managers are responsible for appropriate data-driven, data-informed, or data-inspired decisions based on appropriate measures. Sport managers who achieve a proficient level of data fluency enjoy a marketplace advantage. A fundamental understanding and application of analytics in sport provides a competitive advantage for sport organizations and managers alike; however, those who fail to embrace analytics may find themselves at a competitive disadvantage in the future. Knowing when, where, and how to use analytics to inform strategies and decisions is essential to making data analytics valuable for sport managers and their organizations. Sport managers should understand current analytical tools, methodologies, and results relative to KPIs. They should be able to ask the right questions and interpret the data needed to generate the best decisions. The sport managers who are prepared to engage data analytics to support strategy development and decision-making are the future leaders of the sport industry.

ONLINE ACTIVITIES HKPropel »

Visit HK*Propel* to access the welcome video, exercises, and a key terms review activity for this chapter. Your instructor may also release the assignment, assignment form, and quiz available for this chapter through HK*Propel*. These tutorials, activities, and exercises are designed for interactive learning and to assist students as they learn the material.

REFERENCES

Baker, R.E., and T. Kwartler. 2015. "Sport Analytics: Using Open Source Logistic Regression Software to Classify Upcoming Play Type in the NFL." *Journal of Applied Sport Management* 7 (2): 40-63.

Benbow, J. 2021. "The Sports Analytics Community Is Overwhelmingly White and Male. What Is Being Done to Make It More Diverse?" *Boston Globe*, February 19.

Chelladurai, P. 2014. *Managing Organizations for Sport and Physical Activity: A Systems Perspective.* 4th ed. New York: Routledge.

Coakley, J. 2017. *Sports in Society: Issues and Controversies.* New York: McGraw Hill.

Durning, S.J., and P.A. Hemmer. 2010. "Program Evaluation." In: Ende J, editor. *ACP Teaching Internal Medicine.* Philadelphia: American College of Physicians.

Fullan, M. 2008. *The Six Secrets of Change.* San Francisco: Jossey-Bass.

Galov, N. 2021. "77+ Big Data Stats for the Big Future Ahead." Accessed September 3, 2021. https://hostingtribunal.com/blog/big-data-stats/#gref.

Gerrard, B. 2018. "Winning With Analytics" (blog). https://winningwithanalytics.com/about/

Grand View Research. 2021. *Global Sports Analytics Market Size Report*, 2021-2028. Market Analyst Report GVR-4-68038-128-3. Last modified April 2021.

Knowlton, L.W., and C.C. Phillips. 2012. *The Logic Model Guidebook: Better Strategies.* 2nd ed. Los Angeles: Sage.

Lewis, Michael. 2003. *Moneyball: The Art of Winning an Unfair Game.* 1st ed. New York: W.W. Norton.

MIT Sloan. 2021. "Show Me the Data: 15th Annual MIT Sloan Sports Analytics Conference to Bring Together Leading Figures in Sports Analytics, Business and Technology on April 8 and 9, 2021." Office of Media Relations news release, March 29. https://mitsloan.mit.edu/press/show-me-data-15th-annual-mit-sloan-sports-analytics-conference-to-bring-together-leading-figures-sports-analytics-business-and-technology-april-8-and-9-2021.

Pfeffer, J., and R. Sutton. 2006. "Evidence-Based Management." *Harvard Business Review* 84:62-74, 133.

Plunkett Research, Ltd. 2019. Sports & Recreation Business Statistics Analysis, Business and Industry Statistics. https://www.plunkettresearch.com/statistics/sports-industry/

Sawyer, R.D. 1994. *Sun Tzu: The Art of War.* Boulder, CO: Westview Press.

Sherman, R. 2014. *Business Intelligence Guidebook: From Data Integration to Analytics.* Waltham, MA: Morgan Kaufmann.

Stewart, S. 2019. "Are You Data-driven, Data-informed or Data-inspired?" Last modified March 21, 2019. https://blog.amplitude.com/data-driven-data-informed-data-inspired.

Senge, P. 1990. *The Fifth Discipline: The Art and Practice of the Learning Organization.* New York: Currency Doubleday.

Stavros, J.M., and G. Hinrichs. 2009. *The Thin Book of SOAR: Building Strengths-Based Strategy.* Bend, OR: Thin Book Publishing.

Wolf, E.R. 1990. Distinguished Lecture: Facing Power - Old Insights, New Questions. *American Anthropologist* 92 (3): 586–596. http://www.jstor.org/stable/680336

Xia, B.S., and P. Gong. 2015. "Review of Business Intelligence Through Data Analysis." *Benchmarking* 21 (2): 300-311. doi:10.1108/BIJ-08-2012-0050.

## 2

WORKING WITH QUANTITATIVE DATA IN R

Doug Stroud/NCAA Photos via Getty Images

CHAPTER OBJECTIVES

After completing this chapter and the associated online exercises, you will be able to do the following:

· Develop and execute R coding scripts.

· Import and manipulate datasets using R.

· Explore datasets in R using applicable functions.

· Filter and subset datasets to isolate specific cases and variables for analysis.

· Perform counting and ordering tasks in R.

· Create and apply custom functions in R.

· Analyze data using descriptive statistics.

· Conduct relationship testing between variables using inferential statistics

KEY TERMS

alpha level
bivariate correlation
categorical variable
character
College Sports Supermodel
degrees of freedom
descriptive statistics
factors
filtered data
frequencies (n counts)
global environment
independent samples t-test

inferential statistics
integers
levels
mean
measured variable
median
numeric
observations
one-way analysis of
   variance (ANOVA)
operators
packages

Pearson method
percentages
post-hoc tests
quartiles
regression analysis
scripts
Spearman method
standard deviation
subsetted data
T- statistic
type I error

R FUNCTIONS

```
~                      colnames()           library()            rowSums()
#                      colSums()            lm()                 sapply()
$                      cor.test()           mean()               sd()
abline()               count()              ncol()               setwd()
aggregate()            ctrl+enter           nrow()               str()
aov()                  df[r,c]              order()              sum()
apa.reg.table()        function()           plot()               summary()
apply()                getwd()              prop.table()         t.test()
as.factor()            head()               quantile()           table()
as.numeric()           install.packages()   read.csv()           tail()
c()                    lapply()             round()              TukeyHSD()
colMeans()             levels()             rowMeans()
```

At first blush, working with RStudio and the programming language of R may be an intimidating concept, particularly for those who are used to more traditional platforms for data analysis and data visualization such as Excel, SAS, and SPSS. The lack of drop-down menus, and the ability to search for the correct solutions contained therein, will be an uncomfortable process for people who have limited knowledge or no knowledge of coding. The learning curve for working in R can be steep, but once users gain a certain level of comfort with R, few go back to what they were previously using. The advantages of R in terms of rapid data analysis and superior data visualization quickly lead users to explore deeper and bring the data vividly to life. The versatility of R will soon have you working at a higher level in the field of applied sport business analytics.

Throughout this chapter and the next, you will be guided through a series of R scripts for working with data that is provided as part of this book and its supplemental web-based materials. **Scripts** are lines of code that operate at the functional level to execute functions in RStudio. By the end of the book, you will have a set of "master scripts" that you can save and use on future projects by making simple adjustments to suit your needs. The purpose is to give you a solid foundation for working in R that you can use to further develop your skills in the future.

The entirety of chapters 2 and 3 are based on the *css.csv* file provided in the HK*Propel* online supplement. The file found there, *css.csv*, is a trimmed-down version of the **College Sports Supermodel** that was developed to track NCAA Division I schools over a series of variables on an annual basis. The dataset, provided by Dr. Atwater, was developed using a variety of data sources to look for trends in athletics, such as spending versus performance over time. Some of these variables are independent or **categorical variables** such as conference affiliation, the state the school is located in, and the classification of the school (state school or private school). Other variables are dependent or **measured variables** such as total athletics expenses, points earned in the Learfield IMG College Directors' Cup competition, and the number of athletes at schools included in the dataset. Overall, you will be working with data that covers two years (2016 to 2018) and contains approximately 17,000 data points. Using this data throughout the two chapters allows for consistency in developing scripts and will allow you to develop a comfort level using R.

Visit HK*Propel* to access the video tutorial for downloading and installing R and RStudio.

R BASICS

Before you import the *css.csv* file, however, it is important to first discuss using hashtags to take notes in R.

Taking Notes in R

For many, the hashtag is something used on social media, but from an R perspective, # is a way in which users can keep track of what each script or line of code they have created does. Using the # allows users to take notes. When scripts are run, R ignores anything that is proceeded by a hashtag, even though it appears in the coding. For example, you can start by using your script panel in the top left of RStudio to type the following:

```
# I am super excited to finally be learning R!
```

If you were to run this line of code, you would see that nothing happens. Taking notes is particularly useful because of the many areas covered in chapters 2 through 5. Whenever a new function is introduced, it is recommended that you label it by taking notes.

Importing Data Into R

While it is possible to create datasets in R, most users at the introductory level import their data from other sources more familiar to them. One of the ways in which data is frequently organized is through the use of Excel spreadsheets. When users create a spreadsheet in Excel (or another comparable application), they generally have an option to save or export the data as a comma-separated value file known as a *.csv* file. The *.csv* format is an easy format to import into R. Start by saving the *css.csv* file from the online study guide to a location on your computer where it will be easy to find, such as the desktop. Once you have the *css.csv* file saved, you are ready to begin by creating the following line of code to execute the **read.csv()** function.

```
# Importing .csv files into R
css <- read.csv(file.choose(),)
```

In this instance, the code accomplished the following:

- You have applied a name to the dataset, in this case *css*.
- The less than sign followed by a dash is an "equals sign" used for creating objects.
- `read.csv` describes the type of data file R is looking for.
- `file.choose` tells R that the file will be manually selected from any location on your computer.

To execute the command, place the cursor anywhere within the line of code and do one of two things: (1) hit **ctrl+enter** or (2) click on the run button in the top of the script panel. The recommendation is to get used to using ctrl+enter for executing code because it is easier and quicker. When you run this line of code, a window will appear where you can browse for the *css.csv* file. Select the file, and the data will appear in the top right panel of RStudio. This panel is known as your **global environment**, and it is where you store, create, and remove objects as your project evolves. Figure 2.1 displays this step in RStudio when done correctly.

Note that if the window to browse for your file did not appear, it is more than likely hiding behind RStudio. Minimize the RStudio window and you should see it. If not, verify you have created and executed the line of code properly.

In the global environment panel (top right of figure 2.1), you will see that the *css.csv* file has been successfully imported. There are 348 **observations**. This number represents the number of schools included in the dataset organized by row. Of the 351 schools that comprise Division I of the NCAA, all but three are included. The three schools that are not included are Army, Air Force, and Navy. This is because much

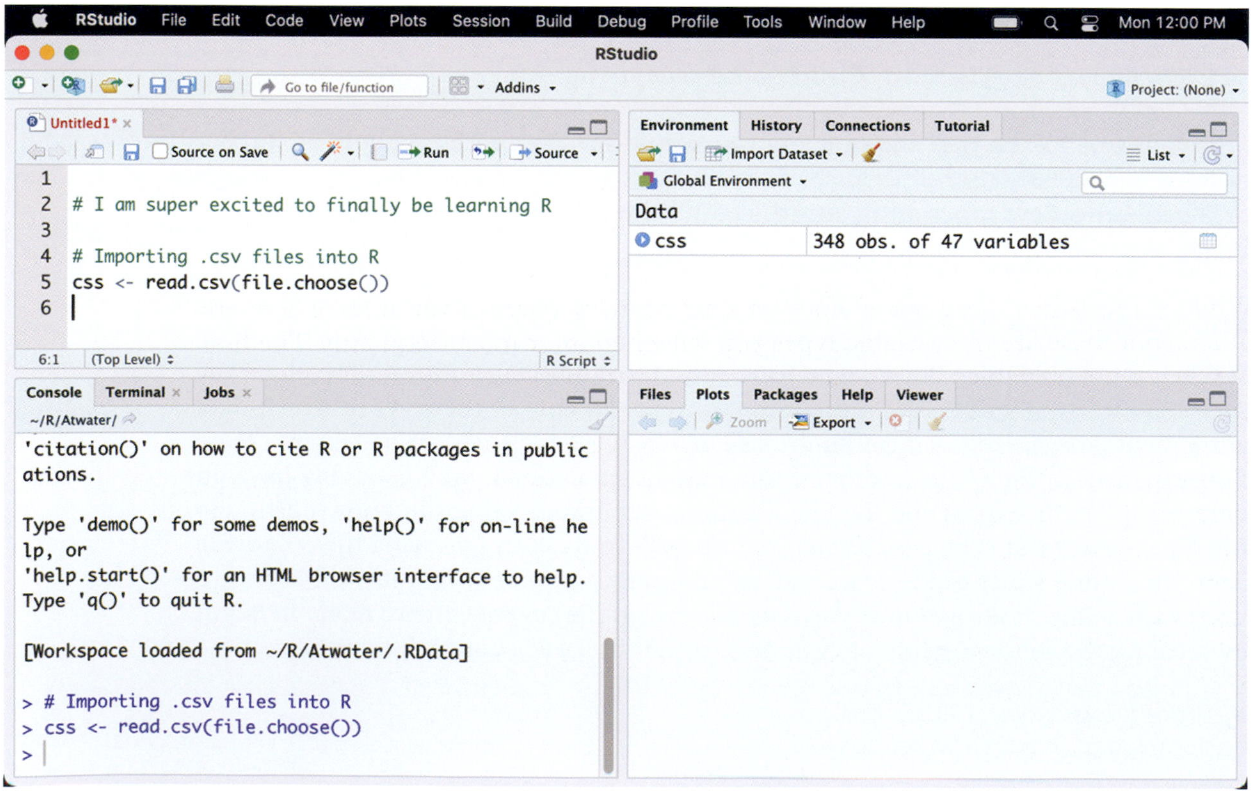

FIGURE 2.1 Imported *css* dataset in RStudio.

of the data in the *css* dataset is mined from the Department of Education's Equity in Athletics database, which does not collect data from the military. The number of variables included in this trimmed-down version of the College Sports Supermodel is 47. These variables (either categorical or measured variables) are organized in columns.

Identifying Your Working Directory and Saving Your Work

At this point, it is a good idea to start saving your work. By default, R will have created a working directory for you where all your work will be saved. To identify the location of your working directory, execute the **getwd()** function.

Visit HK*Propel* to access the video tutorial for importing data into R and the College Sports Supermodel (css) dataset.

```
# Identifying the location of the working directory
getwd()
```

While it is possible to change your working directory using the set working directory function **setwd()**, it is probably easier initially to use the default directory created by R. In the future, whenever you are looking for saved materials, they will be in your working directory. There are two items that can be saved for future use. The first is the panel where you have been developing all your scripts. The second is an option to save your global environment (the objects you have created in the global environment panel). Above each panel is a small blue disk. Simply tap on the disk, give your item a name, and it will be saved. Scripts will be saved as *.R* files, and the global environment will be saved as *.RData* files.

It is recommended that you occasionally create a backup of the scripts (*.R* files) as you progress, because it will continue to grow as more coding is added. The global environment can always be re-created using the scripts you have already developed, so saving the global environment is more for convenience. Lastly, once you have identified your working directory, you can move the *css.csv* file from your desktop or other selected location into the working directory. This will allow you to import the file without using the `file.choose` method. Once you have your *css.csv* file saved in the working directory, you can simply execute the following code to import the data.

Visit HK*Propel* to access the video tutorials for locating and setting your working directory and saving your work.

```
# Importing .csv files from the working directory
css <- read.csv("css.csv")
```

Types of Variables

While working in R, you will encounter four primary types of variables. There are others, but these are the variable types you will encounter most frequently. The first are **character** variables. These may be nominal variables such as school name. The second are grouping variables, such as the athletics conference the school belongs to. When analyzing the structure of the dataset, these variables will be labeled as **factors**. The other two primary types of variables are measured variables. Measured variables will typically be broken down into two categories. The first category is **integers**, which looks at whole numbers for, as an example, female enrollment, where you would not want a result with a decimal (representing a fraction of an individual). The second category is referred to as double variables, but simply stated, they are **numeric** variables that may include fractional data or decimal points as part of the result, such as total athletics expenses in millions. When analyzing the structure of the dataset, the output will indicate **character**, **factor**, **integer**, and **numeric** data.

It is critical to check your dataset when you import it into RStudio to ensure that the variable types are correct. If the variable types are incorrect, you may not be able to analyze the data in a way that achieves your goals. To examine the structure of a dataset, use the structure **str()** function.

```
# Examining the structure of a dataset
str(css)
```

The output from running the str() function appears in the bottom left panel of RStudio known as the console. The first five variables included in the dataset are labeled either as chr (character) or factor. If they are factor, no further structural work needs to be completed. If the result indicates chr, then an adjustment to the variable type will *need* to be made using the **as.factor()** function to change the variable type from chr to factor.

```
# Changing a character variable into a factor variable
css$school <- as.factor(css$school)
```

You can practice by using this function to change the remaining character variables into factor variables. An **as.numeric()** function also exists, but for our purposes, it will not be required.

Once you have converted the first five character variables in the *css* dataset to factor variables, check to make sure they are correct by running the str() function again. Your dataset should now indicate that all the variables in the *css* dataset are either factors, integers, or numeric variables.

Each factor variable has a number of **levels** that are associated with the variable. This tells you how many different options each categorical or factor variable includes. For instance, you will see that the factor of conference (conf) has 32 levels, which is indicative of the 32 possible athletics conferences a school can belong to. The remaining 42 variables in the dataset are measured variables. Variables measured in whole numbers, such as average total enrollment per year at a school (aten), are labeled as integer (int). Variables that include fractional data with decimals, such as total athletics expenses from 2016 to 2018 (expmf), are labeled as numeric (num).

Visit HK*Propel* to access the video tutorials on variables, operators, and as.factor(), as.character(), and as.numeric() functions.

Operators

Operators serve a number of purposes in R. The following common **operators** can be used in a variety of ways to achieve desired results and will be discussed extensively throughout the book.

```
+     Addition
-     Subtraction
*     Multiplication
/     Division
>     Greater than
<     Less than
>=    Greater than or equal to
<=    Less than or equal to
==    Equals
!=    Does not equal
&     And
|     Or
```

Installing and Activating Packages

Installing and activating packages in R allows users to complete a number of specified tasks. **Packages** are sets of functions and data that are replete with well-defined code (Datacamp, 2019). Some packages come standard with RStudio, and others can be downloaded and installed. To see a list of the packages that came standard with your RStudio download, click on the packages tab in the bottom right panel. If you see the name of the package you would like to use, check the box to activate it. If you do not see the package you would like to use, it will need to be installed. Two packages that will be used throughout this chapter and the next are *plyr* and *ggplot2*. To install these packages, use the **install.packages()** function.

```
# Installing packages
install.packages("plyr")
install.packages("ggplot2")
```

Once the packages are installed, you can go back to the packages tab in the bottom right panel of RStudio and make sure their boxes are checked, thus indicating they are activated. It is usually faster and easier, however, to use the **library()** function to activate your packages. Unlike the install.packages() function, the library() function does not require you to use quotation marks around the package name.

Visit HK*Propel* to access the video tutorial on installing and activating packages.

```
# Activating packages
library(plyr)
library(ggplot2)
```

The $ Sign

The final step before tackling the *css* dataset involves the dollar sign. The **$** sign in R is used to identify the data and the variables that are to be used at a functional level. Because you will be creating multiple objects in the global environment, R first needs to know which data to access for analysis. For instance, if you wanted to know the total of all recruiting expenses in millions of dollars in Division I of the NCAA for the years 2016 to 2018, you would first have to identify the dataset to be used (*css*) and then identify the variable for total recruiting expenses in millions of dollars for 2016 to 2018 (tcruitmf). The data being referenced will be represented by the input prior to the $ sign (*css*). The variable being referenced will be represented by the input following the $ sign (tcruitmf). Applying the **sum()** function to the data and variable will produce the result you are looking for.

```
# Creating a total using the sum() function
sum(css$tcruitmf)
```

If you ran the code correctly, you will see the result in the bottom left panel of RStudio known as the console panel. The answer should be $468.25 million. This is the amount of money that all the NCAA Division I schools spent on recruiting from 2016 to 2018. If you want to round the result to a single decimal point, you can wrap the **round()** function around the original coding. The number of decimal places you would like to use is indicated by using the digits= setting.

```
# Rounding
round(sum(css$tcruitmf), digits=1)
```

Visit HK*Propel* to access
the video tutorial
on the $ sign.

Rounding the result will change the output in your console panel to $468.2 million. The sum() function and round() function will be further explored in this chapter in the section on descriptive statistics. For now, the critical concept to understand is that the input before the $ sign represents the data that R will reference for analysis, and the input following the $ sign represents the variable contained in the data for analysis.

EXPLORING DATASETS

Visit HK*Propel* to access
the video tutorial on
exploring datasets.

Now that you have the *css* dataset imported into RStudio and have an understanding of operators as well as how the $ sign works, you can begin to explore the data. There are several exploratory functions that help serve as a baseline for data analysis. The first exploratory function displays the number of rows and columns contained in the dataset. Results appear in the console panel of RStudio and should match the number of observations and the number of variables indicated in the global environment panel. To determine the number of rows and columns in the *css* dataset, use the **nrow()** and **ncol()** functions.

```
# Identifying the number of rows and columns in a dataset
nrow(css)
ncol(css)
```

In the console panel, the results should indicate that there are 348 rows and 47 columns, which matches the number of observations and variables in the global environment panel. Later, you will be adding and removing columns of data in your dataset based on operators. As you do so, the number of variables and the result of the ncol() function will continue to shift. If you were to add cases to your dataset, the number of observations and the result of the nrow() function would also change.

Understanding the levels contained in the categorical variables of the dataset is also important. Knowing the different levels or categories included in different categorical grouping variables allows you to represent data using n counts and percentages. Additionally, if you were to encounter data that is labeled as No Response, or if there is some other identifier that the data is missing such as NA, it would be important to remove those cases when conducting relationship testing among various groups. To learn the different levels or categories contained in the variables, use the **levels()** function. In this case, practice on the classification of school (state school or private school) labeled in the dataset as class.

```
# Determining the levels involved in a categorical variable
levels(css$class)
```

The result indicates that there are two levels involved in this categorical variable. The two levels are private schools and state schools.

The next way in which data can be explored is by using the head() and tail() functions. By default, the **head()** function will show you the first six cases of data, and the **tail()** function will show you the last six cases of data. If you would like to see more than six cases, or fewer cases, you can add the n= setting. However, it is important to know that initially, the cases shown will be in the order of the imported data. For example, if you had your data organized in alphabetical order by school name when you imported it into R, the head() function by default would show you data for Abilene Christian, Akron, Alabama, Alabama A&M, Alabama State, and Albany. The tail() function in this example would show you data for Wofford, Wright State,

Wyoming, Xavier, Yale, and Youngstown State. Later in the chapter you will learn how to sort and order data using different independent factor variables and dependent measured variables. Once data is ordered in a way that demonstrates the results you are seeking, the head() and tail() functions become very useful. To execute the head() and tail() functions, use the following:

```
# head() and tail() functions
head(css)
tail(css)

# head() and tail() functions - Setting the number of cases
displayed
head(css, n=20)
tail(css, n=14)
```

The **summary()** function is the next useful tool for understanding data in your dataset. By default, R will display summary statistics for all the measured variables included in your dataset when the summary() function is applied to the dataset as a whole. For categorical factor variables with six or fewer levels, summary counts will be provided for all the levels. For categorical factor variables with more than six levels, the summary() function will provide summary counts for the first six levels.

```
# Applying the summary() function to an entire dataset
summary(css)
```

If you are interested in seeing summary data for a single variable, you simply add the $ sign and variable name. Remember, the input before the $ sign represents the data being referenced for analysis, while the input following the $ sign represents the specific variable referenced for analysis. By way of example, use the variable that lists the state each school is located in (state). This is a categorical factor variable, so the output will show you summary counts for each level or category included in the variable—in this case, number of NCAA Division I schools per state.

```
# Summary data for a single variable
summary(css$state)
```

You can also use the summary() function to develop summary statistics for any measured variable included in the dataset. Try developing summary statistics for aid for female athletics, in millions of dollars, for 2016 to 2017 at NCAA Division I schools, using the faidm1 variable name.

```
# Summary statistics for measured variables
summary(css$faidm1)
```

The next step in exploring the dataset is a particularly important function that is used to identify the column number and column name of the categorical and measured variables included in the dataset. To this point, variable names have been provided, but moving forward, you will find that as the data evolves, this function will be very useful to keep track of it. To learn the column number and column name of each variable in the dataset, use the **colnames()** function.

```
# Identifying the column number and column name of variables in a
dataset
colnames(css)
```

The `colnames()` function is important because it allows you to home in on specific columns of data you would like to view or analyze instead of having to look at the dataset in its entirety every time a function is run.

Table 2.1 presents the column numbers, column names, and what they represent in the *css* dataset. All financial measures are represented in millions of dollars. A downloadable chart is available in the online study guide.

Visit HK*Propel* to access the College Sports Supermodel variables chart

TABLE 2.1   College Sports Supermodel Variables

Variable	Names	Definitions
1	school	School name
2	state	State where school is located
3	class	Classification of school (state school or private school)
4	conf	Athletics conference school belongs to
5	div	Division of school (DI, FCS, FBS, Power 5)
6	ms	Number of men's sports
7	ws	Number of women's sports
8	ts	Total number of sports
9	amen	Average full-time male undergraduate enrollment
10	afen	Average full-time female undergraduate enrollment
11	aten	Average full-time undergraduate enrollment
12	amath	Average number of male athletes
13	afath	Average number of female athletes
14	atath	Average number of total athletes
15	maidm1	Male athletic aid 2016-2017
16	maidm2	Male athletic aid 2017-2018
17	maidmf	Total male athletic aid 2016-2018
18	faidm1	Female athletic aid 2016-2017
19	faidm2	Female athletic aid 2017-2018
20	faidmf	Total female athletic aid 2016-2018
21	taidm1	Total athletic aid 2016-2017
22	taidm2	Total athletic aid 2017-2018
23	taidmf	Total athletic aid 2016-2018
24	mcruitm1	Male recruiting expenses: 2016-2017
25	mcruitm2	Male recruiting expenses: 2017-2018
26	mcruitf	Total male recruiting expenses: 2016-2018
27	fcruitm1	Female recruiting expenses: 2016-2017
28	fcruitm2	Female recruiting expenses: 2017-2018

Variable	Names	Definitions
29	fcruitmf	Total female recruiting expenses: 2016-2018
30	tcruitm1	Total recruiting expenses: 2016-2017
31	tcruitm2	Total recruiting expenses: 2017-2018
32	tcruitmf	Total recruiting expenses: 2016-2018
33	expm1	Total athletics expenses: 2016-2017
34	expm2	Total athletics expenses: 2017-2018
35	expmf	Total athletics expenses: 2016-2018
36	nf1	Directors' Cup points: fall 2016-2017 season
37	nf2	Directors' Cup points: fall 2017-2018 season
38	nff	Directors' Cup points: fall 2016-2018 seasons
39	nw1	Directors' Cup points: winter 2016-2017 season
40	nw2	Directors' Cup points: winter 2017-2018 season
41	nwf	Directors' Cup points: winter 2016-2018 seasons
42	ns1	Directors' Cup points: spring 2016-2017 season
43	ns2	Directors' Cup points: spring 2017-2018 season
44	nsf	Directors' Cup points: spring 2016-2018 seasons
45	ntot1	Total Directors' Cup points: 2016-2017 season
46	ntot2	Total Directors' Cup points: 2017-2018 season
47	ntotf	Total Directors' Cup points: 2016-2018 seasons

Note. The four divisions of classification further defined are DI (schools who participate in Division I but do not sponsor football), FCS (Football Championship Subdivision), FBS (Group of 5 schools who participate in the Football Bowl Subdivision), and Power 5 (Power 5 schools who participate in the Football Bowl Subdivision).

Once you have identified the column numbers and names, you have a clear idea of what the dataset contains. Once you have ascertained the contents of the dataset, you can make decisions as to whether or not you would like to add some columns of data or perhaps even remove some columns of data if you do not need them for analysis.

Suppose you would like to know the average athletic aid for male athletes at each school for the years 2016 to 2018. You can achieve this quickly and efficiently by adding a column. To get started, type the name of the column as though it already exists. We will name this column *ama*, which stands for average male aid. Then you simply provide the calculation R needs to complete the task using the variable for total male athletic aid for 2016 to 2018 (maidmf) divided by the variable for average number of male athletes (amath) multiplied by 2, so as to cover the number of years in the dataset. When done correctly, you will see that the columns and variables will rise from 47 to 48.

```
# Adding a column of data
css$ama <- (css$maidmf/(css$amath*2))

# Checking the result
css$ama
```

When you type the new variable name to check the result, it is apparent there is a problem. The number for the total male athletic aid column of the dataset is represented in millions. As such, the results are also displayed in millions, generally represented as long decimal values such as 0.008736059, which are difficult to read and make sense of. There are a couple of ways this problem can be remedied. The easiest is to multiply the total male athletic aid variable by a million prior to dividing it by the average number of male athletes over the two-year period being analyzed. To do this, you can simply overwrite the newly created *ama* column using the same name.

```
# Altering the column
css$ama <- (css$maidmf*1000000)/(css$amath*2)

# Checking the result
css$ama
```

At this point, the results are far more readable and easy to understand, but one last alteration will make a significant difference. Since these figures are now represented in thousands of dollars, having two decimal places does not make a lot of sense. We can remove them easily, again by overwriting the current column using the same name and including the round() function.

```
# Getting rid of the decimals using the round() function
css$ama <- round(css$ama, digits=0)
```

Knowing the process and what needs to be done allows you to create columns quickly using a single line of code. This time, create the new column of data for the css$ama variable using all the parameters detailed above in a single line of code.

```
# Getting it all accomplished in a single line of code
css$ama <- round((css$maidmf*1000000)/(css$amath*2), digits=0)
```

The importance of the parentheses in coding is now probably becoming apparent. Remember how they are used from a mathematical perspective. The first parentheses and end parentheses are used to wrap the round function around the other elements. The processes that need to take place first are wrapped in the internal sets of parentheses. That single line of code has been understood by R in the following way:

- css$maidmf is first converted to be represented in full number format, in this case millions of dollars in male athletic aid for 2016 to 2018.
- css$amath is multiplied by 2 so as to cover the number of years represented by millions of dollars in male athletic aid for 2016 to 2018.
- Now that those conversions have taken place, the css$maidmf figure is divided by the css$amath figure for each case included in the dataset.
- Lastly, the round function takes the css$ama results and removes the decimal points by setting digits= to zero.

Conversions and rounding are not always necessary when creating new columns of data, but it is important to check the results each time you do create a new column to ensure that the figures are being represented in a way that makes sense.

Removing columns of data is an even easier process. Suppose there is a column of data you do not find useful or necessary for the analysis you are conducting. If this is the case, you can set the value of the variable to NULL. Start by removing the column of data you just created since it can be easily re-created with the script you just developed.

```
# Removing a column of data
css$ama=NULL
```

Now that you have an understanding of how to add new columns of data to your dataset, let's add columns for average male athletic aid per athlete, average female athletic aid per athlete, average total athletic aid per athlete, average male recruiting expenses per athlete, average female recruiting expenses per athlete, and average total recruiting expenses per athlete. We will name these variables (cssama, cssafa, cssata, cssamr, cssafr, cssatr). Only minor changes to the css$ama code you developed are required. The changes are highlighted in red per each line of code.

```
# Average male athletic aid per athlete
css$ama <- round((css$maidmf*1000000)/(css$amath*2), digits=0)

# Average female athletic aid per athlete
css$afa <- round((css$faidmf*1000000)/(css$afath*2), digits=0)

# Average total athletic aid per athlete
css$ata <- round((css$taidmf*1000000)/(css$atath*2), digits=0)

# Average male recruiting expenses per athlete
css$amr <- round((css$mcruitmf*1000000)/(css$amath*2), digits=0)

# Average female recruiting expenses per athlete
css$afr <- round((css$fcruitmf*1000000)/(css$afath*2), digits=0)

# Average total recruiting expenses per athlete
css$atr <- round((css$tcruitmf*1000000)/(css$atath*2), digits=0)

# Check the results
css$ama
css$afa
css$ata
css$amr
css$afr
css$atr
```

To verify the number of columns is correct, you can use the ncol() function.

```
# Checking the number of columns contained in the css dataset
ncol(css)
```

The results indicate that all the columns have been added, thus bumping the total number of variables from 47 to 53. In essence, you have added 2,088 data points to your dataset by simply changing a couple of letters per line of code. It is a fast and easy process. All the numbers look to be represented in a way that is easy to understand and describe to others when reporting. You may notice there are some zero values in the ama, afa, and ata variables. These zeros represent the Ivy League schools that do not offer aid for participation in intercollegiate athletics. You will learn how to remove cases such as these from the analysis in the next section, which focuses on filtering and subsetting data.

ISOLATING VARIABLES WITH BRACKETS, C(), AND OPERATORS

Frequently in analytics, there is a need to isolate specific cases or variables for analysis. For instance, you may want to analyze specific groups in the dataset that are represented as factors or categorical variables. You can be specific, looking at a single case or a group of cases by filtering the nominal or grouping variables contained in the data. Additionally, you can easily limit the number of columns or measured variables you are analyzing. The process of filtering and subsetting data in R is easy and allows for rapid data manipulation by simply changing small pieces of text or, in many instances, only column numbers. Operators can also be used to filter data or to create subsets of data for analysis.

To get started, a discussion of how brackets are used in R coding is necessary. The bracket base is essentially represented as **df[r,c]**. The first value is the name of the df (dataset) that will be used in the filtering and subsetting process. In this case the dataset that will be used is the *css* dataset. The second value precedes the comma within the brackets. The values entered before the comma represent rows (cases) in your dataset. In the *css* dataset, each row represents a school. The third value appears after the comma within the brackets. The values entered after the comma represent columns in your dataset. In the *css* dataset, each column contains categorical or measured data representative of the schools included in the dataset. To filter or subset the data, you can limit the rows or columns in an endless variety of ways. The key is to limit the data in a way that produces the results you are looking for.

Column combinations and filtering allow you to compare expenses across programs.
Don Juan Moore/Getty Images

Filtering Data

As is the case with the $ sign, brackets need to reference a dataset before filtering and subsetting data. The name of the dataset is entered first and is followed by [,] where you will filter the cases and variables. In this section, you will start small and build from the base up. Start by limiting the data to the first 10 cases of the dataset. If you have used Excel in the past, you are familiar with the use of a colon to select a set of values.

```
# First 10 cases of the css dataset
css[1:10,]
```

You will see that the result of the output in the console panel is limited to the first 10 cases (rows) of the dataset. You will also see that all the variables in the dataset are included. This is because the value after the comma was left blank. A blank value appearing before the comma indicates that all cases (schools) should be included. A blank value appearing after the comma indicates that all variables (columns of data) should be included.

Sticking with the blank column value after the comma, you can change the cases included to look at a single school across all variables. In this example, select Troy University as the school you are interested in. Earlier in the operators section, you probably noticed that the equals value when writing code in R is the double equals sign of == when selecting a specific value such as a name. If you do not know how the schools are labeled, you can use the levels() function you learned earlier and apply it to the css$school variable. It is also important to note that R is case sensitive. Lastly, when specifying a case by name, the use of quotation marks is required. Using Troy as the example, we can isolate this specific case quickly and easily using the css$school variable.

```
# Isolating a single case in R - Troy University
css[css$school=="Troy",]
```

You will see that the complete list of categorical and measured variables for Troy University is included in the output, while all other schools are eliminated from the analysis.

Aside from a single school, you may want to look at a group of schools. Suppose you were interested in not only seeing Troy but also all the other schools in the state of Alabama. This alteration can be made quickly using the css$state variable instead of the css$school variable to limit the cases included in the analysis.

```
# Isolating a group of cases in R - Alabama schools
css[css$state=="AL",]
```

In the console panel, you will see the results are limited to the nine Alabama schools included in the *css* dataset. The extent to which you include and exclude cases is entirely up to you. At this point you may decide to just look at schools in Alabama that spent more than $60 million on athletics from 2016 to 2018. This can be achieved by adding the & operator and the > operator using the css$expmf variable.

```
# Isolating Alabama schools who spent more than $60 million on
athletics for 2016-2018
css[css$state=="AL" & css$expmf > 60,]
```

Now you have pared the result down to the four Alabama schools that spent more than $60 million in the two-year span from 2016 to 2018. Included in the group are Alabama, Auburn, Troy, and the University of Alabama Birmingham (UAB). A final adjustment could be made to highlight the schools in Alabama that spent more than $60 million in the two-year span from 2016 to 2018 and that belong to Power 5 conferences by adding another & operator and the css$div variable.

```
# Isolating Alabama schools who spent more than $60 million
on athletics for 2016-2018 and who are members of a power 5
conference
css[css$state==“AL” & css$expmf > 60 & css$div==“Power 5”,]
```

The results are now limited to the two Power 5 schools in the state: Alabama and Auburn. The ability to quickly manipulate data with a few keystrokes is a major advantage of working in R.

The value after the comma, as discussed earlier, represents the columns in the dataset. This is particularly important because oftentimes analysts are not interested in looking at every column of data when looking for specific results. Earlier in the chapter, you also learned the value of the colnames() function because it gives you the variable number and name in the dataset. When isolating data by columns, the combine **c()** function plays a central role. The c() function will create a collection of the columns you want included in the analysis. Going back to the earlier example of Alabama schools, you may simply want to know what each school spent on athletics during the years 2016 to 2018. This is a remarkably simple result to achieve and is one of the reasons R is so efficient when working with numbers. Using either the colnames() function or the variable sheet from the online study guide, you see that the column number for the expmf variable is 35. Therefore, to get the desired result, that is the column number to use with the c() function.

```
# Isolating total athletics expenses of Alabama schools for the
years 2016-2018
css[css$state==“AL”, c(35)]
```

When you execute the line of code, however, you probably notice a fundamental problem. There are no school names, just the athletics expenses. To include the school names, simply add column 1 to your c() function. This is the column number associated with the variable school. All columns you want included in the output are separated by a comma.

```
# Adding the school name to the output
css[css$state==“AL”, c(1,35)]
```

Like the filtering options for cases to be included in the analysis, the column combinations can be anything you like and are rapidly interchangeable. One could get the same output for average number of total athletes instead of total athletics expenses for 2016-2018 by changing a single column number in the c() function, in this case changing 35 to 14.

```
# Changing total athletics expenses to average number of total
athletes
css[css$state==“AL”, c(1,14)]
```

You can select whichever rows and columns you want to analyze with minimal input and effort. By way of an example, try isolating the results to a specific state of your choice by filtering the rows for state and the columns for school name, conference, division, total athletics expenses for 2016 to 2018, and total Directors' Cup points for 2016 to 2018 (columns 1, 4, 5, 35, and 47 of the *css* dataset). Sticking with Alabama as the example, the results are presented in table 2.2.

TABLE 2.2   NCAA Division I Schools in Alabama

Name	Conference	Division	Total athletics expenses in $millions	Total Directors' Cup points (2016-2018)
Alabama	SEC	Power 5	293.2	1,681.75
Auburn	SEC	Power 5	258.2	1,568.25
Troy	Sun Belt	FBS	61.2	221.50
Jacksonville State	OVC	FCS	28.9	216.00
Samford	SoCon	FCS	39.9	316.50
UAB	Conference USA	FBS	63.7	25.00
South Alabama	Sun Belt	FBS	49.5	155.00
Alabama State	SWAC	FCS	19.8	180.00
Alabama A&M	SWAC	FCS	18.8	0.00

Using brackets, operators, and the `c()` function to narrow down the cases and variables you are analyzing produces quick results. If you are wondering what the profile of any NCAA Division I school looks like based on the variables included in this dataset, you now have the power to do that.

Visit HK*Propel* to access the video tutorials on filtering, subsetting, and ordering data.

Subsetting Data

Filtering data is a particularly useful approach to looking at specific cases and variables in datasets. In many instances, however, analysts are interested in conducting multiple data manipulations and creating visualizations using specific subsets of data. To perform multiple data manipulations and create visualizations without applying the same filters repeatedly, it is oftentimes helpful to create an object in the global environment with set parameters. When done correctly, these become smaller versions of datasets based on the data contained in the complete *css* dataset.

To create subsets of data, the same filtering rules apply. There are a couple of additional operators aside from the & sign that will also be used in this section, including the | (or) operator and the != (does not equal) operator. To get started, let's create a new object in the global environment panel that is subset of data that will only look at schools located in New England. The New England states are Maine, New Hampshire, Vermont, Massachusetts, Connecticut, and Rhode Island. This new subset of data will be named *ne*, which stands for New England. Using the `css$state` variable to limit the cases included in the analysis in conjunction with the | (or) operator will achieve the desired result.

```
# Creating the New England subset
ne <- css[css$state=="ME" | css$state=="NH" |
          css$state=="MA" | css$state=="VT" |
          css$state=="CT" | css$state=="RI",]

# Checking the result and running the summary() function
ne
summary(ne)
```

The newly created subset should have appeared as an object in the global environment panel to indicate that the *css* dataset, which contains 348 observations (schools), has now been narrowed down to 22 observations (schools) in a new subsetted dataset called *ne*. Because the value after the comma within the brackets was left blank, all columns of data have been included from the *css* dataset. This number should match the number of variables indicated in the *css* dataset. The variable labels remain unaffected and are therefore the same for both datasets.

Two important things must be noted at this point. First, you will see that when writing the code, three lines were used. This is not mandatory. Using the return or enter key simply drops the code down a line to preserve horizontal space and keep everything nicely organized and visible in the script panel. As coding develops in length, keeping it organized and visible can be very helpful. The other item of note is that moving forward you must remember to use the new subsetted dataset name when conducting an analysis. For example, variables will now be prefaced with the name *ne* rather than *css* if you are looking to analyze just the New England schools. For instance, if you would like to look at total athletic aid in millions of dollars for the years 2016 to 2018 at just the New England schools, this would be achieved by manipulating the `ne$taidmf` variable rather than the `css$taidmf` variable.

```
# Total athletic aid in millions at New England schools for 2016-
2018
sum(ne$taidmf)
```

Like the filtering of datasets, the combinations of subsetted datasets you can create are only limited by your imagination and the data contained in the overall dataset of *css*. Subsetting data does not require much time or effort. For instance, if you wanted to look at all schools with the exception of the Power 5 schools, that subsetted dataset could be created very quickly using the `!=` (does not equal) operator in conjunction with the `css$div` variable. Let's use the name *nonp5* for this new subsetted dataset.

```
# Creating a subset that eliminates power 5 schools
nonp5 <- css[css$div != "Power 5",]
```

The new subsetted dataset appears in your global environment panel and indicates that the 65 schools in Power 5 from the *css* dataset have been removed leaving the other 283 schools in the new *nonp5* dataset. You can create as many subsetted datasets as you like for future use. The original *css* dataset will never go away or be altered negatively by creating new subsets of data. The last twist on creating subsets will be to decide which columns of data you want to include. If you were simply interested in looking at the school name, total athletics expenses for 2016 to 2018, and total Directors' Cup points for 2016 to 2018, you would use the `c()` function along with the column numbers for the variables `school`, `expmf`, and `ntotf` (1, 35, and 47).

```
# Altering nonp5 subset to limit variables included in the dataset
nonp5 <- css[css$div != "Power 5", c(1,35,47)]
```

You will see that the number of observations or schools has remained steady at 283 in the new altered dataset, but the number of variables included in the dataset has been reduced to three. You will learn how to order the data later in the chapter, which is a particularly helpful tool for answering questions such as "Who spent the most money outside of the Power 5 schools for the years 2016 to 2018?" As is usually the case in R, the answer to this question is only a few keystrokes away.

Now that you have a clear understanding of how to subset data, you can create a few new objects in your global environment to make analysis of certain variables more representative of the data contained in the dataset. For instance, if you wanted to look at which schools offered the most male athletic aid per athlete, female athletic aid per athlete, and total athletic aid per athlete at the NCAA Division I level, it would make sense to remove schools that spent zero dollars on athletic aid. As discussed earlier, these are the Ivy League schools. There are two easy methods to remove the Ivy League schools from the analysis by creating a subsetted dataset. Call this new dataset *nonivy*.

```
# Removing the Ivy League Schools from aid analysis - Method 1
nonivy <- css[css$conf != "Ivy League",]
```

```
# Removing the Ivy League Schools from aid analysis - Method 2
nonivy <- css[css$taidmf > 0,]
```

Whether you limit the data by setting the value as != "Ivy League" or by setting the value of total aid in millions of dollars for 2016 to 2018 to > 0, they both achieve the same result. You will see that the eight Ivy League schools have been removed from the *css* dataset, leaving you with 340 observations. Now, when conducting analysis or data visualization on athletic aid, you can use the newly created *nonivy* dataset instead of the *css* dataset.

Like the athletic aid analysis, another core component of the *css* dataset examines total points scored in the Directors' Cup competition. Regrettably, not all schools included in the dataset scored points for the 2016-2018 seasons. Thus, when analyzing results based on Directors' Cup scoring, schools that scored zero points during this time period should be removed. Later you can limit the results even further, but for now, you should at least eliminate the non-scorers. As you have learned, the process simply involves limiting the number of cases included in the subsetted dataset by manipulating the `css$ntotf` variable. You can use the name *nac* for this newly created subset of data.

Visit HK*Propel* to access the video tutorials on removing objects from the global environment, creating and removing columns of data, and saving a new *.csv* file.

```
# Removing the non-scorers from the css dataset
nac <- css[css$ntotf > 0,]
```

DESCRIPTIVE STATISTICS

Now that you have a fundamental understanding of how R operates, you can begin to quantitatively analyze the data using **descriptive statistics**. Common descriptive statistics include frequencies (n counts), percentages, sum totals, means, standard deviations, and quartiles, all of which will be examined here.

Visit HK*Propel* to access the video tutorial on common statistical functions in R.

Frequencies and Percentages

A common first step in most data analysis includes working with the factor variables included in your dataset. The factor variables are categorical in nature and therefore are usually represented in a character format that is not amenable to statistical analysis. They are, however, important in describing the cases included in the dataset as well as for ordering factor data. Commonly, the first table presented in a report is a "demographics table" that describes who or what is included in the dataset and to what extent. This table is broken down by categories that will impact how the reader interprets the results.

The two most important items that are required in a table of this nature are **frequencies (n counts)** and **percentages**. In other words, how many of each category are included in the dataset and what percentage of the overall population that category represents. You do not need to create a section in the demographics table for every factor variable included in the dataset, but you should create one for the variables that have some meaning moving forward. For instance, if you conducted a frequency count and percentage analysis for the variable of css$school, the result would indicate that each school has an n count of 1 and represents approximately 0.003 percent of the total population. This is not a particularly useful finding. The same is true for the category of conference affiliation. Because there are 32 conferences, the overall n counts and percentages of representation will be similar and not very useful for interpreting the results. Though there is some variation between n counts and percentages in the css$conf factor variable, they are essentially negligible.

For the purposes of analyzing the *css* dataset, the two factor variables of interest are the css$class variable (state school and private school classification) and the css$div variable (DI, FCS, FBS, and Power 5 categories). In these factor variables, the n counts and percentages will be larger and therefore more meaningful when looking at relationships between categorical variables and measured variables such as css$expmf (total athletics expenses for the years 2016-2018). Because these factor variables are represented in a character format, performing statistical functions will not be possible. Instead, you will rely on the **table()** and **prop.table()** functions. Using these functions will allow you to quantify the n counts and percentages of the categorical factor variables contained in the dataset.

To get started, identify the categorical variable of interest that you would like to include in the demographics table. The first variable to attack is the classification variable that describes whether each school in the dataset is classified as a private school or as a state school. The overall goal is to determine how many schools are private schools and how many schools are state schools. Once the n counts have been generated, they can be converted to percentages to determine the percentage of the classifications in relation to the overall sample. To begin, create an object called class using the table() function to identify the n count for each classification contained in the *css* dataset.

```
# Producing the n count for the classification variable and
checking the result
class <- table(css$class)
class
```

The result indicates there are 118 private schools and 230 state schools included in the *css* dataset. This result makes sense because there are 348 Division I schools included in the dataset. The next step is to determine the percentages that these figures represent in relation to the total number of schools included in the *css* dataset. To develop the percentages for each of the n counts, you can use the `prop.table()` function in conjunction with the `class` object you just created.

```
# Producing percentages for the classification variable
prop.table(class)
```

When you execute the code, you will see that the n count data is transformed into percentages. If you would like to make a small adjustment to the coding to make the result easier to read and report, you can multiply the `prop.table` function by 100 to shift the decimal two spaces to the right and include a rounding function to reduce the final figure to a single decimal point.

```
# Making the prop.table percentages easier to read and report
round(100*prop.table(class), digits=1)
```

The results indicate that 33.9 percent of the schools included in the dataset are classified as private schools, while 66.1 percent are classified as state schools. Having undertaken this simple process, you can make minor alterations to the code to develop the n counts and percentages for the `css$div` variable. The minor alterations required are indicated in red.

Visit *HKPropel* to access the video tutorials on n counts and percentages, ordering factor variables, and counting and ordering data.

```
# Creating n counts and percentages for the category of division
div <- table(css$div)
div
round(100*prop.table(div), digits=1)
```

Having the n counts and percentages for the categories of classification and division allows you to report the findings using a demographics table (see table 2.3).

Aside from developing a demographics table to describe the characteristics of the cases included in the dataset separately, there may be times when you want to table factor variables as combined groupings. For instance, you may want to look at the categorical variables of classification and division together to determine how many state schools and how many private schools exist in each of the four divisions.

Using the same coding as above, you can create a cross table (see table 2.4) by simply adding a comma after the first variable being tabled (`css$class`) and including the second variable (`css$div`) after the comma in the function. You can name this new object cd to stand for classification and division. Aside from the comma and additional variable being added, the coding remains the same as before. The changes in the new object are indicated in red.

```
# Cross table with 2 categorical variables
cd <- table(css$class, css$div)
cd
round(100*prop.table(cd), digits=1)
```

TABLE 2.3   Characteristics of NCAA Division I Institutions

Variable	Category	n	%
Classification	Private school	118	33.9
	State school	230	66.1
Division	Division I	97	27.9
	FCS	125	35.9
	FBS	61	17.5
	Power 5	65	18.7

TABLE 2.4   NCAA Division I Schools by Classification and Division

Division	Private schools		State schools	
	n	%	n	%
Division I	51	14.7	46	13.2
FCS	49	14.1	76	21.8
FBS	6	1.7	55	15.8
Power 5	12	3.4	53	15.2

Counting and Ordering Data

As previously stated, it does not always make sense to table factor variables by providing n counts and percentages. The earlier example of tabling factor variables such as css$school and css$conf demonstrated that these calculations would be of minimal value. There are, however, times when analysts would like to count instances of occurrence based on factor variables and order them in a way that paints a stronger picture of the overall results. To achieve this goal, most analysts can use a simple **count()** function and then create ordered objects that are amenable to analysis. To use the count() function, start by activating the *plyr* package you installed earlier.

```
# Activating the plyr package
library(plyr)
```

Once you have activated the *plyr* package, you are able to use the count() function to create frequency counts that indicate the number of times each case in the dataset contains a particular designation. You can start by using the count() function to determine how many NCAA Division I schools are located in each of the 50 states included in the dataset.

```
# Using the count() function to determine how many schools are
located in each state
count(css$state)
```

The above function produces a list of states and the associated number of Division I schools located in each state in the console panel. The information is useful, but you will find that after getting the listing of states and number of schools in those states, there is not much else you can do with the data. Because much of sport business analytics relies on ordering data, the better course of action would be to create an object that captures the counts as frequencies. In this example, create an object called states by using the same coding as above.

```
# Creating an object using the count() function
states <- count(css$state)
```

When you have run this line of code, you will see that a new object has been created in your global environment panel. There are 50 observations (one for each state included in the dataset) and two variables (the state abbreviation and the frequency count associated with each state abbreviation). Again, the advantage to creating an object is that it easily allows you to make a comparison of Division I school state affiliations using the **order()** function as well as the head() and tail() functions discussed earlier in the chapter.

To order data, the bracket configuration will be used (as discussed earlier), most notably in the filtering and subsetting of data section. The variable to be referenced will be the new frequency count variable states$freq you just created contained in the new states object you added to the global environment. Using the name sord, which stands for state order, you can now create an object listing the states with the most schools first using the order() function. You will need to use a minus sign ahead of the variable name to create an object in descending order. If you do not use a minus sign in front of the variable name, the data will be ordered in ascending order. Also, remember to use the comma after the parentheses to include all columns in the sord object.

```
# Creating an ordered object listing states with the most schools
first (descending order)
sord <- states[order(-states$freq),]
```

If you have executed the line of code correctly, you will see that you have again created an object with 50 observations and two variables. However, these observations are now listed in order of most to least in relation to number of schools per state contained in the dataset. You can verify your results by employing one of two methods. The first method would be to simply type the new object's name into the scripts panel and hit ctrl+enter. This produces the list from top to bottom.

```
# Viewing the ordered results - method # 1
sord
```

This method, however, oftentimes produces a list that is too long to easily navigate. For instance, if you ordered the *css* dataset by most money spent to least money spent, you would have 348 distinct entries to sift through. Therefore, the second method of using the head() and tail() functions to view the results is preferable.

Using the sord object you have created, let's just look at the top 20 in terms of number of schools per state and the bottom 5 in terms of number of schools per state. Remember, when using the head() and tail() functions, R will default to the first six or last six cases unless you include the n= statement to specify the number of cases you would like to include in the output.

```
# Using the head() and tail() functions to view the ordered
results - method # 2
head(sord, n=20)
tail(sord, n=5)
```

The previous order() function was demonstrated using factor data developed using the count() function, but the order() function is also easily applied to numeric data. Oftentimes, people want to develop top-25 lists. In this way, ordering data becomes an essential tool for sport analysts. If somebody were to ask you to develop a list of the top-25 schools spending the most on Division I athletics for the 2017-2018 season, you could develop the list very quickly using the order() function along with the c() function to isolate the variables of school name (column 1 of the *css* dataset) and grand total athletics expenses for 2017 to 2018 (column 34 of the *css* dataset).

```
# Using the order() function to determine the top-25 spending
schools in Division I athletics
spend <- css[order(-css$expm2), c(1,34)]
head(spend, n=25)
```

To view the bottom 25 in spending, you can use the tail() function instead of the head() function, or you can simply remove the minus sign proceeding the css$-expm2 variable to re-create the spend object in ascending order. The decision comes down to how you would like to view the data. Using the tail() function instead of the head() function will produce a list starting with the highest-spending school in the bottom 25 and the values will dwindle as you move down through the list. This is because the original spend object was created in descending order. If you change the order by removing the minus sign to re-create the spend object, the results will start with the lowest-spending school in the bottom 25 and rise. Let's try both methods.

```
# Using the tail() function to determine the bottom-25 spending
schools in descending order
tail(spend, n=25)

# Re-creating the spend object determine the bottom-25 spending
schools in ascending order
spend <- css[order(css$expm2), c(1,34)]
head(spend, n=25)
```

Ordering data is a powerful technique for analysts to employ when exploring factor data and measured data, particularly when used in tandem with filtered or subsetted datasets.

Basic Statistical Functions in R

Now that you have an understanding of how to work with factor data, it is time to look at some of the basic statistical functions you can use to analyze measured data. As you learned in the section dedicated to exploring the dataset, the `summary()` function can return some immediate results of interest.

```
# Using the summary() function to get some basic descriptive
statistics
summary(css)
```

Visit HK*Propel* to access the video tutorials on `sum()`, `colSums()`, `mean()`, `colMeans()`, `rowSums()`, `rowMeans()`, `sapply()`, `lapply()`, and `aggregate()` functions and the tutorial on quartiles.

The statistics that are produced using the `summary()` function on numeric variables will provide you minimum and maximum values, first and third quartiles, as well as the **median** (middle value) and **mean** (average value). This can be a good jumping off point for understanding the measured variables in your dataset, but they are incomplete and inadequate for presenting data in a formal manner. For instance, traditionally one would like to include the **standard deviation** along with the mean for a reported result to see the extent to which the values vary in a dataset, but standard deviation is not included in the `summary()` function output. Producing the results you are looking for will require you to look at each of these elements separately, at least to begin with. Later you will learn to write functions that can produce a customized set of statistics for variables of interest.

Sums and colSums

A common starting point for analyzing numeric data is to look at the sums of specific measured variables. For instance, you may wish to report the total amount of money spent in Division I athletics for the years 2016 to 2018. This can be easily achieved by using the `sum()` function in conjunction with the `css$expmf` variable.

```
# Calculating the total amount of money spent on Division I
athletics for 2016-2018
sum(css$expmf)
```

The result indicates that $26,426.1 million was spent on Division I college athletics from 2016 to 2018. This result is a good reminder that data should always be altered to present the findings in a palatable manner. For many, imagining the meaning of $26,000 million is a bit of a stretch. Because of the flexibility of the operators in R, this result can be quickly modified to be represented in billions of dollars rather than millions of dollars by simply dividing the initial result by 1,000. Additionally, reporting money in the billions of dollars to the fourth decimal point does not make a great deal of sense, so the round() function will also be included to reduce the final number to a single decimal point.

```
# Changing the result from millions to billions and rounding to a
single decimal point
round(sum(css$expmf)/1000, digits=1)
```

The final result indicates that $26.4 billion was spent on Division I college athletics for the years 2016 to 2018. The same calculation can be applied to the categories of css$maidmf, css$faidmf, and css$taidmf describing the total amount spent on male athletic aid, female athletic aid, and total athletic aid, respectively. These amounts can be calculated by making small adjustments to the code. For the purpose of this exercise, just focus on the total athletic aid for 2016 to 2018. The adjustment to the code is indicated in red.

```
# Calculating total athletic aid for 2016-2018 in billions
round(sum(css$taidmf)/1000, digits=1)
```

The result indicates that $5.2 billion was spent on total athletic aid for the years 2016 to 2018. However, the same code should not be used when calculating male athletic recruiting expenses, female athletic recruiting expenses, and total athletic recruiting expenses because the final result would be represented as fractions of billions. When analyzing the css$mcruitmf, css$fcruitmf, and css$tcruitmf variables, they should be reported in millions. Therefore, the minor adjustment made to the previous code would be to remove the division by 1,000 calculation. You can also eliminate the round() function if you wish because the result will only include two decimal places. That final option is up to you.

```
# Calculating total athletics recruiting expenses for 2016-2018 in
millions
sum(css$tcruitmf)
```

The sum() function is a quick way to understand the totals of measured variables and present data that is representative of the entire sample included in a dataset. Often, however, there are instances when you will want to use the sum() function on multiple columns of data at the same time. Using the sum() function on each measured variable individually would be time-consuming and tedious. Therefore, there is a way in which analysts can combine the filtering and subsetting techniques learned earlier in the chapter with the **colSums()** function to produce totals for multiple measured variables in a single line of code.

Suppose you wanted to know the totals for all the athletics recruiting expenses variables included in the dataset simultaneously. The variables are represented in columns 24 to 32 of the *css* dataset. Using the colSums() function in conjunction with the bracket structure to isolate the selected columns will produce the result you are looking for.

```
# Multiple column sums for athletics recruiting expenses
colSums(css[ ,24:32])
```

The colSums() function does not require the use of ranges of variables. Each variable to be used can be selected by the user, who can include as many or as few of the variables desired using the same strategy employed in the filtering and subsetting of data section. For example, if you wanted to look only at male athletics recruiting expenses, female athletics recruiting expenses, and total athletics recruiting expenses for the 2016-2017 year, the code can easily be modified to isolate columns 24, 27, and 30 of the dataset. These are the columns associated with the variables `css$mcruitm1`, `css$fcruitm1`, and `css$tcruitm1`. Because the selected columns are not a consecutive range of columns, the `c()` function will also need to be added. The modifications to the code are indicated in red.

```
# Changing range of columns 24-32 to only include columns 24,27,
and 30
colSums(css[ ,c(24,27,30)])
```

Means and colMeans

Another common statistic generated from measured variables is the mean value. To determine the mean value of any measured variable, you can simply use the **mean()** function. In this instance, you can determine the mean number of sports sponsored at Division I institutions. You can also add the `round()` function to remove the decimal places altogether if you would like total sports represented as a whole number.

```
# Calculating the mean value of total sports sponsored in Division
I
mean(css$ts)
```

```
# Rounding total sports sponsored to the nearest whole number
round(mean(css$ts), digits=0)
```

Like the `colSums()` function presented earlier, the **colMeans()** function allows users to calculate the mean value of multiple columns of data simultaneously.

```
# Calculating the mean values of male, female, and total athletic
aid 2016-2017
colMeans(css[ ,c(15,18,21)])
```

This is the point when many people ask if standard deviation works the same. The answer is yes and no. You can use the **sd()** function to determine the standard deviation of any measured variable of interest, but there is no colSds() function that would be comparable to the `colSums()` and `colMeans()` functions. We will address the standard deviation calculation applied over multiple columns when we get to using statistical functions with the `apply()`, `sapply()`, and `aggregate()` functions.

Another common question is whether or not similar functions exist for calculating the sums and means of rows of data. The answer is absolutely. The functions of **rowSums()** and **rowMeans()** can be very useful and are operationalized the same as the `colSums()` and `colMeans()` functions from a coding perspective.

Quartiles

Quartiles are a popular way of understanding the distribution of data within a dataset. The functions used for determining the quartiles of a dataset or specific selected variables are the `summary()` function and the `quantile()` function. The `quantile()` function will produce what is essentially an exact replica of the `summary()` function output with a couple of small differences. When using the `summary()` function, you will receive the minimum and maximum values, the first and third quartiles, and the mean and median values for either the entire dataset or for selected variables. For the purposes of this example, use the summary() function in conjunction with the css$ntotf variable, which refers to the total points earned in the Directors' Cup competition for the years 2016 to 2018.

```
# Quartile data using the summary() function
summary(css$ntotf)
```

The **quantile()** function produces the same results as the summary() function minus the mean value and does not label the output in the same way as the summary() function. Regardless of which method you ultimately choose to use, it will be reported the same to include the first and third quartiles along with the range of values and median value. The 25 percent and 75 percent quartiles reported in the quantile() function output will match the first and third quartiles reported in the summary() function output. These are referred to as the lower and upper quartiles. The 0 percent and 100 percent values reported in the quantile() function output will match the minimum and maximum values reported in the summary() function output. This provides analysts with the range they need to report. Lastly, the 50 percent quartile reported in the quantile() function output will match the median value reported in the summary() function output.

```
# Quartile data using the quantile() function
quantile(css$ntotf)
```

apply() and sapply() Functions

The apply() and sapply() functions are powerful tools for maximizing efficiency in data analytics. They are a malleable set of features capable of running mass amounts of quantitative statistical analyses simultaneously. You can employ core functions such as mean(), sd(), and sum() over large quantities of data. The extent to which you employ the apply() and sapply() functions is up to you, but understanding the core parameters of apply() and sapply() will empower you to take great strides.

EXERCISING CAUTION WHEN USING STATISTICAL ANALYSIS

At this point, you have been able to develop code that produces meaningful statistical results. However, relying on these figures may produce a biased report. It is important to check that the cases you are including in the analysis are appropriate. By way of an example, we can look at the mean value of total athletic aid in Division I athletics for the years 2016 to 2018. If you were to use the summary() function or the mean() function to report the mean value, you would get a result of $14.97 million. The problem with using the mean value reported from the summary() or mean() functions is that those functions include all the schools in the dataset. This can be problematic when you encounter instances of zero value.

When looking at the dataset, we determined earlier that there are eight schools that reported zero values for male, female, and total athletic aid. These eight schools comprise the Ivy League, a conference that does not offer aid for athletics participation. Including these eight schools when producing the mean values for athletic aid skews the results. It is important to make decisions about which data will be included in any given analysis. If you determine that these eight schools should be eliminated from the analysis to produce a more accurate mean value for the athletic aid variables, then that should be done before conducting the test. Whereas the result earlier indicated that the mean value of athletic aid in Division I was $14.97 million, removing these eight zero values yields a mean value of $15.32 million.

Without getting too technical, the `apply` family of functions was developed to streamline coding and remove the need to create loops (Fanara, 2019). This allows analysts to minimize coding and maximize efficiency. The primary difference between `apply()` and `sapply()` is the objective of the analysis and the formatting of the input and output of data. While the difference in formats of data such as vectors, lists, and matrices has not been a focal point of this chapter, it is something that can (and should) be explored at a deeper level as you progress in your R capabilities throughout your career. For the sake of simplicity and consistency, however, we will continue to work with *css* in a dataset format with outputs in a vector format. Both the `apply()` function and the `sapply()` function will accept the dataset format for input and produce vector format results as output.

apply() Function

The **`apply()`** function uses a set structure that requires three elements for analysis.

1. The data that is to be analyzed.
2. MARGIN—A determination as to whether the data will be analyzed by row or by column. `MARGIN=1` indicates that the data will be analyzed by row. `MARGIN=2` indicates that the data will be analyzed by columns.
3. The function that is to be applied to the data.

As an example, suppose you wanted to know the sum totals for every column of data included in the *css* dataset. The simple coding structure is as follows:

```
# Sum totals for all variables included in the css dataset
apply(css, MARGIN=2, sum)
```

When you run this line of code, however, you will find that you get an error message. This is because the `sum()` function (as well as all the other statistical functions) can only be applied to numeric variables. There are two ways to deal with this situation. You can either create a subset of data to eliminate all the factor variables or you can filter the data to only include the numeric variables. Both approaches will require the use of the bracket structure.

```
# Creating a subset of the css dataset to only include the numeric
variables
css2 <- css[ ,c(6:47)]
```

When you run this line of code, you will see a newly created object appear in the global environment. The `css2` object includes all the same schools (observations = 348), but the variables have dropped from 53 to 48. The columns that have been removed from the *css* dataset to create the *css2* dataset are `css$school`, `css$state`, `css$class`, `css$conf`, and `css$div`. These are the five factor variables that the `sum()` function cannot be applied to. Now when you use the `apply()` function in conjunction with the *css2* dataset, you will achieve the desired result.

```
# Sum totals for all variables included in the css2 dataset
apply(css2, MARGIN=2, sum)
```

If you do not feel you will need a subsetted dataset for future analysis, you can simply embed the code into the `apply()` function to let R know that you only want to run the function on selected variables. This approach should also be familiar to you from earlier in the chapter. Knowing that the first five variables in the *css* dataset are factor variables, you can create the appropriate code for the `sum()` function to be applied only to the numeric variables.

```
# Sum totals for only numeric variables included in the css
dataset
apply(css[ ,c(6:47)], MARGIN=2, sum)
```

Both approaches are effective ways of obtaining results for large amounts of data with minimal coding effort.

Working with row data may involve an additional step. If you were to run the `sum()` function with the `apply()` function and set the margin to 1, you would get the results, but you would not necessarily know which school each result represented. Remember, each row corresponds to a specific case included in the dataset—in this case, individual schools. The schools are not the names of the rows; rather, they are considered a factor variable with 348 levels. The row names are actually the row numbers 1 to 348. Knowing the sum total and mean value of a measured variable for row 127 would probably not mean anything to you. To deal with this issue, you can simply create a new dataset called *css3* that contains all the *css* data, but this time you would include the argument of `row.names=1` to the script. In other words, you will import the data again using the `read.csv()` function, but this time use column 1 of the dataset as row names instead of importing column 1 as a factor variable.

```
# Creating a new dataset using column 1 data for row names
css3 <- read.csv("css.csv", row.names=1)
```

You will see that the new *css3* dataset has one less variable than the original *css* dataset. The variable that has been removed is `css$school`, which is now represented as row names. Now that the row names are represented, you can go ahead and use the statistical functions with the `apply()` function to produce the results you desire. Because the columns of data per row in the *css3* dataset range from number of sports sponsored to average enrollment to total expenses in millions, it would be somewhat silly to produce sums and means for the rows of the *css3* dataset. However, you may want to look at data that matches. For the purposes of this exercise, use the `apply()` function along with the *css3* dataset to get sum totals for athletic aid from 2016 to 2018 for each school. The columns of data included in the analysis will be `css3$-maidm1`, `css3$maidm2`, `css$faidm1`, and `css$faidm2`. These are columns 14, 15, 17, and 18 of the new *css3* dataset.

```
# Sum totals for athletic aid by school 2016-2018
apply(css3[ ,c(14,15,17,18)], MARGIN=1, sum)
```

At this point, you have probably noticed that the `sum()` functions you just ran with the `apply()` function are remarkably similar to the `colSums()` and `rowSums()` functions discussed earlier in the chapter. The same is true if you were to use the `apply()` function to determine the mean values for multiple columns or rows of data. It is essentially the same as the `colMeans()` and `rowMeans()` functions. The `apply()` function, however, can be used with an array of statistical functions that are not available as `col` or `row` functions. In the earlier sections on `colSums` and `colMeans`, you learned that there is no `colSds` function for standard deviation or `colMedians` function for getting the median value. The same is true of the row functions. Using the `apply()` function, however, all of these statistical measures are able to be applied to multiple columns or rows simultaneously. Some popular statistical measures used with the `apply()` and `sapply()` functions are as follows:

sum—total value

mean—mean value

sd—standard deviation

median—median value

min—minimum value

max—maximum value

range—range of values

quantile—quartile data

Sapply() Function

The **sapply()** function is similar to the `apply()` function but does not include a `MARGIN=` setting to determine whether you want to analyze rows or columns of data. All that is required is the data name and the function that will be applied to the data. The `sapply()` function uses a set structure that requires the following two elements for analysis:

1. The data that is to be analyzed
2. The function that is to be applied to the data

To get started, you can create a simple line of code to produce quartile data for athletic aid for both males and females for periods 2016 to 2017 and 2017 to 2018. In the *css* dataset, these variables are associated with columns 15, 16, 18, and 19. Because of the eight Ivy League schools that do not offer athletic aid for participation, you can also include a filter to eliminate those schools from the final results.

```
# Quartile data for male and female athletic aid 2016-2017 and
2017-2018
sapply(css[css$conf != "Ivy League" ,c(15,16,18,19)], quantile)
```

Both `apply()` and `sapply()` are efficient ways for developing descriptive statistics over large amounts of data. Whether you are looking to develop results by row or by columns, these tools will help you achieve your goals.

aggregate() Function

The **aggregate()** function is the final tool you will develop in this chapter for working with descriptive statistics. The `aggregate()` function works in much the same way as the `sapply()` function but allows you to break down results based on categorical factor variables. In the `sapply()` section, we applied the desired functions to develop results for entire groups of data as a whole. By employing the `aggregate()` function and adding a `by=list()` setting, we can further break down the results. The `aggregate()` function uses a set structure that requires three elements for analysis.

1. The data that is to be analyzed.
2. `by=list()`—A determination of how you would like the results aggregated.
3. The function that is to be applied to the data.

In this instance, suppose you wanted to develop the mean value for number of male sports, female sports, and total sports (columns 6, 7, and 8 of the *css* dataset) but break the results down by the classification variable of private schools versus state schools. By using the `aggregate()` function, you can see how the results differ for the two levels of the categorical factor variable `css$class`.

```
# Average number of male, female, and total sports offered at
private and state schools
aggregate(css[,c(6:8)], by=list(css$class), mean)
```

The `aggregate()` function is a useful tool for taking a deeper look at data and providing some contextual meaning to the results.

Creating and Applying Custom Functions

Now that you have developed some critical core skills for working with quantitative data in R, you are ready to take it to the next level. At this point, you should feel comfortable with coding and writing scripts to achieve desired results. However, creating custom functions will speed up your work even more. As of now, each statistic you have produced has been singular in nature. This means that every time you would like to create a table that requires multiple statistics, you would have to create a separate line of code for each statistic. For instance, if you were asked for the mean and standard deviation for a set of variables, you would have to run functions on each variable twice, once to produce the mean value and once to produce the standard deviation. Creating functions allows analysts to apply a series of statistics to individual or multiple variables simultaneously. To begin, create a function called `f1` that incorporates the three elements of n counts, means, and standard deviations by combining them using the `c()` function in conjunction with the **function()** function.

Creating custom functions expedites analysis, such as isolating for expenses by division, sex, or league.
Timothy Nwachukwu/NCAA Photos via Getty Images

Visit HK*Propel* to access
the video tutorial on
creating and using
custom functions.

```
# Creating a function in R - f1
f1 <- function(x) c(n=length(x), mean=mean(x), sd=sd(x))
```

You will see that the function you have created appears in the global environment panel. If you would like to keep the formatting you have developed throughout the chapter by including the round() function with the mean= and sd= settings to increase or decrease the decimal places, this too can be embedded in the code.

```
# Creating a function in R with rounding embedded - f2
f2 <- function(x) c(n=length(x),
          mean=round(mean(x), digits=2),
          sd=round(sd(x), digits=2))
```

Once you have created the function, it can be applied to individual variables or within the parameters of the apply(), sapply(), and aggregate() functions to produce the desired results.

```
# Using the f2 function to produce the n count, mean, and SD for
average number of female athletes at Division I schools
f2(css$afath)
```

```
# Using the f2 function to produce the n count, mean, and SD for
average number of female athletes at Division I schools who have
an average total enrollment greater than 10,000
f2(css[css$aten>10000, c(13)])
```

```
# Using the f2 function in the apply() function to produce n
counts, means, and SD for multiple columns of data
apply(css[ ,c(6:47)], MARGIN=2, f2)
```

```
# Using the f2 function in the sapply() function to produce n
counts, means, and SD for male and female athletic aid without
including the Ivy League schools
sapply(css[css$conf !="Ivy League",c(15,16,18,19)], f2)
```

```
# Using the f2 function in the aggregate() function to produce n
counts, means, and SD for grand total athletics expenses 2016-2018
aggregated by division
aggregate(css$expmf, by=list(css$div), f2)
```

Creating functions and applying them to individual variables or within the parameters of apply(), sapply(), and aggregate() functions offers tremendous flexibility for analysts to manipulate data in an efficient and effective manner.

At this point, the power of creating and applying functions in the domain of sport analytics is apparent, but there is an additional tweaking of the code that can take your current f2 function to the next level. In the past, you have created filters to eliminate zero values of data from specific analyses. To do this, you have used the bracket structure. For instance, you have been filtering the Ivy League schools out of the equation to make sure that the athletic aid measures are more representative of Division I as a whole. The problem with continually applying filters is that it requires many lines of code that must constantly be altered to suit each unique situation.

If you were asked to create a table that shows the n counts, means, and standard deviations for the items listed below, you should be able to produce it relatively quickly with minimal coding. However, seven of the eight variables contain zero values, which would skew the results. This means that each script produced must be sensitive to changes in the dataset depending on the variable being examined. In this scenario, you are tasked with reporting the n counts, means, and standard deviations for the following measured variables:

1. Male athletic aid: 2017-2018
2. Female athletic aid: 2017-2018
3. Total athletic aid: 2017-2018
4. Grand total athletics expenses: 2017-2018
5. Directors' Cup points: fall 2017-2018
6. Directors' Cup points: winter 2017-2018
7. Directors' Cup points: spring 2017-2018
8. Total Directors' Cup points: 2017-2018

Variables 1 to 3 involve athletic aid. There are eight schools that reported zero values for male, female, and total athletic aid for the period of 2017 to 2018. Variable 4 is grand total athletics expenses and is the one variable required in this table that will include every case in the dataset. Variables 5 to 8 involve Directors' Cup points. Each of the four reporting spans have schools that earned zero Directors' Cup points for the fall, winter, and spring seasons as well as for the entire 2017-2018 season. Whereas the athletic aid measures can be easily remedied by removing the Ivy League schools, the Directors' Cup measures present a new challenge. Because the schools with zero values are not necessarily the same for each of the four reporting spans, the Directors' Cup measures will have to be calculated individually.

To clarify, school A may have scored points in the fall but not during the winter or the spring. This means that school A has values for fall Directors' Cup points (css$nf2) and total Directors' Cup points (css$ntot2), but nothing for the css$nw2 or css$ns2 variables. School B, on the other hand, may have scored points in the winter and in the spring but not during the fall. This means that school B has values for winter Directors' Cup points (css$nw2), spring Directors' Cup points (css$ns2), and total Directors' Cup points (css$ntot2) but nothing for the css$nf2 variable. The issue is apparent that we cannot simply create a filter that eliminates a set of specific schools, again, because they fluctuate. To achieve the goals set forth by the challenge and produce a table with what you have learned to this point (see table 2.5), the following scripts would be required:

```
sapply(css[css$conf != "Ivy League",c(16,19,22)],f2)
f2(css$expm2)
f2(css[css$nf2>0, c(37)])
f2(css[css$nw2>0, c(40)])
f2(css[css$ns2>0, c(43)])
f2(css[css$ntot2>0, c(46)])
```

While this is not a bad way to achieve your goals, it is a bit clumsy and slow, and as the number of variables increases, it can become unmanageable. Therefore, we will add a simple tweak to your f2 function that can produce everything you need for the table in one line of code. This function will not only save you a significant amount of time, but it can also be quickly applied to other areas of data with minor tweaks to produce results in seconds. The adjustment that is required is to add a !=0 setting to the n count, means, and standard deviation arguments when creating the new function f3. The changes made to the f2 function are highlighted in red.

TABLE 2.5   NCAA Division I Athletic Aid, Recruiting Expenses, Grand Total Expenses in Millions of Dollars, and Total Directors' Cup Points (2017-2018)

Measure	n	M	SD
Male athletic aid	340	4.17	2.59
Female athletic aid	340	3.65	2.10
Total athletic aid	340	7.83	4.56
Grand total athletics expenses	348	39.21	38.06
Directors' Cup points—fall	204	91.0	78.5
Directors' Cup points—winter	191	124.4	125.0
Directors' Cup points—spring	217	123.7	139.5
Total Directors' Cup points	289	239.4	289.5

```
# Tweaking the f2 function to ignore zero values during
statistical analysis - f3
f3 <- function(x) c(n=length(x[x!=0]),
          mean=round(mean(x[x!=0]), digits=2),
          sd=round(sd(x[x!=0]), digits=2))
```

The columns of data incorporated into the table requirements are columns 16, 19, 22, 34, 37, 40, 43, and 46. Using the f3 function with the sapply() function and setting the column values using the c() function will produce every element of the table at the same time with the proper n counts, means, and standard deviation for each measure.

```
# Creating the table using the new f3 function
sapply(css[ ,c(16,19,22,34,37,40,43,46)],f3)
```

The advantage of having developed the f3 function becomes even more impressive when you would like to apply it to a slightly different set of data. This can be done by making the smallest of changes. Suppose you decided you only want to look at the Football Championship Subdivision (FCS) schools included in the *css* dataset (see table 2.6). This can be done by adding a simple filter to the script you just created. The changes to the script are indicated in red.

```
# Changing the table to just include the FCS schools
sapply(css[css$div=="FCS",c(16,19,22,34,37,40,43,46)],f3)
```

As a final wrinkle, you may want to compare the data by the classification variable css$class (see table 2.7). For this, you need only use the aggregate() function and add the by=list() setting. For simplicity's sake, just include the athletic aid measures. Additionally, you do not need to include the n counts in this table because they will be the same for each category.

```
# Comparison of Division I athletic aid between private schools
and public schools
aggregate(css[ ,c(16,19,22)], by=list(css$class),f3)
```

TABLE 2.6   FCS Athletic Aid, Recruiting Expenses, Grand Total Expenses in Millions of Dollars, and Total Directors' Cup Points (2017-2018)

Measure	n	M	SD
Male athletic aid	117	3.37	1.56
Female athletic aid	117	2.73	1.47
Total athletic aid	117	6.10	2.89
Grand total athletics expenses	125	19.72	8.80
Directors' Cup points—fall	58	64.6	45.9
Directors' Cup points—winter	50	63.8	51.0
Directors' Cup points—spring	65	55.4	38.9
Total Directors' Cup points	95	111.0	100.0

TABLE 2.7   Comparison of Athletic Aid Between Private Schools and State Schools (2017-2018)

Measure	Private schools		State schools	
	M	SD	M	SD
Male athletic aid	4.68	2.88	3.93	2.40
Female athletic aid	4.52	2.21	3.23	1.92
Total athletic aid	9.19	4.89	7.17	4.25

INFERENTIAL STATISTICS

Having a clear understanding of how to develop descriptive statistics in R, it is now time to start conducting tests to examine relationships between data using **inferential statistics**. There are a number of tests that can be used to examine relationships between variables, but the four most commonly used are the t-test, analysis of variance (ANOVA), correlation, and regression. Each test has specific parameters for usage which will return results that can be used to determine the strength of relationships between variables or whether or not a relationship between variables is statistically significant. To start, we will establish an alpha level of 0.05 for significance testing between variables. For most relationship testing, an alpha level of 0.05 is commonplace and is in fact the default value for inferential statistics tests in R. This value can be changed depending on the goals of your analysis, but for the purposes of this book, using the preset alpha level of 0.05 is appropriate.

Independent Samples T-Test

Independent samples t-tests can be used when examining relationships between independent variables and dependent variables. The t-test is concerned with hypothesis testing to determine whether or not a measured variable is related to an independent variable in a statistically significant manner.

An **independent samples t-test** can be used when exploring the relationship between an independent variable comprised of two levels and a dependent variable.

Visit HK*Propel* to access the video tutorials on the t-test, one-way ANOVA, and bivariate correlation.

A core element contained in the t-test is the **alpha level**, which is the level at which an analyst determines the threshold for rejecting the null hypothesis. The alpha level is important because it sets the bar for an acceptable level of type I error. Without getting too technical, **type I error** involves rejecting the null hypothesis and accepting an alternative hypothesis when in fact the null hypothesis is correct. From a statistical perspective, the alpha level is the probability that type I error can occur (McLeod, 2019).

To get started, review the five independent (factor) variables included in the *css* dataset. From working with the data, you are probably aware that the only factor variable with two levels is the css$class variable. The two levels are private schools and state schools. Now that you have identified an independent factor variable with two levels, you can run a t-test to determine whether or not there is a statistically significant relationship between the css$class variable and one of the measured variables in the dataset. To this point, you have been able to compare the means of measured variables between different groups using the aggregate() function, but you have not been able to determine whether those differences are statistically significant.

Suppose you wanted to know the difference in means between private schools and state schools in terms of average total enrollment and whether or not that relationship is statistically significant. We can hypothesize that private schools probably have a lower average enrollment than state schools. Using the aggregate() function you learned earlier, you can examine the difference in means.

```
# Using the aggregate() function to look at average enrollment at
private and state schools
aggregate(css$aten, by=list(css$class), mean)
```

The results indicate that the average total enrollment at private schools is approximately 5,914 students versus 15,053 students at state schools. This is where the t-test becomes useful. In this instance you are looking to determine whether there is a statistically significant relationship between the css$class variable and the css$aten variable, and this is where the alpha level comes into play.

The working hypothesis suggests there is a difference in means in average total enrollment based on school classification. Conversely, this means the null hypothesis suggests there is no difference. Using the alpha level of 0.05, the relationship between the css$class variable and the css$aten variable can be tested. To perform a t-test in R, use the **t.test()** function. Within the parentheses, you will first add the measured css$aten variable followed by the tilde ~ symbol. The ~ symbol is used to link the measured variable to the factor css$class variable. All the other elements required to conduct the t-test are preset, but if you need to modify the t-test parameters to suit particular needs, the settings can be easily modified.

```
# Conducting a t-test to determine if there is a statistically
significant relationship between average total enrollment and
school classification
t.test(css$aten~css$class)
```

As part of the results, you will see the same mean number of students per classification as you saw when using the aggregate() function: 5,914 students on average at Division I private schools and 15,053 students on average at Division I state schools. In addition to the means, there are three other numbers of consequence that are required when reporting the results. The requirements for reporting the results of a t-test are as follows:

- **t-statistic**—Examines the difference in means between the null hypothesis and sample data. If the t-statistic is zero, the null hypothesis is supported. The greater the difference in means between the null hypothesis and the sample data, the larger the t-value becomes. Large t-values combined with small p-values indicate the null hypothesis should be rejected (Minitab, 2016).

- **degrees of freedom**—Estimate of the mean and variability of the mean. Degrees of freedom are tied to the number of independent values within a sample (Frost, n.d.).

- **p-value**—The probability value that is linked to the alpha level. Oftentimes in sports, research is conducted using an alpha level of 0.05; p-values that are less than the alpha level indicate a statistically significant relationship. The smaller the p-value, the less likely it is that you are seeing a false positive, which provides strong evidence for rejecting the null hypothesis (Glen, n.d.).

The reporting structure for t-test results is $t(\text{df}) = ?, p = ?$ so all the values required are contained in the output. For the degrees of freedom, you can round to the nearest whole number. For the t-statistic, you can use two decimal points. For the p-value, if it is .000 or less, the result can be reported as $p < .001$. If the p-value is greater than .001 you will report the actual number—for example, $p = .065$. Using the results from the t-test, the write-up would read something along these lines: "Based on the difference in means in average total enrollment between private schools and state schools, an independent samples t-test was run. The relationship between average total enrollment and the classification of schools is significant at the 0.05 level $t(346) = -12.54, p < .001$."

One-Way Analysis of Variance

A **one-way analysis of variance (ANOVA)** can be used when exploring the relationship between an independent variable comprised of three or more levels and a dependent variable. The parameters for reporting the results of an ANOVA are very similar to the t-test, except you will have an f-statistic rather than a t-statistic and you will have two values for degrees of freedom. The p-value will be reported the same. A final difference required when reporting the results of an ANOVA will involve running post-hoc tests when p-values indicate statistically significant relationships.

Post-hoc tests are used to determine which relationships are significant. In the t-test, there is no question as to which relationships are significant because there are only two levels. To perform an ANOVA, it is best to create an object using the **aov()** function. The structure within the aov() function will be the same as the t.test() function (dependent$variable~independent$variable). Sticking with average total enrollment as our measured variable of choice, let's examine the relationship between the four different divisions that are represented in the *css* dataset. The four divisions—DI, FCS, FBS, and Power 5—and are represented by the css$div variable. We will call the new object a1, which stands for ANOVA 1.

```
# Creating an object using the aov() function
a1 <- aov(css$aten~css$div)
```

The reporting structure for ANOVA results is $F(\text{df}_1, \text{df}_2) = ?, p = ?$ which is very similar to the reporting structure for t-test results. To get the required figures, run the summary() function on the a1 object.

```
# Generating the results of a one-way ANOVA using the summary()
function
summary(a1)
```

The f-value, degrees of freedom, and p-value are all present in the output. The next step is to look at the overall significance. Because the p-value is so small, far less than .05, there is a statistically significant difference in average total enrollment between the four groups represented in the css$div variable. However, this does not necessarily mean that the difference between each of the four groups is significant. To determine which groups differ significantly, post-hoc tests must be performed. A popular way of doing this is to employ the **TukeyHSD()** function.

```
# Using the TukeyHSD() function to perform post-hoc tests
TukeyHSD(a1)
```

You can see from the results that significance testing has taken place between each of the groups. Each p-value that is lower than the 0.05 alpha level indicates a significant relationship. The results of the post-hoc tests indicate that the difference in average total enrollment at the four different groups of schools is statistically significant from each other except for one. When examining the difference in means between the DI division and the FCS division, we see that the results indicate a p-value of .637, which exceeds the threshold for determining a significant relationship.

Using the results from the ANOVA, the write-up would read as something along these lines: "Based on the difference in means in average total enrollment between the different divisions of DI, FCS, FBS, and Power 5, a one-way ANOVA was run. The relationship between average total enrollment and the division of schools is significant at the 0.05 level $F(3,344) = 82.99$, $p < .001$. Based on this significance testing, post-hoc tests were run to examine which groups differed significantly in average total enrollment. The post-hoc tests indicate that all of the mean differences between the four divisions are significant with the exception of the DI and FCS divisions."

Bivariate Correlations

A **bivariate correlation** can be used to examine the extent to which two dependent measured variables are related. If there is a relationship between the two variables, it can be positive or negative. For example, we could look at the relationship between hours spent partying per week and grade point average (GPA). In this scenario, one would assume that as the level of one variable rises (partying), the other drops (GPA). In other words, the more hours you devote to partying, the lower your GPA will be. This would be referred to as a negative correlation. If we were to swap hours spent partying with hours spent studying, one would assume that as the level of one variable rises (studying), so too does the other (GPA). In other words, the more hours you devote to studying, the higher your GPA will be. This would be referred to as a positive correlation.

The **Pearson method** is used to examine the relationship between two continuous scale variables. If you are interested in examining the relationship between variables using an ordinal scale, it would be more appropriate to use the **Spearman method** (Ramzai, 2020). The scale of a bivariate correlation ranges from −1 (perfect negative correlation) to 1 (perfect positive correlation). A value of 0 indicates no correlation. A general rule of thumb for describing the strength of a correlation would be to use the following:

```
Less than 0.3      Weak Correlation
0.3-0.5            Weak to Medium Correlation
0.5-0.7            Medium to Strong Correlation
Greater than 0.7   Strong Correlation
```

There are a couple of different methods for conducting correlations in R, but because of the American Psychological Association (APA) style requirements used in most scholarly work, the **cor.test()** function is the easiest. The cor.test() function will not only produce a value for Pearson's *r* but will also produce a value for degrees of freedom and the p-value used for significance testing. These are all elements required for APA reporting. Additionally, the default method assigned to the cor.test() function in R is the Pearson method, so a method="" setting is not required.

After sifting through all of this data, I am sure you are curious about whether or not earning Directors' Cup points is strongly correlated with spending. To analyze this relationship, first remove the schools who scored zero Directors' Cup points during the 2016-2018 seasons by creating an object named ndcp, which stands for no Directors' Cup points. Then run the cor.test() function by placing the variables within the function separated by a comma.

```
# Examining the correlation between athletics expenses and
Directors' Cup points 2016-2018
ndcp <- css[css$ntotf >0,]
cor.test(ndcp$expmf , ndcp$ntotf)
```

Comparing the results to the guide presented above, it is clear there is a very strong correlation between total Directors' Cup points and grand total athletics expenses. The APA reporting structure for correlation results is $r(\text{df}) = ?, p = ?$ so all the values required are contained in the output. Using the results from the correlation, the write-up might read as follows: "A bivariate correlation was run to demonstrate the strength of the relationship between grand total athletics expenses and total Directors' Cup points for the 2016-2018 seasons. The two variables are strongly correlated $r(316) = 0.91, p < .001$."

Introduction to Regression Analysis

Correlation results are oftentimes presented along with a scatterplot demonstrating the distribution of values. Even though we are not covering plotting in this chapter, a demonstration of how to develop a simple scatterplot and add the regression line to it is provided. To avoid dense clustering of data in the bottom left area of the scatterplot, further limit the data to schools that spent at least $100 million and scored at least 300 Directors' Cup points during the 2016-2018 seasons by creating a new subset called *dc300*.

```
# Creating the dc300 subset
dc300 <- css[css$expmf >= 100 & css$ntotf >= 300,]
```

You will see the *css* dataset has been narrowed to 72 schools that fit the criteria. To plot the data, use the **plot()** function and input the two dependent measured variables (x-axis variable goes first and y-axis variable goes second). After you have input the variables, add an xlab="" setting and a ylab="" setting to set labels for the x-axis and y-axis.

```
# Creating a simple scatterplot using the plot() function
plot(dc300$expmf,dc300$ntotf,
    xlab="Grand Total Athletics Expenses in Millions 2016-2018",
    ylab="Total Directors' Cup Points 2016-2018")
```

You can now see how the data is distributed within the *dc300* subset. To add a regression line, you first need to fit the model using the linear model **lm()** function. **Regression analysis** is something you will continue to come across in applied sport business analytics, and it will be a topic you will cover in your statistics courses as you advance your skill set, but for now, it is most important to know that it is used in a predictive capacity.

To fit the model, the input required is the dependent variable being predicted (dc300$ntotf) followed by the tilde ~ symbol, which will link the predicted variable to the predictor variable (dc300$expmf). Call this model r1. What the model does is determine the extent to which total Directors' Cup points can be predicted by grand total athletics expenses.

```
# Creating the r1 object using the lm() function
r1 <- lm(dc300$ntotf~dc300$expmf)
```

After the r1 object has been created, the regression line can be added to the scatterplot using the **abline()** function (see figure 2.2). To make the line stand out, use the col= setting to make the line color blue (the number 4 in R) and increase the thickness of the line using the lwd= setting.

```
# Adding the regression line to the scatterplot with the abline()
function
abline(r1, col=4, lwd=2)
```

A final helpful hint to get you started down the path of working with regression analysis is to install the *apaTables* package and run the **apa.reg.table()** function. Because many people prefer to report their regression results in a table format, this is a particularly useful package and function. To use the apa.reg.table() function, input the name of the regression object you have created (r1) and a filename="" setting that must end in .*rtf* or .*doc* for formatting purposes.

Visit HK*Propel* to access the video tutorial on basic scatterplots.

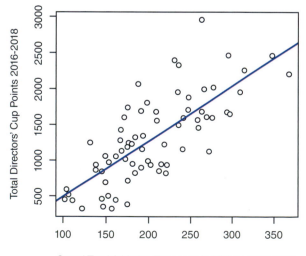

FIGURE 2.2   Scatterplot of total Directors' Cup points and grand total athletics expenses.

FANTASY BASKETBALL DRAFT STRATEGY

Fantasy sports are a significant entertainment outlet for many people. As fantasy managers try to create rosters that will help them win their leagues, many rely on the advice given by experts on websites or through other means such as television. There are a number of different draft styles, but the style of this one was an auction draft in which league members participate in a live auction to create their teams. This can lead to bidding wars for top players. The key to this analysis was to use filters to find players who may be less coveted than the top (and most expensive) players, who could be rostered for less money.

STRATEGY

- Run all player statistics from the 2019-2020 season through a set of 12 statistical filters to create a draft target list of players with the highest overall filter scores (4 of the 12 filters are included in the list below).
- Roster as many players from the final primary target list as possible using the $200 allotted to each team manager for the draft.
- As players demonstrate value, trade them for more expensive players, thus adding approximately $50 to the draft day budget retroactively while building a serious contender moving toward the playoffs.

Name	Pos	Cost	FGP	FTP	PPG
Anthony Davis	PF-C	75.4	0.503	0.846	26.1
Nikola Jokic	PF-C	74.1	0.528	0.817	19.9
Damian Lillard	PG	67.9	0.463	0.888	30.0
Karl-Anthony Towns	C	67.0	0.508	0.796	26.5
Jayson Tatum	SF-PF	57.8	0.450	0.812	23.4
Kawhi Leonard	SG-SF	52.9	0.470	0.886	27.1
Bradley Beal	SG-SF	51.8	0.455	0.842	30.5
Joel Embiid	PF-C	45.5	0.477	0.807	23.0
Jimmy Butler	SF-PF	43.2	0.455	0.834	19.9
Devin Booker	SG-SF	43.2	0.489	0.919	26.6
Shai Gilgeous-Alexander	SG-SF	30.0	0.471	0.807	19.0
Pascal Siakam	PF-C	27.3	0.453	0.792	22.9
Nikola Vucevic	C	26.0	0.477	0.784	19.6
Khris Middleton	SF-PF	21.5	0.497	0.916	20.9
Zach LaVine	SG-SF	20.3	0.450	0.802	25.5
Jamal Murray	PG-SG	19.0	0.456	0.881	18.5
Brandon Ingram	SF-PF	17.2	0.463	0.851	23.8
CJ McCollum	PG-SG	14.1	0.451	0.798	22.2
DeMar DeRozan	SG-SF	13.7	0.531	0.845	22.1
Gordon Hayward	SG-SF	11.9	0.500	0.855	17.5
Tobias Harris	SF-PF	10.6	0.471	0.806	19.6
TJ Warren	SF-PF	9.1	0.536	0.819	19.8
Collin Sexton	PG-SG	9.0	0.472	0.846	20.8
Malcolm Brogdon	PG-SG	9.0	0.438	0.892	16.5
Eric Bledsoe	PG-SG	7.0	0.475	0.790	14.9
Richaun Holmes	PF-C	3.9	0.648	0.788	12.3
Mikal Bridges	SG-SF	3.1	0.510	0.844	9.1

Notes: Pos = position; FGP = field goal percentage; FTP = free throw percentage; PPG = points per game.

(continued)

FANTASY BASKETBALL DRAFT STRATEGY [CONTINUED]

DRAFT RESULTS

On draft night, the Alabama Sweat Storm entered the auction draft with a list of 27 draft targets. Based on budget constraints, players ranked in the top 10 of the draft target list were in essence removed from realistic consideration, thus leaving 13 primary targets and 4 secondary targets. The players in the middle section of the list were considered primary targets, while those in the bottom third of the list were considered secondary targets. The cost variable included in the chart was an estimate of what Yahoo Fantasy Sports believed players would be auctioned for. It is also important to note that these estimates are oftentimes lower than what players actually cost to roster. For instance, in this auction draft, both Anthony Davis and Nikola Jokic were rostered for $80. The manager of the Alabama Sweat Storm was able to roster 9 of the team's 13 primary targets and one secondary target on draft night within the $200 budget limit set by the league. The Alabama Sweat Storm selections are highlighted in green. Players lost during the bidding process are highlighted in pink. Player concerns (i.e., areas where players failed filters) are highlighted in yellow. On draft night, the Alabama Sweat Storm achieved the first two elements of their overall strategy: (1) Draft players of high value based on a statistical filtering system, and (2) roster as many primary targets as possible within the allocated budget of $200. The last element of the strategy involved leveraging lesser-valued players who demonstrated value throughout the beginning of the season and trading them for more expensive players in an attempt to add approximately $50 to the draft day budget retroactively while building a serious contender moving toward the playoffs.

ADDING VALUE

- **Players Traded Away**: CJ McCollum, Jamal Murray, DeMar DeRozan, and Brandon Ingram—Total Value on Draft Night = **$68**
- **Players Traded For**: Jimmy Butler, Lonzo Ball, and Karl-Anthony Towns—Total Value on Draft Night = **$131**
- **Value Added** = **$63**

```
# Creating a regression analysis results table in APA format using
the apaTables package
install.packages("apaTables")
library(apaTables)
apa.reg.table(r1, filename = "r1.doc")
```

You will find your perfectly formatted APA table in your working directory, which you can cut and paste into your own document, as shown in table 2.8.

TABLE 2.8   Regression Results Using dc300$ntotf as the Criterion

Predictor	b	b 95% CI [LL, UL]	beta	beta 95% CI [LL, UL]	sr²	sr² 95% CI [LL, UL]	r	Fit
(Intercept)	−279.31	[−619.66, 61.04]						
dc300$expmf	7.73**	[6.13, 9.34]	0.75	[0.60, 0.91]	.57	[.41, .67]	.75**	
								R^2 = .568**
								95% CI[.41,.67]

Notes: A significant b-weight indicates the beta-weight and semi-partial correlation are also significant. b represents unstandardized regression weights. beta indicates the standardized regression weights. sr² represents the semi-partial correlation squared. r represents the zero-order correlation. LL and UL indicate the lower and upper limits of a confidence interval (CI), respectively.

** indicates $p < .01$.

SUMMARY

Throughout the course of this chapter, you have developed the skills you need to work with quantitative data in R. These skills have allowed you to import data files and manipulate them in a variety of ways. By working with a consistent dataset throughout the chapter, you have been able to focus on the R scripts and functions to develop a sense of comfort and ease working in a new environment.

Important functions you have learned to execute in R include filtering and subsetting data, counting and ordering data, and creating custom functions to improve your efficiency and effectiveness as an analyst. Finally, you have learned how to develop descriptive statistics and engage in inferential statistics testing to examine relationships between different variables. The next step is to bring the data to life in chapter 3, Plotting Data in R.

ONLINE ACTIVITIES   HK*Propel* 》

Visit HK*Propel* to access the video tutorials, *css* dataset, College Sports Supermodel Variables Chart, exercises, and a key terms review activity for this chapter. Your instructor may also release the assignments, assignment forms, and quiz available for this chapter through HK*Propel*. These tutorials, activities, and exercises are designed for interactive learning and to assist students as they learn the material.

REFERENCES

Datacamp. 2019. "R Packages: A Beginner's Guide." Last modified March 25, 2019. https://datacamp.com/community/tutorials.

Fanara, Carlo. 2019. "Tutorial on the R Apply Family." Last modified January 15, 2019. https://datacamp.com.

Frost, Jim. n.d. "Degrees of Freedom in Statistics." Accessed June 14, 2021. https://statisticsbyjim.com.

Glen, Stephanie. n.d. "P-Value in Statistical Hypothesis Tests: What Is It?" Accessed June 14, 2021. https://statisticshowto.com.

McLeod, Saul. 2019. "What Are Type I and Type II Errors?" Last modified July 4, 2019. https://simplypsychology.org.

Minitab. 2016. "What Are T Values and P Values in Statistics?" Last modified November 4, 2016. https://blog.minitab.com.

Ramzai, Juhi. 2020. "Clearly Explained: Pearson V/S Spearman Correlation Coefficient." Last modified June 25, 2020. https://towardsdatascience.com.

PLOTTING DATA IN R

Justin Tafoya/NCAA Photos via Getty Images

## 3

CHAPTER OBJECTIVES

KEY TERMS

boxplot	ggplot2	line plot	scatterplot
density plot	histogram	regression line	violin plot

R FUNCTIONS

```
aes()              ggtitle()              plot_usmap()
boxplot()          geom_boxplot()         scale_fill_continuous()
coord_flip()       geom_histogram()       scale_fill_discrete()
element_blank()    geom_jitter()          scale_x_continuous()
element_line()     geom_line()            scale_y_continuous()
element_rect()     geom_point()           theme()
element_text()     geom_text()            write.csv()
factor()           geom_text_repel()      xlab()
ggplot()           geom_violin()          ylab()
```

A primary goal in reporting data is the ability to convey it in a meaningful way that can lead to actionable decision-making. To achieve this goal, it is rarely effective to make a presentation that demonstrates your ability to do statistics. Many of the listeners in data presentations will not be moved to action based on reports indicating statistically significant relationships between independent and dependent variables. However, if you can convey the results to the listener in a way that helps them comprehend where they stand from a graphical perspective, the graphical displays can be very impactful. Data visualization is compelling because it allows a client or end user to easily comprehend where they stand in relation to their competitors, a task that is far more challenging when only reading statistical reports and tables.

Throughout the chapter, you will develop a set of plotting structures to keep and modify as you see fit for working on future projects. There are endless combinations of how one can prepare and plot data in RStudio. Every element in an R plot can be manipulated, changed, modified, and customized to suit individual needs. Furthermore, there are a large number of packages available for RStudio that exist to minimize an analyst's efforts when coding and creating plots. Packages that will be installed, activated, and used throughout this chapter include *ggplot2*, *ggrepel*, and *usmap*. The use of these packages allows for rapid plotting employing advanced visualization techniques that will paint a meaningful picture for the client or end user in a way that can lead to action. Being able to bring data vividly to life and convey the results in a useful manner is the focus of this chapter.

BASE PLOTTING STRUCTURES IN R

Before you begin to work with the packages previously mentioned, it is important to learn some of the settings for working with the base elements that are involved in plotting data in R. There are many settings available for plotting in R. The settings covered in this section are for

- entering data on the x-axis and y-axis,
- creating a custom order for factor variables,
- creating a main plot title,
- creating labels for the x-axis and y-axis,
- setting the color of plot elements, and
- customizing tick mark intervals and orientation.

The difference between setting elements and mapping elements will be discussed later in the chapter.

For the sake of continuity, the first plot you create will build on what you learned toward the end of chapter 2, when you created a simple **scatterplot** with a **regression line**. Scatterplots are helpful for demonstrating the distribution of data between two measured variables. At the end of chapter 2, you examined the correlation between grand total athletics expenses and total Directors' Cup points for the 2016 to 2018 seasons. You limited the data to a specific range of numeric values in the plotting structure and, by doing so, were able to demonstrate with clarity how far the data points deviated from the regression line. Lastly, when you analyzed the relationship between grand total athletics expenses and total Directors' Cup points, there was a strong correlation between the two variables. Being able to demonstrate the relationship graphically made a significant difference in the impact of the findings.

The second plot you will develop in this chapter is a **boxplot**. Unlike a scatterplot, which presents the distribution of data based on two dependent measured variables, a boxplot presents the distribution of data within groups based on independent factor variables. The boxplot you develop will be created from scratch to ensure you understand how each element is being modified or added to the plot in a stepwise fashion. Understanding the individual steps in plotting is important when you begin to work with larger code blocks. Code blocks can become extensive, so dropping down a line in the coding script each time you introduce a new element is recommended to help you keep your work organized.

Before we get started, it is important to examine the geometry of boxplots in general. Boxplots follow the model of quartiles, which you learned during the basic statistical functions portion of chapter 2. Individual data points represent outliers. You see one in the Atlantic Coast Conference (ACC) and one in the Big 12 in figures 3.2 and 3.3. The top of the vertical line represents the maximum value (excluding outliers) and the bottom of the vertical line represents the minimum value (excluding outliers). The horizontal line within the box represents the median value. The bottom of the box represents the first (lower) quartile, while the top of the box represents the third (upper) quartile. The space within the box is referred to as the interquartile range. Understanding the anatomy of a boxplot is helpful when describing your findings to a client or end user and for customizing the boxplot to represent your findings in the best way possible (Galarnyk, 2018).

To develop the basic boxplot, start with the **boxplot()** function. For this plot, the distribution of data will represent the average number of athletes per school by division in the *css* dataset. The average number of athletes per school is represented as the `css$atath` variable. This measured variable will be grouped by the `css$div` factor variable that has four levels (DI, FCS, FBS, and Power 5). The measured data that will appear on the y-axis will be entered into the `boxplot()` function first and the groups that will appear on the x-axis will be entered second. The two entries are connected by a tilde ~ symbol. Remember to include the $ sign to link the overall dataset to the variables of interest.

Visit HK*Propel* to access the College Sports Supermodel (*css*) dataset and to review the video tutorials on statistics and scatterplots.

```
# Creating a basic boxplot using the boxplot() function
boxplot(css$atath~css$div)
```

If you executed the line of code correctly, the boxplot should have appeared in the bottom right panel of RStudio. You are probably a bit underwhelmed by what you see, but remember, this is just the beginning. As you continue to change and alter the appearance of the plot, the new lines of code being added will be highlighted in red. With each addition, the boxplot will continue to morph until it is presentable and ready for export.

Before you go any further, however, you probably noticed the order in which the factor variable groups appeared on the x-axis. This creates an interesting dilemma. It would be nice to have the different levels of the css$div variable in an escalating order more natural to how people analyze Division I athletics. The natural order would be to start with DI and proceed through the FCS, FBS and Power 5 levels. However, because R defaults to alphabetical order, it presents the FBS division before the FCS division. To customize the order of the css$div factor variable, you can simply overwrite the existing variable by employing the **factor()** function along with a levels= setting.

```
# Overwriting the `css$div` variable to customize the order of the
levels
css$div <- factor(css$div, levels=c("DI","FCS","FBS","Power 5"))
```

Now, if you re-execute the line of code used to create the boxplot, the new customized order should be reflected on the x-axis. The next thing to add is a main title for the boxplot. This can be achieved using the main="" setting. As a reminder, each new element in the parentheses will be separated by a comma, and it is advisable that you drop a line each time you enter a new element by hitting the return key to keep the code in a manageable layout.

```
# Adding a main title to the boxplot
boxplot(css$atath~css$div,
   main="Average Number of Athletes at Division-I Schools")
```

You should see the main title appear above the plot. The next step is to add some labels to the x-axis and the y-axis. This can be achieved using the xlab="" and ylab="" settings. The x-axis in this instance, however, is self-explanatory, so you may decide to eliminate an x-axis label altogether. You can do this by leaving the space within the quotations blank, or you can set the value to NULL. The y-axis will be labeled using the same technique as the main title.

```
# Adding labels to the x-axis and y-axis
boxplot(css$atath~css$div,
   main="Average Number of Athletes at Division-I Schools",
   xlab=NULL,
   ylab="Average Number of Athletes")
```

The next element you may wish to change is the color of your data to make it stand out. In this plot, start by changing the color of the data from its default color to blue. The color of the data can be changed using the col= setting, and the end result can be achieved using one of two methods. You can set the color to the actual name you want such as "blue" or you can use the number associated with the color to complete the col= setting. A brief color setting guide is included below. When you get further along in the chapter, your choices of colors will expand tremendously, but for now, these core eight will get you started.

```
1       black
2       red
3       green
4       blue
5       cyan
6       magenta
7       yellow
8       gray
```

```
# Changing the color of data using the col= setting
boxplot(css$atath~css$div,
    main="Average Number of Athletes at Division-I Schools",
    xlab=NULL,
    ylab="Average Number of Athletes",
    col=4)
```

Here you should see that all the boxes within the boxplot have turned blue. However, for presentation sake, it is probably better to assign a different color for each box. This can be achieved a few different ways, but if you decided the box colors should be yellow, red, blue, and green, the col= setting would incorporate the c() function to set the desired colors.

```
# Assigning different colors to each box in the boxplot
boxplot(css$atath~css$div,
    main="Average Number of Athletes at Division-I Schools",
    xlab=NULL,
    ylab="Average Number of Athletes",
    col=c(7,2,4,3))
```

The last element you may want to tackle are the tick marks. Currently, R has chosen to default to an interval of 200 athletes between each tick mark on the y-axis. If you would like to have tighter spacing, such as a tick mark for every 100 athletes, this can be achieved using the yaxp= setting. You can use the xaxp= setting on the x-axis as well, but it does not make sense to do so in this scenario because the x-axis is currently associated with factor variable groupings.

To use the yaxp= setting, three values are required. These values are the minimum value (in this case 0), the maximum value (in this case 1,200), and the number of intervals desired. Since the desired interval between tick marks is 100 athletes, the number of intervals required is 12. Additionally, adding tick marks and shrinking the margins between tick mark labels may result in some crowding on the y-axis. To avoid this problem, you can rotate the tick labels 90 degrees using the las= setting. The default value for las is 0. To rotate the y-axis tick marks 90 degrees, the value for las= is 1.

Visit HK*Propel* to view the RStudio basic customized boxplot, which you should see if you have completed all the steps properly, and to watch the video tutorial on boxplots.

```
# Changing the tick mark intervals and orientation on the y-axis
boxplot(css$atath~css$div,
    main="Average Number of Athletes at Division-I Schools",
    xlab=NULL,
    ylab="Average Number of Athletes",
    col=c(7,2,4,3),
    yaxp= c(0, 1200, 12),
    las=1)
```

SETTING AND MAPPING PLOT ELEMENTS

Before moving on to create more advanced plots with *ggplot2*, it is important to understand the difference between setting and mapping plot elements. To this point, you have used settings to alter the appearance of your plots. The settings you have learned thus far include the `main=""` setting for adding a plot title, `xlab=""` and `ylab=""` settings for adding labels to the x-axis and y-axis, `col=` setting for customized colors, `xaxp=` and `yaxp=` settings for customized intervals between tick marks, and the `las=` setting for tick mark label orientation. Though these settings will not be exactly the same in the *ggplot2* plotting structures, they are at the core of plotting in R and will continue to play a central role.

However, many plot elements such as color, size, and shape can be mapped rather than set. When a plot element is mapped, it means the plot element is tied to a variable within the dataset. For instance, suppose you would like to use four different colors for your boxplot based on the four levels of division (DI, FCS, FBS, and Power 5). When you set the boxplot colors using the `col=c(7,2,4,3)` coding script, you set the colors as yellow, red, blue, and green. If, on the other hand, you mapped the `color=` setting to the `css$div` factor variable in the plotting structure, R knows to assign four different colors to the output automatically. Mapping aesthetic values will feature prominently as you continue to take your plotting to the next level.

PLOTTING DATA WITH GGPLOT2

ggplot2 is a powerful package used by analysts for plotting data in R. It features robust capabilities that allow users to modify every element of a plot. At its core, *ggplot2* requires only a few attributes to get started. These attributes are

- data to be used for plotting,
- inputs for the x-axis and y-axis, and
- geometry to be applied to the plot.

There are a myriad of different geometry options available to you in *ggplot2*, but the options covered in this chapter include the following:

```
geom_point()
geom_boxplot()
geom_jitter()
geom_histogram()
geom_density()
geom_line()
geom_text()
geom_text_repel()
geom_violin()
```

The ggplot function allows you to identify and plot boundless comparisons from the *css* dataset.
Justin Tafoya/NCAA Photos via Getty Images

Before getting started, make sure the *plyr, ggplot2, ggrepel,* and *usmap* packages are installed and activated using the `install.packages()` and `library()` functions.

geom_point()

Having created both a scatterplot and boxplot using the basic plotting functions contained in R, you have an understanding of what the output demonstrates to the end user in relation to the distribution of data contained in the plots. Although you have been able to develop these plots in a way that makes them visually appealing and easy to convey and understand, there are a number of tweaks that you can make to improve their appearance and impact.

To get started, you will first build a scatterplot to demonstrate the distribution of data in the Power 5 division of the *css* dataset based on grand total athletics expenses and total Directors' Cup points for the 2016 to 2018 seasons. The core settings of the x-axis and the y-axis will be essentially the same as what you created for your previous scatterplot when using the `plot()` function. The difference, however, is that you will be adding these settings within the **`ggplot()`** function.

The `ggplot()` function allows you to create a seemingly endless set of custom modifications to suit your needs by allowing for the setting and mapping of each plot element. At bare minimum, *ggplot2* requires you to identify the data that is to be referenced and then set the values using the **`aes()`** function, which stands for aesthetics. Before you get started with *ggplot2*, however, first create a subset of data based on the *css* dataset called *power5* to isolate the 65 Power 5 schools associated with Division I athletics.

```
# Creating the power5 subset
power5 <- css[css$div=="Power 5",]
```

Having isolated the set of schools you wish to analyze, the core elements of the ggplot() and aes() functions can now be set.

```
# Core settings for the x-axis and y-axis using ggplot2
ggplot(data=power5, aes(x=expmf, y=ntotf))
```

With this line of code, you have set the x-axis and y-axis data within the aes() function and associated those settings with the *power5* data subset being referenced within the ggplot() function. However, when you execute this line of code, nothing appears to happen. This is because unlike the basic plot() function in R, *ggplot2* does not work under the assumption that you would like the data graphically represented as points. Instead, *ggplot2* will require you to set the geometry of the output as you desire.

The geometric parameter used to create a scatterplot in *ggplot2* is the **geom_point()** function. The geom_point() function is a way of demonstrating the trend that as the level of athletics expenses increases, so too does the level of total Directors' Cup points. The geom_point() function creates a traditional-looking scatterplot. As you continue to develop the plot, changes to the coding will be indicated in red. To add the geom_point() geometry, use the + sign.

```
# Adding geometry to a plot in ggplot2 using geom_point()
ggplot(data=power5, aes(x=expmf, y=ntotf)) +
 geom_point()
```

Adding the geometry should have produced a scatterplot that looks similar to the scatterplot you created using the base plotting structure of R. When creating this scatterplot, you may have noticed that the geom_point() function has the traditional parentheses structure of all functions. This is because each geometry function and the overall ggplot() and aes() functions are customizable. For instance, you can easily make the points green by adding a color=3 setting within the geom_point() function rather than within the plotting structure itself. You probably noticed that a color= setting was used rather than the col= setting you have been working with. It is a good idea at this point to start working with the color= setting rather than the col= setting because the col= setting will not work in all *ggplot2* plotting applications.

The nice thing about using the ggplot() function is that once you have developed plotting structures with defined parameters that you like and will use multiple times, those plotting structures can be saved as objects in the global environment. This will save you a massive amount of time when working on projects. For instance, create an object based on the plotting structure above to preserve the data that the plot is referencing (*power5*) and the aesthetics settings (x=expmf, y=ntotf). Name this new object p1, which stands for plot 1.

```
# Creating the p1 object to preserve the developed plotting
structure
p1 <- ggplot(data=power5, aes(x=expmf, y=ntotf))
```

In the future, when you want to use the parameters contained in the p1 object to plot data, you can simply call it up and add onto it. For the purposes of this exercise, we will again add the geometry as geom_point() and change the color of the points to green (see figure 3.1).

```
# Using the p1 object with the geom_point() function
p1 + geom_point(color=3)
```

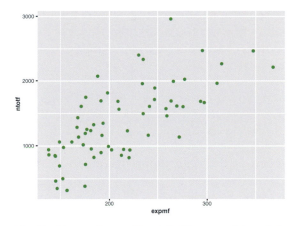

FIGURE 3.1   Using the `p1` object to create a scatterplot with green data points.

Now that you have created the `p1` object and used it to develop a scatterplot with data points set to the color green using the `color=` setting, the difference between setting and mapping plot elements can be demonstrated. On the plot above, data is distributed in a uniform color. Suppose, however, that you would like to know which conference each of the data points belongs to. Power 5 is comprised of the Southeastern, Big 10, Pac 12, Big 12, and Atlantic Coast conferences. The goal of differentiating the data points by conference can be achieved by mapping the color setting to the `css$div` factor variable within the `aes()` function. To save this change, you can overwrite the existing `p1` object or create a new object. For the purposes of this exercise, overwrite the existing `p1` object. The required change to the coding script is indicated in red.

```
# Overwriting the p1 object to map the color setting to conference
p1 <- ggplot(data=power5, aes(x=expmf, y=ntotf,
            color=conf))
```

You have now mapped the color to the `css$conf` factor variable. Using the new `p1` plotting structure along with the `geom_point()` function will produce the desired result.

```
# Creating a scatterplot with data point color mapped to
conference
p1 + geom_point()
```

The plot yields some interesting insights for individuals who represent the Power 5 conferences. For instance, the plot demonstrates that the Pac 12 had three schools in the top 5 of the Directors' Cup competition for the combined 2016 to 2018 seasons, despite not having a single school with a top-10 budget over that same time span.

An additional way to enhance your scatterplot is to modify the shape and size of the data points. For instance, you may not like having a solid data point, and perhaps you think the data points are too small. Because of the flexibility of *ggplot2*, these issues are easily remedied. There are 25 different shapes that can be used in R, and there are online lists readily available for reference. You can also play around with the different shapes in R by changing the `shape=` number setting in the coding. Personal favorites are shapes 1 and 21, which are hollow rings and fillable rings. These are the shapes used in the following examples. For both examples, you will also make the

Visit HK*Propel* to view the resulting scatterplot with color mapped to conferences and to watch the video tutorial on next level scatterplots.

data points larger by using the `size=` setting, and in the fillable rings example, you will introduce the `alpha=` setting that deals with transparency (a particularly useful setting for when data points overlap). The changes made to the coding script between each step are indicated in red.

```
# Changing the data point shape to hollow rings and increasing
their size to 3
p1 + geom_point(shape=1, size=3)
```

You now see that each of the data points has been changed into a hollow ring shape and enlarged. If you would like to tweak the appearance of the data points even further, you can change the shape to fillable rings, meaning the rings will be filled with color. Because you would like to preserve the core color mapped to the `css$conf` factor variable, you will need to change the `p1` object `color=` setting to a `fill=` setting. Other than that, and changing the `shape=` number from 1 to 21, the rest of the coding will look the same.

```
# Changing the color= setting to a fill= setting in p1 to use on
fillable ring data points
p1 <- ggplot(data=power5, aes(x=expmf, y=ntotf,
              fill=conf))

# Changing scatterplot data points to fillable rings mapped to
conference
p1 + geom_point(shape=21, size=3)
```

The final tweak to the data points is to make them a bit transparent. Currently, their appearance is relatively heavy and some of the data points are covering up other data points. To change the transparency of plot elements, use the `alpha=` setting. The `alpha=` setting ranges from 0 (completely transparent) to 1 (completely opaque). For the purposes of this example, use the `alpha=` setting of 0.6 to set the transparency of the data points. Another thing to remember is the `color=` setting. This is an example of how the mapping and setting of plot elements can work together. The fill is mapped to conference, but you can set the color of the rings separately in the `geom_point()` function. To demonstrate, set the ring color to black.

Visit HK*Propel* to view the scatterplot that has enlarged fillable rings, fill color mapped to conferences, and transparency and ring color set outside the parameters of the p1 object.

```
# Adding transparency and setting the ring color separately from
p1 parameters
p1 + geom_point(shape=21, color=1, size=3, alpha=0.6)
```

Previously, when working with the base plotting structures, you encountered an option to customize your tick marks and intervals on the x-axis and y-axis. This, too, is possible in *ggplot2*. However, instead of using the `xaxp=` and `yaxp=` settings, the process will rely on the use of the **scale_x_continuous()** and **scale_y_continuous()** functions. Despite the difference, the inputs are essentially the same. These functions require a minimum value, maximum value, and the desired interval between tick marks. The biggest difference is that instead of determining the number of intervals, you will determine the length of each interval. For the x-axis (because no school in the Power 5 spent less than $100 million or more than $400 million for the combined seasons of 2016 to 2018), set the minimum value to 100, the maximum value to 400, and the intervals to 50 using the `breaks=seq` setting and `by=` setting.

For the y-axis, set the minimum value to 0, the maximum value to 3,000, and the intervals to 500 using the `breaks=seq` setting and `by=` setting.

```
# Customizing tick marks using the scale_x_continuous() and
scale_y_continuous() functions
p1 + geom_point(shape=21, color=1, size=3, alpha=0.6) +
 scale_x_continuous(breaks=seq(100, 400, by = 50)) +
 scale_y_continuous(breaks=seq(0, 3000, by=500))
```

The next elements to modify are the x-axis and y-axis labels. Accomplishing this requires using the **xlab()** and **ylab()** functions. These functions operate the same as the `xlab=` and `ylab=` settings you learned in the base plotting section of this chapter.

```
# Adding x-axis and y-axis labels using the xlab() and ylab()
functions
p1 + geom_point(shape=21, color=1, size=3, alpha=0.6) +
 scale_x_continuous(breaks=seq(100, 400, by = 50)) +
 scale_y_continuous(breaks=seq(0, 3000, by=500)) +
 xlab("Grand Total Athletics Expenses in Millions 2016-2018") +
 ylab("Total Directors' Cup Points 2016-2018")
```

Lastly, this is a good place to introduce the **theme()** function. So far, you have been making all your modifications within a parentheses structure as opposed to a simple `setting=` format. This is because all the elements can be further modified in a myriad of ways within the context of the `theme()` function. Using the `theme()` function, the final element to tackle is the legend.

There are two issues to address with this particular legend. First, the legend title is redundant and therefore unnecessary. It is clear that the different colors and names refer to the Division I Power 5 conferences. Aside from that, the legend is also taking up a significant amount of space in its current position on the right-hand side of the plot. In this plot, the legend is better suited to a position above the plot where it will be rendered horizontally. Removing the legend title and changing the position of the legend requires two small modifications. For the title, use the **element_blank()** function to eliminate various plot elements. To change the position of the legend, use the `legend.position=` setting. Both of these changes are made within the `theme()` function.

```
# Removing the legend title and moving the legend above the plot
p1 + geom_point(shape=21, color=1, size=3, alpha=0.6) +
 scale_x_continuous(breaks=seq(100, 400, by = 50)) +
 scale_y_continuous(breaks=seq(0, 3000, by=500)) +
 xlab("Grand Total Athletics Expenses in Millions 2016-2018") +
 ylab("Total Directors' Cup Points 2016-2018") +
 theme(legend.title = element_blank(),
   legend.position="top")
```

Visit HK*Propel* to see the plot for the grand total athletics expenses and the total Directors' Cup points in the Power 5 conferences for the 2016 to 2018 seasons.

geom_boxplot()

Now that you have learned some techniques for enhancing your plots, the flexibility of data visualization in R is probably becoming apparent. To continue building your skill set, it is time to revisit boxplots and add some more tools to your arsenal using the same *power5* subset that you used previously. The base coding provided has been used to create the p2 object and a boxplot employing the **geom_boxplot()** function. This coding includes elements you have already worked with and should recognize. The base coding includes the following parameters:

- x-axis aesthetic set to conference
- y-axis aesthetic set to grand total athletics expenses in millions of dollars (2016-2018)
- fill color aesthetic mapped to conference
- geometry set with boxplot() function
- alpha level of 0.4 to make the boxplot partially transparent
- boxplot outline color set to black
- x-axis label left blank (inclusion is unnecessary in this boxplot)
- y-axis label added
- custom y-axis tick marks set with a range of 100-400 in intervals of 50
- legend.position= set to "none" to remove it (inclusion is unnecessary in this boxplot)

These parameters have been developed to produce a boxplot that demonstrates the distribution of grand total athletics expenses in each of the Power 5 conferences (see figure 3.2).

```
# Creating the p2 object
p2 <- ggplot(data=power5, aes(x=conf, y=expmf,
             fill=conf))

# Creating the boxplot using the p2 object and geom_boxplot()
function
p2 + geom_boxplot(alpha=0.4, color=1) +
 xlab("") +
 ylab("Athletics Expenses in Millions") +
 scale_y_continuous(breaks=seq(100,400, by=50)) +
 theme(legend.position = "none")
```

Understanding the anatomy of a boxplot is helpful when describing your findings to a client or end user and for customizing the boxplot to represent your findings in the best way possible. Being familiar already with the geom_point() function, the first thing you can do to elevate the effectiveness of this boxplot is to add the individual data points representing the different schools that comprise the Power 5 conferences. You can also increase their size to make them stand out on the vertical line of the boxplot structure. The changes required to add the data points and make them larger are indicated in red.

```
# Adding individual data points to the boxplot
p2 + geom_point(size=2) +
 geom_boxplot(alpha=0.4, color=1) +
 xlab("") +
 ylab("Athletics Expenses in Millions") +
 scale_y_continuous(breaks=seq(100,400, by=50)) +
 theme(legend.position = "none")
```

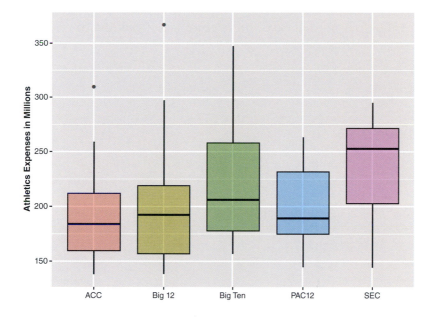

FIGURE 3.2 First draft. Boxplot demonstrating Power 5 athletics expenses in millions of dollars by conference (2016-2018).

You now see that data points representing the different schools have appeared in the plot. There are a few important things to note at this point before moving forward. First, you will notice that the geom_point() function was added before the geom_boxplot() function. This technique is known as layering, and it is something you will engage in frequently as you continue to hone your plotting skills. The most important thing to remember about layering is that the first layer will be the bottom layer. Layers added thereafter using other geometry functions will be added on top of previous layers.

Therefore, if you had added the geom_point() function after the geom_boxplot() function, the individual data points would always be visible in their full color saturation format because they would be a layer above the boxplot layer, thus defeating the purpose of using the alpha= setting to make the boxplot somewhat transparent. This is why the boxplot was set up with a transparency setting to begin with. You will see that the data points appearing in the interquartile range in the boxplot structure are visible, but not as much as the data points appearing outside the interquartile range. This is because the boxplot layer is above the data point layer and has been set to have some transparency. If the alpha= setting did not exist, the only data points visible on the plot would be those outside the interquartile range.

The next item that can be enhanced is the appearance of the x-axis and y-axis text. As this plot has been developed, these labels appear to be a bit on the small side. To grant them a better audience, you can use an axis.text.x= setting within the **element_text()** function, which will be embedded in the theme() function. The same will be true of the y-axis except for .x, which is changed to .y to indicate the text element on the y-axis.

As indicated earlier in the chapter, the utility of the theme() function is immense and will be used frequently to adjust a vast amount of aesthetic plot qualities. Within this plot, add a size= setting as well as a face= setting within the theme() function.

While the `size=` setting for text elements is self-explanatory, the `face=` setting is probably not. This setting refers to the appearance of the text in relation to the following font-style settings guide:

1. Standard
2. **Bold**
3. *Italics*
4. ***Bold Italics***

For the purpose of enhancing this plot, use a font size of 11 and set the `face=` setting to bold.

```
# Modifying the size and font style of x-axis and y-axis text
elements
p2 + geom_point(size=2) +
 geom_boxplot(alpha=0.4, color=1) +
 xlab("") +
 ylab("Athletics Expenses in Millions") +
 scale_y_continuous(breaks=seq(100,400, by=50)) +
 theme(legend.position = "none",
   axis.text.x=element_text(size=11, face=2),
   axis.text.y=element_text(size=11, face=2))
```

Now that the x-axis and y-axis text elements make the plot easier to read, the y-axis title is disproportionally sized. The process for adjusting the size and font style of the y-axis title is almost exactly the same as the process used for adjusting the size and font style of the x-axis and y-axis text elements. The difference is that you will use the `axis.title.y=` setting rather than an `axis.text.y=` setting. The rest of the arguments remain the same. Additionally, you probably would like the axis title to stand out even more than the axis text, so this time, make the `size=` setting 13 and add a `face=` setting to set the font style to bold.

```
# Modifying the y-axis title
p2 + geom_point(size=2) +
 geom_boxplot(alpha=0.4, color=1, size=0.7) +
 xlab("") +
 ylab("Athletics Expenses in Millions") +
 scale_y_continuous(breaks=seq(100,400, by=50)) +
 theme(legend.position = "none",
   axis.text.x=element_text(size=11, face=2),
   axis.text.y=element_text(size=11, face=2),
   axis.title.y=element_text(size=13, face=2))
```

Before moving on to the `geom_jitter()` function, finish off this boxplot by making the following final adjustments:

- Increase the size of the boxplot frames to give them better presence.
- Add a customized main title including position, size, and font style.
- Change the panel background of the plot from the standard gray to something warmer in appearance.
- Change the panel grid lines to match the new panel background.

Though that sounds like a number of items that may take some time to accomplish, the adjustments are actually quite simple. To increase the physical presence of the boxplots, simply add a `size=` setting inside the `geom_boxplot()` function. To add a main title to the plot, you will use the **ggtitle()** function. To change the aesthetics of the main title, you will use the `plot.title=` setting in conjunction with the `element_text()` function. The `size=` and `face=` settings required to alter the appearance of the main title are already familiar to you. In relation to the positioning of the main plot title, you will use the `hjust=` setting. The `hjust=` setting deals with the horizontal alignment of the title. The default value of 0 is align left, the value of 0.5 is align center, and the value of 1 is align right. For this plot, the preference is align left, but you can alter this setting if you would like. These adjustments are all made within the context of the `theme()` function.

To change the panel background, you will use the `panel.background=` setting in conjunction with the **element_rect()** function. To change the panel grid lines, you will use the `panel.grid=` setting in conjunction with the **element_line()** function. Both the panel background and panel grid adjustments will be made within the context of the `theme()` function.

As a final note, the color palette in R is rather expansive. To get a full list of color options, there are a number of resources available online that will show you the full spectrum of colors in R. For this example, however, try using "`slategray1`" for the panel background and "`cornsilk`" for the panel grid lines. Making these final adjustments (indicated in red) will bring your plot to life (see figure 3.3).

```
# Bringing it all together
p2 + geom_point(size=2) +
 geom_boxplot(alpha=0.4, color=1, size=0.8) +
 ggtitle("Power 5 Athletics Expenses by Conference 2016-2018") +
 xlab("") +
 ylab("Athletics Expenses in Millions") +
 scale_y_continuous(breaks=seq(100,400, by=50)) +
 theme(legend.position = "none",
   plot.title = element_text(hjust=0,
          size=16,face="bold"),
   axis.text.x=element_text(size=11, face=2),
   axis.text.y=element_text(size=11, face=2),
   axis.title.y=element_text(size=13, face=2),
   panel.background = element_rect(fill="slategray1"),
   panel.grid = element_line(color="cornsilk"))
```

Visit HK*Propel* to access the video tutorial on next level boxplots.

geom_jitter()

Having mastered the `geom_boxplot()` function, it is time to move on to the `geom_jitter()` function. The **geom_jitter()** function is particularly useful in instances where the number of data points contained in a plot is so great that it is nearly impossible to distinguish one from another. In other words, it paints a muddy picture of how the data is distributed. In the boxplot you just created, this is not an issue. Because each boxplot represents a range of 10 to 15 schools, each data point is distinct and recognizable. When you are looking at data with a greater number of data points, however, they are often overlapping and cover one another. To demonstrate the utility of the `geom_jitter()` function, create a new plotting structure called p3. This new

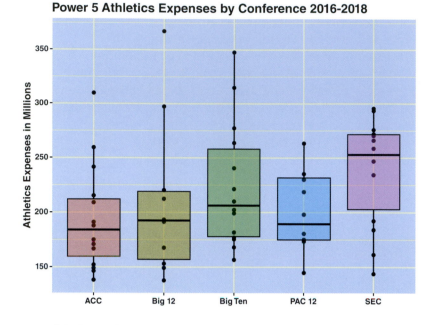

FIGURE 3.3   Final draft. Boxplot demonstrating Power 5 athletics expenses in millions of dollars by conference (2016-2018).

plotting structure will include the entire *css* dataset to look at the average number of total athletes at NCAA Division I schools by division (DI, FCS, FBS, and Power 5). If your *css* dataset has retained the custom order you created for the `css$div` factor variable, the order of the output on the x-axis will be correct. Otherwise, you can create the custom order again using the `levels=` setting in conjunction with the `factor()` function before creating the p3 plotting structure.

```
# Creating the p3 plotting structure
p3 <- ggplot(data=css, aes(x=div, y=atath,
            fill=div))
```

Now that you have created the p3 object, you can make some very minor alterations to the final boxplot rendered above to look at the distribution of data in each of the four divisions. Simply cut and paste the coding in RStudio and make the required changes. The required changes to the coding are indicated in red and include

- swapping the referenced plot structure from p2 to p3,
- changing the plot title and y-axis title, and
- altering the y-axis scale (now using a range between 100 to 1,200 with intervals of 100).

```
# Making minor alterations to the previous boxplot
p3 + geom_point(size=2) +
 geom_boxplot(alpha=0.4, color=1, size=0.8) +
 ggtitle("Average Number of Athletes at D-I Schools by Division")
 +
 xlab("") +
 ylab("Average Number of Athletes") +
```

```
scale_y_continuous(breaks=seq(100,1200, by=100)) +
theme(legend.position = "none",
   plot.title = element_text(hjust=0,
            size=16,face="bold"),
   axis.text.x=element_text(size=11, face=2),
   axis.text.y=element_text(size=11, face=2),
   axis.title.y=element_text(size=13, face=2),
   panel.background = element_rect(fill="slategray1"),
   panel.grid = element_line(color="cornsilk"))
```

As you can see, the boxplots themselves look fine, but the data points are a mess. There are so many overlapping data points that you cannot tell where one starts and the other ends or, for that matter, how many data points are simply buried beneath others. This is where the utility of the geom_jitter() function comes in handy.

What geom_jitter() will do is scatter these data points around to minimize the crowding of currently overlapping data points. To get a strong sense of how each individual data point is distributed within the plot, swap the geom_point() function for the geom_jitter() function. You can give the data a further advantage by changing the shape= setting to 1 (hollow rings). This way, if there are still overlapping data points, it will be absolutely clear. To present your data in an accurate manner, you also need to remove the outliers that come standard with the geom_boxplot() function. This is because those particular cases will now be shown twice, once as an outlier and once as a geom_jitter() data point. To remove the outliers from the geom_boxplot(), use the outlier.shape= setting and set it to NA. Lastly, for variety's sake and practice, change the panel background color to "ghostwhite" and remove the panel grid lines altogether using the element_blank() function.

```
# Uncovering individual data points using geom_jitter() instead of
geom_point()
p3 + geom_jitter(shape=1, size=2) +
 geom_boxplot(alpha=0.4, color=1, size=0.8, outlier.shape=NA) +
 ggtitle("Average Number of Athletes at D-I Schools by Division")
 +
 xlab("") +
 ylab("Average Number of Athletes") +
 scale_y_continuous(breaks=seq(100,1200, by=100)) +
 theme(legend.position = "none",
   plot.title = element_text(hjust=0,
            size=16,face="bold"),
   axis.text.x=element_text(size=11, face=2),
   axis.text.y=element_text(size=11, face=2),
   axis.title.y=element_text(size=13, face=2),
   panel.background = element_rect(fill="ghostwhite"),
   panel.grid = element_blank())
```

Visit HK*Propel* to see the figure for using geom_jitter() to better understand the distribution of crowded and overlapping data points.

geom_histogram()

Histograms are popular plotting methods and are effective in demonstrating the distribution patterns of data within a given dataset. You can conceptualize this distribution in terms of a classic bell curve. Histograms are capable of demonstrating whether data reflects a normal distribution, negatively or positively skewed distribution, bimodal distribution, or random distribution. Before jumping into histograms,

however, make sure the new variables you created for the *css* dataset in chapter 2 have been retained. If you do not still have these variables in your current *css* dataset, please re-create them at this point. They are as follows:

```
# Average male athletic aid per athlete
css$ama <- round((css$maidmf*1000000)/(css$amath*2), digits=0)

# Average female athletic aid per athlete
css$afa <- round((css$faidmf*1000000)/(css$afath*2), digits=0)

# Average total athletic aid per athlete
css$ata <- round((css$taidmf*1000000)/(css$atath*2), digits=0)

# Average male recruiting expenses per athlete
css$amr <- round((css$mcruitmf*1000000)/(css$amath*2), digits=0)

# Average female recruiting expenses per athlete
css$afr <- round((css$fcruitmf*1000000)/(css$afath*2), digits=0)

# Average total recruiting expenses per athlete
css$atr <- round((css$tcruitmf*1000000)/(css$atath*2), digits=0)
```

When you are sure you have made the necessary adjustments to the original *css* dataset, you can save it in your working directory using the **write.csv()** function. The input required for the write.csv() function is a reference to the dataset (*css*) followed by a comma and the new file name you would like to use in quotation marks. You will add another comma after the new file name and add a row.names=F setting to maintain the integrity of the original *css* dataset structure.

```
# Saving the new css dataset using the write.csv() function
write.csv(css,"css.csv", row.names = F)
```

Your *css* dataset should contain 348 observations and 53 variables. To get started with histograms, create the p4 plotting object using the ggplot() function. The inputs required for the p4 plotting object are the dataset being referenced and the data that will appear on the x-axis. Other elements that can be included in the aes()

function embedded in the `ggplot()` function are attributes such as color and fill; for now, though, start with the basic structure. The dataset to reference in the `ggplot()` function is the *css* dataset, and the x-axis data will be populated using the average total athletic aid per athlete `css$ata` variable.

```
# Creating the p4 object
p4 <- ggplot(data=css, aes(x=ata))
```

Now that the plotting structure has been created and saved as an object in the global environment, add the geometry using the **geom_histogram()** function along with a `binwidth=` setting. The purpose of the `binwidth=` setting is to set a series of ranges that will be captured on the x-axis. For instance, the minimum value for average total athletic aid per athlete is approximately $4,000 whereas the maximum value for average total athletic aid per athlete is approximately $47,000. Using a `bin-width=1000` setting, all the cases that fall within $1,000 ranges will be captured. By way of example, all the schools that averaged between $20,000 and $20,999 in total athletic aid per athlete will be in one bin, while all schools averaging between $21,000 and $21,999 in total athletic aid per athlete will be in another bin. Each school in a bin adds to the overall total represented as a frequency count on the y-axis. The frequency count details how many schools are represented per bin.

```
# Generating a histogram for average total athletic aid per
athlete with binwidth=1000
p4 + geom_histogram(binwidth=1000)
```

As you can see, the output is relatively rudimentary and uninspiring from a visual perspective. The plot, however, is still compelling in the sense that it provides a clear sense of the distribution of average total athletic aid per athlete. As was the case with descriptive and inferential statistics (covered in chapter 2), you immediately notice the Ivy League schools are all represented on the $0 line, so eliminating them is the first thing you need to do. You can remove the Ivy League schools by creating the *nonivy* subset. You may still have this subsetted dataset in your global environment from the work you did in chapter 2.

```
# Creating the nonivy subset
nonivy <- css[css$conf != "Ivy League",]
```

You can now substitute the *nonivy* data for the *css* data in the p4 plotting structure and use the altered plotting structure to create the first draft of your average total athletic aid per athlete histogram.

```
# Histogram depicting average total athletic aid per athlete
p4 <- ggplot(data=nonivy, aes(x=ata))
p4 + geom_histogram(binwidth=1000)
```

While this is not the most impactful data plot as it stands, this histogram demonstrates positively skewed data. The tail of the histogram gets smaller as the average total athletic aid per athlete increases. Most of the schools are clumped in the $10,000 to $22,000 range. If you were to check the histogram against the dataset, you would verify this conclusion. Of the 340 Division I schools represented in the *nonivy* dataset, 237 of them averaged between $10,000 and $22,000 in total athletic aid per athlete—in other words, approximately 68 percent of the schools—so even in this relatively unattractive form, the histogram still has value.

To make the histogram more visually appealing and easier to read, some basic alterations can be made. To start, create a border around each of the bins in the histogram using a color= setting. It can be anything you like. The border color is set to "blue" for this example.

Remember that when working with aesthetic elements such as fillable rings, boxplots, or in this case histograms, there is a difference between the color= setting and the fill= setting. The color= setting in these instances refers to the frame of the geometry whereas the fill= setting refers to the color contained within the frame. In this instance, the fill= setting is set to "lightsteelblue1" to add some visual contrast between the frame and the fill.

At this stage, it is also a good idea to tighten up the scale intervals using the scale_x_continuous() and scale_y_continuous() functions that you learned earlier in the chapter. For the x-axis data, set the minimum value to 0 and the maximum value to 50,000; for the intervals, use a value of 5,000. For the y-axis data, set the minimum value to 0, the maximum value to 30, and a value of 2 for the intervals. You can also add a main title, x-axis title, and y-axis title.

```
# Modifying the Histogram - phase 1
p4 + geom_histogram(binwidth=1000, color="blue",
        fill="lightsteelblue1") +
 scale_x_continuous(breaks=seq(0,50000,by=5000)) +
 scale_y_continuous(break=seq(0,30,by=2)) +
 ggtitle("Frequency Distribution of Average Total Athletic Aid") +
 xlab("Average Total Athletic Aid Per Athlete") +
 ylab("Frequency Count")
```

The histogram is beginning to take shape from an aesthetics standpoint. The breaks between the bins are much easier to read, and the frequency counts are easier to comprehend having moved to an interval of 2 on the y-axis. Additionally, changing the x-axis tick marks to every $5,000 rather than $10,000 makes that portion of the data easier to read. The final alterations to make are purely aesthetic in nature and involve using the theme() function. Within the theme() function, you will do the following:

- Add a custom color line to the x-axis and y-axis.
- Change the x-axis and y-axis text color.
- Set the panel background color.
- Remove the panel grid from the plot.
- Move the main title into the plot.

To achieve these tasks, a series of functions and settings will be used in tandem within the theme() function. The changes to the coding script are highlighted in red below. For this example, make the custom color line for the x-axis and y-axis "blue" as well as the x-axis and y-axis text. For the panel background, use the color "linen" (see figure 3.4). The groupings of theme() settings, functions, and function settings for making the necessary changes are as follows:

theme() settings

- axis.line=
- axis.text.x=
- axis.text.y=

- panel.background=
- panel.grid=
- plot.title=

functions

- element_line()
- element_text()
- element_text()
- element_rect()
- element_blank()
- element_text()

function settings

- color=
- color=
- color=
- fill=
- N/A
- hjust= and vjust=

```
# Final adjustments to the average athletic aid per athlete
histogram
p4 + geom_histogram(binwidth=1000, color="blue",
        fill="lightsteelblue1") +
 scale_x_continuous(breaks=seq(0,50000,by=5000)) +
 scale_y_continuous(breaks=seq(0,30,by=2)) +
 ggtitle("Distribution of Average Total Athletic Aid") +
 xlab("Average Total Athletic Aid Per Athlete") +
 ylab("Frequency Count") +
 theme(axis.line = element_line(color="blue"),
   axis.text.x = element_text(color="blue"),
   axis.text.y = element_text(color="blue"),
   panel.background = element_rect(fill="linen"),
   panel.grid = element_blank(),
   plot.title=element_text(hjust=0.9,
            vjust=-15))
```

Histograms can also serve a deeper purpose in describing the distribution of data within a dataset. Suppose you hypothesized that the average total athletic aid per athlete is higher at private schools than at state schools based on the cost of tuition. You can use the histogram plotting structure to make the comparison with minimal effort. All that is required is to map the fill setting in the p4 plotting structure to the css$class factor variable and remove the color= setting from the geom_histogram() function. The rest is aesthetics. To keep the output distinct, the panel background color will be removed altogether. Because this is a comparative histogram, a legend will be placed in the plot using the legend.position= setting. The legend will be modified using the scale_fill_discrete() function to remove the legend title and customize the classification labels (see figure 3.5). All changes made to the previous coding are indicated in red.

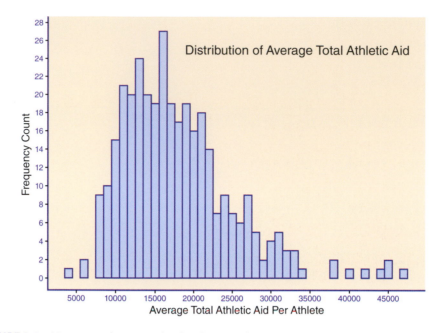

FIGURE 3.4 Histogram depicting the distribution of average total athletic aid per athlete.

```
# Changing the plotting structure to compare private schools and
state schools
p4 <- ggplot(data=nonivy, aes(x=ata,
            fill=class))
p4 + geom_histogram(binwidth=1000, color="blue",
          alpha=0.5) +
  scale_x_continuous(breaks=seq(0,50000,by=5000)) +
  scale_y_continuous(breaks=seq(0,30,by=2)) +
  scale_fill_discrete(name="",
          labels=c("Private Schools",
              "State Schools")) +
  ggtitle("Distribution of Average Total Athletic Aid") +
  xlab("Average Total Athletic Aid Per Athlete") +
  ylab("Frequency Count") +
  theme(axis.line = element_line(color="blue"),
    axis.text.x = element_text(color="blue"),
    axis.text.y = element_text(color="blue"),
    panel.background = element_rect(fill=NA),
    panel.grid = element_blank(),
    plot.title=element_text(hjust=0.9,
          vjust=-15),
    legend.position = c(0.7,0.7))
```

geom_density()

Like a histogram, a **density plot** demonstrates the distribution of data throughout a dataset in a way that indicates whether the data is distributed in a normal, negatively or positively skewed, bimodal, or random manner. However, the primary difference

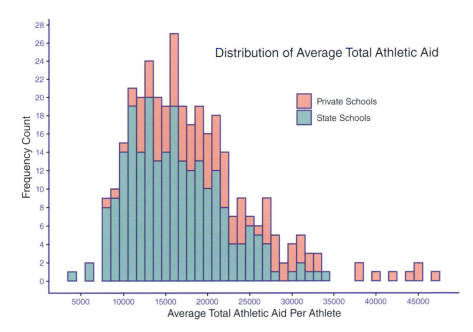

FIGURE 3.5 Histogram depicting the distribution of average total athletic aid per athlete at private and state schools.

is that density plots are not constrained by bin settings and therefore create a smooth distribution curve. Because density plots use incremental decimal measures, the area below the density line adds up to 1, but for simplicity's sake, you can conceptualize this as 100 percent. The rise and fall of the line demonstrates the relative probability of cases being in any given area of the density plot (Analyttica Datalab, 2019).

Density plots are excellent for demonstrating the distribution of any measured variable to a client or end user so that they can understand how and where they stack up when compared to competitors. To examine the similarities and differences between histograms and density plots, the same *nonivy* dataset is used along with the measured variable for analysis, which was average total athletic aid per athlete. This will give you a way of comparing the output of the previous histograms with the current density plots. To create the p5 plotting structure, use the ggplot() and aes() functions. The core coding only requires the data being referenced and a value for the x-axis.

```
# Creating the p5 plotting structure
p5 <- ggplot(data=nonivy, aes(x=ata))
```

Now that the p5 plotting structure is created, you can generate the first density plot using the **geom_density()** function. You can change the histogram you created earlier into a density plot using the same aesthetic qualities coded in the histogram section. You can do this by copying and pasting the code and then making minor adjustments. The minor adjustments include
  • swapping the p4 plotting structure for the p5 plotting structure,
  • swapping the geom_histogram() for the geom_density() function,
  • removing the binwidth=1000 setting,
  • removing the scale_y_continuous() function, and
  • altering the y-axis label.

```
# Changing the histogram coding into density plot coding
p5 + geom_density(color="blue",
            fill="lightsteelblue1") +
 scale_x_continuous(breaks=seq(0,50000,by=5000)) +
 ggtitle("Distribution of Average Total Athletic Aid") +
 xlab("Average Total Athletic Aid Per Athlete") +
 ylab("Density") +
 theme(axis.line = element_line(color="blue"),
   axis.text.x = element_text(color="blue"),
   axis.text.y = element_text(color="blue"),
   panel.background = element_rect(fill="linen"),
   panel.grid = element_blank(),
   plot.title=element_text(hjust=0.9,
            vjust=-15))
```

The same is true of comparing the distribution of average athletic aid between private schools and state schools. Again, the changes made to the coding are minimal and offer you an opportunity to look at the two plots side by side (see figure 3.6). The changes required include

- adding a `fill=class` argument to the p5 plotting structure,
- swapping the p4 plotting structure for the p5 plotting structure,
- swapping the `geom_histogram()` for the `geom_density()` function,
- removing the `binwidth=1000` setting,
- removing the `scale_y_continuous()` function, and
- altering the y-axis label.

```
# Adding a fill=class argument to the p5 plotting structure
p5 <- ggplot(data=nonivy, aes(x=ata,
            fill=class))

# Changing the histogram coding into density plot coding
p5 + geom_density(color="blue", alpha=0.5) +
 scale_x_continuous(breaks=seq(0,50000,by=5000)) +
 scale_fill_discrete(name="",
            labels=c("Private Schools",
               "State Schools")) +
 ggtitle("Distribution of Average Total Athletic Aid") +
 xlab("Average Total Athletic Aid Per Athlete") +
 ylab("Density") +
 theme(axis.line = element_line(color="blue"),
   axis.text.x = element_text(color="blue"),
   axis.text.y = element_text(color="blue"),
   panel.background = element_rect(fill=NA),
   panel.grid = element_blank(),
   plot.title=element_text(hjust=0.9,
            vjust=-15),
   legend.position = c(0.7,0.7))
```

Being able to look at the two distribution plots side by side allows you to determine which would be best for discussing data with a client or end user. You could additionally join the two by adding a density plot line to a histogram, but that may

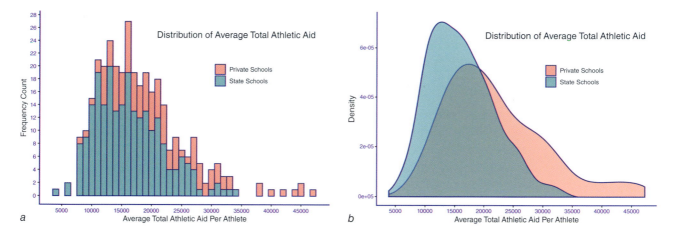

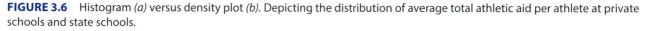

FIGURE 3.6 Histogram *(a)* versus density plot *(b)*. Depicting the distribution of average total athletic aid per athlete at private schools and state schools.

muddy the waters. Either way, being able to describe the distribution of data in a graphical manner to a client or end user is critically important.

geom_line()

Line plots are used to link data points together to demonstrate the relationship between two variables. As x-axis values change for one variable, it is possible to see the result the x-axis changes have on the y-axis variable, and vice versa. It is similar to the concepts covered earlier on scatterplots. In fact, it is recommended that you use a combination of the **geom_line()** function used to create a line plot and the geom_point() function used to create a scatterplot. Using these functions in tandem will produce a plot that effectively demonstrates the relationship between the variables being analyzed.

For the purposes of demonstrating the utility of the geom_line() function, create a subset of data named *difcs*, which stands for the DI and FCS divisions. Adhere to the following parameters to create the *difcs* subset:

- Only include schools from the DI and FCS divisions.

- Schools included must have offered some level of athletic aid for the 2017 to 2018 season.

- Schools must have scored at least 70 points in the Directors' Cup competition for the 2017 to 2018 season.

```
# Creating the difcs dataset
difcs <- css[css$div=="DI" & css$ntot2 >= 70 &
        css$taidm2 > 0 |
        css$div=="FCS" & css$ntot2 >= 70 &
        css$taidm2 > 0,]
```

Your new *difcs* dataset should include 81 observations and 53 variables. The purpose of creating the *difcs* dataset is that it allows analysts to look at similarly situated schools included in the dataset. Oftentimes, individuals analyzing data have little to no interest in comparisons between observations (in this case, schools) that do not naturally compete with one another based on the measures included in the dataset.

Visit HK*Propel* to view and compare the histogram and the density plot depicting the distribution of average total athletic aid per athlete, and to watch the video tutorials on density plots and histograms.

For instance, it makes little sense to compare Power 5 schools to FCS schools on measures such as grand total athletics expenses, total athletics recruiting expenses, total athletic aid expenses, and total Directors' Cup points. However, when conducting inferential statistics, you learned there are few statistically significant differences between DI and FCS schools based on the *css* dataset measures. The salient difference between the DI and FCS divisions is the inclusion of football in the FCS division, which naturally leads to higher numbers in areas such as average number of athletes. However, even with football, there is no statistically significant difference between grand total athletics expenses or total athletic aid.

In this analysis, create a line plot that demonstrates the relationship between the number of total athletes at DI and FCS schools included in the *difcs* dataset and total athletic aid at DI and FCS schools included in the *difcs* dataset for the 2017 to 2018 season. To get started, create the p6 object using the `ggplot()` function. The inputs required for the `ggplot()` function for this form of data plotting will be a reference to the dataset (*difcs*) using the `data=` setting, an x-axis input (taidm2), and a y-axis input (atath). Additionally, to demonstrate the difference between the DI and FCS divisions, map the `color=` setting to the `difcs$div` variable.

```
# Creating the p6 plotting structure
p6 <- ggplot(data =difcs, aes(x=difcs$taidm2,
             y=difcs$atath,
             color=difcs$div))
```

Now that you have created the p6 plotting structure, you can begin to add geometry to it starting with the `geom_line()` function. As you progress through the process of modifying this plot, additional elements will be added to enhance the base plot.

The first new wrinkle to introduce is the ability to use colors other than the default R colors when mapping elements to dataset variables. This can be achieved using a `scale_color_manual()` function with a `values=` setting contained within. You will need the number of manually set colors to match the number of levels contained in the categorical factor variable. In this case, the `difcs$div` variable has two levels (DI and FCS), so two colors will be required in the `values=` setting. For this example, manually set the colors mapped to the `difcs$div` variable as "olivedrab4" and "orchid".

```
# Basic line plot for total athletes and total athletic aid at DI
and FCS schools 2017-2018
p6 + geom_line() +
 scale_color_manual(values=c("olivedrab4", "orchid"))
```

The line plot should include a line for DI schools (olivedrab4 color) and a separate line for FCS schools (orchid color). Naturally, as predicted, FCS schools have more athletes on average than DI schools. What is more important, however, is the relationship between total athletic aid and total athletes for both divisions. You will see that the trajectory of both lines is similar. Both lines demonstrate how much athletic aid rises in comparison to the number of total athletes.

As it stands, the plot is simple but already has utility. To further improve the effectiveness of this line plot, add a layer using the `geom_point()` function. Some additional enhancements are to include a `size=` setting within the `geom_line()` function, as well as a `shape=21` setting, `size=2` setting, `fill="white"` setting, and `stroke=1.3` setting in the `geom_point()` function. These changes to the coding are highlighted in red. What these custom settings accomplish is as follows:

- The lines in the `geom_line()` function will be thicker, thus making them stand out better.
- The shape of the data points in the `geom_point()` function will be changed to fillable rings.
- The data points in the `geom_point()` function will be enlarged.
- The fillable rings produced by the `geom_point()` function will be filled with white.
- The thickness of the rings will be increased.

```
# Enhancing the original line plot
p6 + geom_line(size=0.7) +
 scale_color_manual(values=c("olivedrab4", "orchid")) +
 geom_point(shape=21, size=2,fill="white", stroke=1.3)
```

As you can see, adding data points greatly enhances the impact of this line plot. The additional sizing, and the addition of fillable rings set to white to represent the individual data points, makes a significant difference. At this point, modify the x-axis scale to tighten up the intervals, add a main title, and modify the x-axis and y-axis labels. By now, you should feel comfortable working with the `scale_x_continuous()`, `ggtitle()`, `xlab()`, and `ylab()` functions.

```
# Adjusting the x-axis scale, adding a main title and modifying
the axis labels
p6 + geom_line(size=0.7) +
 scale_color_manual(values=c("olivedrab4", "orchid")) +
 geom_point(shape=21, size=2,fill="white", stroke=1.3) +
 scale_x_continuous(breaks=seq(0,20,by=2)) +
 ggtitle("Athletic Aid by Total Athletes at DI and FCS Schools) +
 xlab("Total Athletic Aid in Millions 2017-2018") +
 ylab("Total Number of Athletes at DI and FCS Schools")
```

The next alterations will be aesthetic changes using the `theme()` function. In this instance, change the background of the plot to the color "oldlace" and the panel grid to "white" using the `panel.background=` setting and the `panel.grid=` setting in conjunction with the `element_rect()` and `element_line()` functions. These settings and functions should be familiar to you from previous exercises.

```
# Changing the plot background color and the plot grid color
p6 + geom_line(size=0.7) +
 scale_color_manual(values=c("olivedrab4", "orchid")) +
 geom_point(shape=21, size=2,fill="white", stroke=1.3) +
 scale_x_continuous(breaks=seq(0,20,by=2)) +
 ggtitle("Athletic Aid by Total Athletes at DI and FCS Schools") +
 xlab("Total Athletic Aid in Millions 2017-2018") +
 ylab("Total Number of Athletes at DI and FCS Schools") +
 theme(panel.background = element_rect(fill="oldlace"),
   panel.grid = element_line(color="white"))
```

The final alterations to this plot all deal with different options available to you for modifying the legend. The first element that is modifiable is the direction of the legend.

By default, the legend has generally appeared in a vertical configuration. There are times, however, where you will prefer a legend that is configured horizontally. This is a simple thing to achieve by using the `legend.direction=` setting within the `theme()` function.

You may also want to modify the position of the legend, which you already have some practice with. To this point, you have moved the plot legend around using settings such as `legend.position="top"` as well as setting coordinates such as `legend.position=c(0.7, 0.7)`, which was the setting you used in the histogram and density plot section. The `legend.position=` setting possesses great utility, so it is important to understand what the different orientations are.

The guide below lists the four different core position settings. From the core position settings, you can make whatever alterations you need for moving the legend around vertically and horizontally based on numbers ranging from 0 to 1. The first number controls horizontal movement and the second number controls vertical movement.

```
legend.position=c(0,1)   Top Left Corner
legend.position=c(1,1)   Top Right Corner
legend.position=c(0,0)   Bottom Left Corner
legend.position=c(1,0)   Bottom Right Corner
```

For the purposes of this plot, use a horizontal figure of 0.2 (moving it 0.2 in from the left) and a vertical figure of 0.8 (moving it 0.8 up from the bottom). Moving the legend into the plot may also lead to the desire to remove the background because the color or aesthetic may not match the plot background you have developed. This can be achieved using the `legend.background=` setting within the `theme()` function. Additionally, you may wish to remove the legend title because it is redundant and unnecessary. This can be achieved using the `legend.title=` setting within the `theme()` function. Both of these elements can be eliminated from the plot by employing the `element_blank()` function that you have become familiar with.

Lastly, you may wish to change the fill color of the legend key elements because they no longer match the panel background (see figure 3.7). You can accomplish this by using the `legend.key=` setting along with the `element_rect()` function within the `theme()` function. This process mirrors the process used to change the plot panel background color. As such, set both the `color=` setting and the `fill=` setting to the "oldlace" color setting. The final alterations to the plot are highlighted in red.

```
# Final alterations - modifying the legend aesthetics
p6 + geom_line(size=0.7) +
 scale_color_manual(values=c("olivedrab4", "orchid")) +
 geom_point(shape=21, size=2,fill="white", stroke=1.3) +
 scale_x_continuous(breaks=seq(0,20,by=2)) +
 ggtitle("Athletic Aid by Total Athletes at DI and FCS Schools") +
 xlab("Total Athletic Aid in Millions 2017-2018") +
 ylab("Total Number of Athletes at DI and FCS Schools") +
 theme(panel.background = element_rect(fill="oldlace"),
  panel.grid = element_line(color="white"),
  legend.direction = "horizontal",
  legend.position = c(0.2,0.8),
  legend.background = element_blank(),
  legend.title = element_blank(),
  legend.key = element_rect(color="oldlace",
            fill="oldlace"))
```

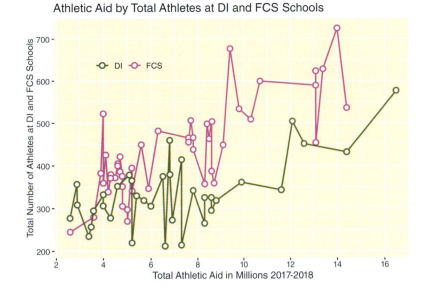

Athletic Aid by Total Athletes at DI and FCS Schools

FIGURE 3.7 | Line plot depicting the relationship between total athletes and total athletic aid at DI and FCS schools.

geom_text() and geom_text_repel()

The geom_text() and geom_text_repel() functions offer analysts an opportunity to label data points. This is a tool that can make a significant impact in the boardroom when one is trying to demonstrate to a client or end user where they stand in relation to their competition. To get started, use the **geom_text()** function to demonstrate the odds a school has of winning the Directors' Cup competition based on its division designation. Very quickly, using a text plot, one can demonstrate unequivocally that if the school is not a member of a Power 5 conference, it has essentially no chance of winning.

To demonstrate this truth, create the p7 plotting structure using the css$div factor variable for the x-axis input and the css$ntot2 variable containing total Directors' Cup points for the 2017 to 2018 season for the y-axis input. To differentiate between the four divisions of DI, FCS, FBS, and Power 5, map the color= setting to the css$div factor variable. To create the text geometry, add a label= setting in the aes() function; alternatively, you can wait and add a separate aes() function within the geom_text() function. Because you have not mapped separate function settings outside your plotting structures up to this point, this is a good opportunity to learn how to do that. Therefore, wait on creating the label= setting required for using the geom_text() function.

```
# Creating the p7 plotting structure
p7 <- ggplot(data=css, aes(x=div,
            y=ntot2,
            color=div))
```

Now that you have the p7 plotting structure, you can add geometry to the plot using the geom_text() function. As previously stated, the only real requirement within the geom_text() function is the label= setting, which in this case will be set to division. This will make each of the data points in the plot take on its mapped label dimension (DI, FCS, FBS, Power 5). If you were to run this, however, you would see a significant amount of overlapping data and it would be a bit of a mess. To eliminate this problem, you can use a `check_overlap=` setting and set it to T or TRUE.

```
# Directors' Cup scoring by division 2017-2018
p7 + geom_text(aes(label=div), check_overlap=T)
```

From the resulting plot, you understand clearly that you have almost no chance of winning the Directors' Cup trophy if you are a DI (non-football), FCS, or non-Power 5 FBS school. The highest-scoring school outside of the Power 5 during the 2017 to 2018 season was Princeton, which finished 40th in the competition and trailed the overall winner by more than 850 points.

To demonstrate the utility of the `geom_text()` function even further, you can apply it to a plot you developed earlier in the chapter. In the earlier section on scatterplots, you created an object named `power5` that contained only schools from Power 5 conferences. You used this object with the `ggplot()` function to create the p1 plotting structure that had the fill color of the data points mapped to conference. This plotting structure along with the `geom_point()` function was used to demonstrate the relationship between grand total athletics expenses and total Directors' Cup points for the 2016 to 2018 seasons. The plot that was generated showed that three of the schools in the top 5 in scoring were from the Pac 12, despite the Pac 12 not having a single school in the top 10 of grand total athletics expenses.

Using the same p1 plotting structure but replacing the `geom_point()` function with the `geom_text()` function will reveal which three Pac 12 schools finished in the top 5 of the Directors' Cup competition. It will also reveal which of the Big 12 schools was the only school to top $350 million in grand total athletics expenses for the 2016 to 2018 seasons. To keep as many data points as possible on the plot with the `check_overlap=` setting set to T, while also maintaining the readability of the school names, set the `size=` setting to 2.5 within the `geom_text()` function. Lastly, remember to map the `color=` setting to conference rather than having the `fill=` setting mapped to conference in the p1 plotting structure, because these data points will no longer be fillable rings.

```
# Changing the p1 plotting structure
p1 <- ggplot(data=power5,
         aes(x=expmf, y=ntotf, color= conf))

# Replacing the geom_point() function with the geom_text()
function
p1 + geom_text(aes(label=school), check_overlap = T,
         size=2.5)+
  scale_x_continuous(breaks=seq(100, 400, by = 50)) +
  scale_y_continuous(breaks=seq(0, 3000, by=500)) +
  xlab("Grand Total Athletics Expenses in Millions 2016-2018") +
  ylab("Total Directors' Cup Points 2016-2018")
```

Visit HK*Propel* to view the geom_point() versus geom_text() scatterplot with Power 5 athletics expenses and total Directors' Cup points for the 2016 to 2018 seasons.

From the plot comparison, you see that the three Pac 12 schools that finished in the top 5 of the Directors' Cup competition were Stanford, USC, and UCLA. The Big 12 school that spent more than $350 million on athletics for the span of 2016 to 2018 was Texas, which to its credit, also finished in the top 10 of the Directors' Cup competition during that time span. In layperson's terms, the `geom_text()` function allows an analyst to put a name to a face, which is a powerful way to graphically present data.

As a final demonstration illustrating the importance of spending and its relationship to earning points in the Directors' Cup competition, return to using the full *css* dataset containing all 348 schools. This dataset will be developed using the css$div variable to label the data points. What this plot will demonstrate beyond a shadow of a doubt is that when it comes to competing in the Directors' Cup, you basically get what you pay for. If your school rank in overall spending is 150, be prepared to finish somewhere around 150 in the Directors' Cup standings. This plot also further demonstrates that anybody outside of the Power 5 essentially has no realistic shot of competing for the top spot.

To complete this plot, create a new p8 plotting structure using the *css* dataset as the data reference, grand total athletics expenses for the 2016 to 2018 seasons (expmf) for the x-axis input, and total Directors' Cup points for the 2016 to 2018 seasons (ntotf) for the y-axis input, and then map the color= setting to the css$div variable.

```
# Creating the p8 plotting structure
p8 <- ggplot(data=css, aes(x=expmf, y=ntotf,
           color=div))
```

There are only a couple of other changes to your previous coding that are required to make this plot complete. The label= setting will be altered from school to div, and the scale_x_continuous() breaks= setting will now have 0 as its lowest value rather than 100 because there are a large number of schools that spent less than $100 million during this time span as opposed to the Power 5, which had no schools spending less than $100 million during this time span. Lastly, because a legend is not necessary for this plot, a legend.position="none" setting will be added to the theme() function.

```
# Using geom_text() to demonstrate the relationship between
spending and Directors' Cup points
p8 + geom_text(aes(label=div), check_overlap = T,
          size=2.5)+
 scale_x_continuous(breaks=seq(0, 400, by = 50)) +
 scale_y_continuous(breaks=seq(0, 3000, by=500)) +
 xlab("Grand Total Athletics Expenses in Millions 2016-2018") +
 ylab("Total Directors' Cup Points 2016-2018") +
 theme(legend.position="none")
```

Visit HK*Propel* to view the scatterplot using the geom_text() function to demonstrate the relationship between spending and total Directors' Cup points by division.

The **geom_text_repel()** function works much the same as the geom_text() function but offers more flexibility in terms of manipulating aesthetics. By way of example, instead of using a check_overlap=T setting, the geom_text_repel() function will shift data labels in a way that accommodates all data points, even if they are overlapping. There are a number of additional settings to be explored as well, but before using the geom_text_repel() function for the first time, introduce a new column of data to the *css* dataset. This new column of data will represent the average total cost per athlete at the schools contained in the dataset for the 2016 to 2018 seasons. Name this new column of data aca, which stands for average cost per athlete.

```
# Creating the `css$aca` average cost per athlete variable
css$aca <- round((css$expmf*1000000)/
          (css$atath*2), digits=0)
```

Now that you have developed the average cost per athlete variable, develop a new subset of data called *mg*, which stands for middle group. This subsetted dataset must accomplish the following goals:

1. Eliminate all Power 5 schools.
2. Include only schools that scored between 100 and 300 points in the Directors' Cup competition for the 2017 to 2018 season.
3. Include only schools that spent between $50,000 and $100,000 on average per athlete.

The purpose of this new subset is to look at some of the schools that appear in the middle of the dataset in terms of measures such as grand total athletics expenses, total Directors' Cup points, average number of athletes at their schools, number of sports at their schools, and so on. By eliminating a number of schools from both ends of the spectrum, schools that are similarly situated (albeit within a healthy range) can begin to see where they truly stand in relation to their true competitors.

```
# Building the mg dataset
mg <- css[css$div!="Power 5" & css$ntot2 >=100 &
          css$ntot2 <=300 & css$aca >= 50000 &
          css$aca <=100000,]
```

Using the *mg* data subset, create the p9 plotting structure with average cost per athlete represented on the x-axis, total Directors' Cup points for the 2017 to 2018 season represented on the y-axis, the `color=` setting mapped to the mg$div variable, and the `label=` setting mapped to the mg$school variable.

```
# Creating the p9 plotting structure
p9 <- ggplot(data=mg, aes(x=aca, y=ntot2,
             color=div, label=school))
```

Now that the plotting structure has been developed, the plot can be modified through a series of alterations based on settings and functions. One thing to note is that based on the amount of physical space required for a plot constructed using the `geom_text_repel()` function, it will need to be exported in a much larger size than the default size in terms of pixels. For the purposes of this plot, export it by checking the box to maintain aspect ratio and setting the width to 1,200 pixels. This will allow for the plot to distribute the inputs more appropriately. However, do not be alarmed if the bottom right plot panel in RStudio looks like a complete mess. Trust that the plot is being developed properly. If at any time you would like to see how it will be rendered in the larger size, try exporting it and you will get a clearer picture. The modifications that will be made to the p9 plotting structure include the following:

1. Adding the `geom_text_repel()` geometry
2. Enlarging the `geom_text_repel()` labels and putting them in a bold italics font
3. Adding individual data points to the labels by layering with the `geom_point()` function
4. Adding labels for the x-axis and y-axis
5. Customizing the x-axis and y-axis scales and intervals
6. Customizing the legend as follows:

a. Removing the legend title

b. Enlarging the legend text

c. Specifying the legend position

d. Removing the legend background

e. Using a custom color and fill for the legend key elements

7. Enlarging the text on the x-axis and y-axis and putting them in a bold font

8. Enlarging the text on the x-axis and y-axis titles

9. Removing the plot panel background

10. Adding a custom color setting for the panel.grid

As these changes are made, the coding that has been added will appear in red. Start with the first five items on the list. In item 2, for the size= setting in the geom_text_repel() function, set it to 5, and for the fontface= setting, set it to bold italics. Items 3 and 4 should not require any explanation. In item 5, when using the scale_x_continuous() function, set the minimum value to 50,000, the maximum value to 100,000, and the intervals to 25,000. When using the scale_y_continuous() function, set the minimum value to 100, the maximum value to 300, and the intervals to 50.

```
# First draft - geom_text_repel() plot
p9 + geom_text_repel(size=5, fontface=4) +
 geom_point() +
 xlab("Average Cost Per Athlete 2017-2018") +
 ylab("Total Directors' Cup Points 2017-2018") +
 scale_x_continuous(breaks=seq(50000, 100000, by = 25000)) +
 scale_y_continuous(breaks=seq(100, 300, by=50))
```

Next, work on meeting the requirements for the legend. This will require you to employ a number of different settings and functions within the theme() function. One of the requirements is to increase the size of the legend text. To achieve this, use the size= setting and set it to 20. For the legend.position= setting, use a horizontal position of 0.15 and a vertical position of 0.93. For the legend.key= setting, use a color=NA setting along with a fill=NA setting.

```
# Second draft - geom_text_repel() plot - working with the legend
settings
p9 + geom_text_repel(size=5, fontface=4) +
 geom_point() +
 xlab("Average Cost Per Athlete 2017-2018") +
 ylab("Total Directors' Cup Points 2017-2018") +
 scale_x_continuous(breaks=seq(50000, 100000, by = 25000)) +
 scale_y_continuous(breaks=seq(100, 300, by=50)) +
 theme(legend.title = element_blank(),
   legend.text = element_text(size=20),
   legend.position=c(0.15,0.93),
   legend.background = element_blank(),
   legend.key = element_rect(color=NA,fill=NA))
```

At this point, you can attack items 7 and 8 on the list. For the x-axis and y-axis text, set the size= setting to 15 and the face= setting to bold. For the x-axis text, also include an `hjust=` setting to make the axis text right-aligned to the axis tick marks. This will prevent the final 100,000 label from running off the edge of the plot. For the x-axis and y-axis titles, set the `size=` setting to 25.

```
# Third draft - geom_text_repel() plot - working with the x-axis
and y-axis text and title settings
p9 + geom_text_repel(size=5, fontface=4) +
 geom_point() +
 xlab("Average Cost Per Athlete 2017-2018") +
 ylab("Total Directors' Cup Points 2017-2018") +
 scale_x_continuous(breaks=seq(50000, 100000, by = 25000)) +
 scale_y_continuous(breaks=seq(100, 300, by=50)) +
 theme(legend.title = element_blank(),
   legend.text = element_text(size=20),
   legend.position=c(0.15,0.93),
   legend.background = element_blank(),
   legend.key = element_rect(color=NA,fill=NA),
   axis.text.x = element_text(size=15, face=2,
           hjust=1),
   axis.text.y = element_text(size=15, face=2),
   axis.title.x = element_text(size=25),
   axis.title.y = element_text(size=25))
```

The previews you are receiving in the plot panel of RStudio are probably a bit unsettling at this point, but trust that you are on the right track. If you are curious as to what all of these alterations look like as you continue to build the plot, remember you can always export it with the larger pixel setting to get a glimpse of your progress. The final items on the list are to remove the plot panel background and use a custom color for the plot panel grid (see figure 3.8). Use "navajowhite" for the grid color.

```
# Final draft - geom_text_repel() plot meeting the 10 stated
requirements
p9 + geom_text_repel(size=5, fontface=4) +
 geom_point() +
 xlab("Average Cost Per Athlete 2017-2018") +
 ylab("Total Directors' Cup Points 2017-2018") +
 scale_x_continuous(breaks=seq(50000, 100000, by = 25000)) +
 scale_y_continuous(breaks=seq(100, 300, by=50)) +
 theme(legend.title = element_blank(),
   legend.text = element_text(size=20),
   legend.position=c(0.15,0.93),
   legend.background = element_blank(),
   legend.key = element_rect(color=NA,fill=NA),
   axis.text.x = element_text(size=15, face=2,
           hjust=1),
   axis.text.y = element_text(size=15, face=2),
   axis.title.x = element_text(size=25),
   axis.title.y = element_text(size=25),
   panel.background = element_blank(),
   panel.grid=element_line(color="navajowhite"))
```

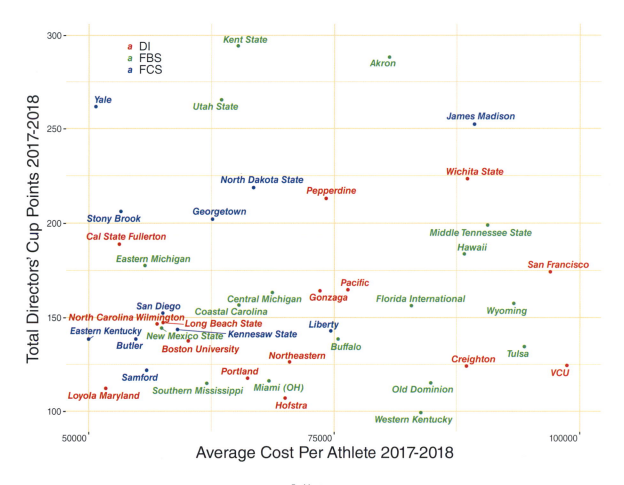

FIGURE 3.8 Scatterplot using `geom_text_repel()` function to demonstrate the relationship between average cost per athlete and total Directors' Cup points by division for selected schools (2017-2018).

geom_violin()

The final plotting structure you will be working with in *ggplot2* utilizes the **geom_violin()** function. **Violin plots**, like boxplots, are ways of analyzing the distribution of measured variables within groups of data. The difference between boxplots and violin plots is similar to how you understand the difference between histograms and density plots. The violin plot not only demonstrates the distribution of data, but it indicates, through curving, where more or less of the distribution of data lies based on how wide or thin the violin is at any point in the plot (Lewinson, 2019). To get started, use the plotting structure you used for the geom_boxplot() section of the chapter. This plotting structure was referred to as p2 and used the *power5* subset of data. You will use the same coding you developed to create the final boxplot; the only required alteration is to replace the geom_boxplot() function with the geom_violin() function (see figure 3.9).

```
# Converting the Power 5 boxplot into a violin plot
p2 + geom_point(size=2) +
 geom_violin(alpha=0.4, color=1, size=0.8) +
 ggtitle("Power 5 Athletics Expenses by Conference 2016-2018") +
 xlab("") +
 ylab("Athletics Expenses in Millions") +
 scale_y_continuous(breaks=seq(100,400, by=50)) +
 theme(legend.position = "none",
   plot.title = element_text(hjust=0,
            size=16,face="bold"),
   axis.text.x=element_text(size=11, face=2),
   axis.text.y=element_text(size=11, face=2),
   axis.title.y=element_text(size=13, face=2),
   panel.background = element_rect(fill="slategray1"),
   panel.grid = element_line(color="cornsilk"))
```

As you can see, the violin plot is a useful tool for better visualizing the distribution of individual data points within a group. From this plot, you can see that the majority of the schools in the ACC are clustered in the $150 million to $200 million range whereas the majority of the schools in the Southeastern Conference (SEC) are clustered between $250 million and $300 million. To finish the *ggplot2* section of this chapter, continue to use the *power5* subset of data and create the p10 plotting structure by altering the p2 plotting structure. The fill= setting needs to be changed to a color= setting, but other than that, the other elements will remain the same. The changes are indicated in red.

```
# Altering the p2 plotting structure to create the p10 plotting
structure
p10 <- ggplot(data=power5, aes(x=conf,
            y=expmf,
            color=conf))
```

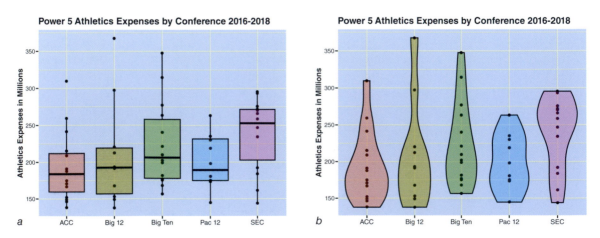

FIGURE 3.9   Boxplot *(a)* versus violin plot *(b)* showing Power 5 athletics expenses in millions of dollars by conference (2016-2018).

Now that the `p10` plotting structure has been created, it is time to tackle the violin plot challenge. The violin plot you will develop contains these requirements:

1. Add the `geom_violin()` geometry and include settings to accomplish the following:
   a. Add transparency to the fill color.
   b. Remove the line border from around the violin plot.
   c. Set a custom fill color.
   d. Provide a scale setting.

2. Layer the `geom_point()` geometry into the `geom_violin()` geometry and include settings to:
   a. Change the shape of the data points to hollow rings.
   b. Increase the size of the rings.
   c. Set a custom color for the rings.

3. Layer the `geom_text_repel()` geometry into the `geom_violin()` and `geom_point()` geometries and include settings to:
   a. Provide a minimum segment length for lines drawn between data points and labels.
   b. Map labels to school names.
   c. Increase the size of the labels and apply a bold font.
   d. Indicate the desired space around the data points (i.e., point padding).

4. Remove the x-axis and y-axis titles.

5. Customize the y-axis scale and intervals.

6. Add a main title to the plot.

7. Use the `theme()` function to do the following:
   a. Center the main title.
   b. Make the main title larger and add a bold font.
   c. Set a custom color for the main title.
   d. Make the x-axis and y-axis labels larger and add a bold font.
   e. Remove the legend.
   f. Provide a custom color for the plot panel background.
   g. Provide a custom color for the plot panel grid.

8. Swap the x-axis and y-axis to flip the plot into a horizontal orientation.

The first item uses an `alpha=` setting of 0.5 to provide some transparency to the fill color. The `linetype=` setting is set to 0 to indicate that lines serving as frames for the violins are not desired. The `fill=` color is set to "gray84". The `scale=` setting is set to "count" because of the different number of schools per group.

```
# Step 1 - Adding the geom_violin() geometry layer
p10 + geom_violin(alpha=0.5, linetype=0,
        fill="gray84",
        scale="count")
```

The next step is to add the `geom_point()` layer. To meet the requirements set forth, use a `shape=1` setting to change the data points to hollow rings. To make the rings stand out, set the `size=` setting to 3, and set the `color=` setting to "black".

```
# Step 2 - Adding the geom_point() geometry layer
p10 + geom_violin(alpha=0.5, linetype=0,
           fill="gray84",
           scale="count") +
  geom_point(shape=1,size=3,color="black")
```

Next, add the `geom_text_repel()` layer. To meet the requirements set forth, use a `min.segment.length=` setting of 0, map the `label=` setting to the `power5$school` variable, add a `size=` setting of 5 and a `fontface=` setting of "bold", and include a `point.padding=` setting of 0.4.

```
# Step 3 - Adding the geom_text_repel() geometry layer
p10 + geom_violin(alpha=0.5, linetype=0,
           fill="gray84",
           scale="count") +
  geom_point(shape=1,size=3,color="black") +
  geom_text_repel(min.segment.length = 0,
           label=power5$school,
           size=5, fontface="bold",
           point.padding=0.4)
```

To accomplish items 4 to 6 in the list, the axis text, scale, and aesthetics will need to be modified. Use a minimum value of 100, a maximum value of 400, and intervals of 50 for the `scale_y_continuous()` function when modifying the plot scale.

```
# Step 4 - Removing x-axis and y-axis titles, providing a custom
y-axis scale, and adding a main title
p10 + geom_violin(alpha=0.5, linetype=0,
           fill="gray84",
           scale="count") +
  geom_point(shape=1,size=3,color="black") +
  geom_text_repel(min.segment.length = 0,
           label=power5$school,
           size=5, fontface="bold",
           point.padding=0.4) +
  xlab("") +
  ylab("") +
  scale_y_continuous(breaks=seq(100,400,by=50)) +
  ggtitle("Power 5 Schools - Total Athletics Expenses in Millions
2016-2018")
```

For item 7, set the plot title text to size 18 and the x-axis and y-axis text to size 14. The colors for the individual settings can be whatever you like. For this example, the main title is "dark blue", the plot panel background is "white", and the plot panel grid lines are "light gray".

```
# Step 5 - Adding the theme() function elements
p10 + geom_violin(alpha=0.5, linetype=0,
          fill="gray84",
          scale="count") +
 geom_point(shape=1,size=3,color="black") +
 geom_text_repel(min.segment.length = 0,
          label=power5$school,
          size=5, fontface="bold",
          point.padding=0.4) +
xlab("") +
ylab("") +
scale_y_continuous(breaks=seq(100,400,by=50)) +
ggtitle("Power 5 Schools - Total Athletics Expenses in Millions
2016-2018") +
theme(plot.title = element_text(hjust=0.5,
            size=18,face="bold",
            color="dark blue" ),
  axis.text.x=element_text(size=14,face="bold"),
  axis.text.y=element_text(size=14,face="bold"),
  legend.position = "none",
  panel.background = element_rect(fill="white"),
  panel.grid.major = element_line(color="light grey"))
```

The final requirement listed is to change the plot orientation from a vertical plot to a horizontal plot by swapping the x-axis and the y-axis. This can be achieved using the coord_flip() function. When you have added that to the coding, you can export your final product. Remember to check the box to maintain aspect ratio and to increase the width to 1,200 pixels.

```
# Step 6 - Using the coord_flip() function to change the plot
orientation
p10 + geom_violin(alpha=0.5, linetype=0,
          fill="gray84",
          scale="count") +
 geom_point(shape=1,size=3,color="black") +
 geom_text_repel(min.segment.length = 0,
          label=power5$school,
          size=5, fontface="bold",
          point.padding=0.4) +
xlab("") +
ylab("") +
scale_y_continuous(breaks=seq(100,400,by=50)) +
ggtitle("Power 5 Schools - Total Athletics Expenses in Millions
2016-2018") +
theme(plot.title = element_text(hjust=0.5,
            size=18,face="bold",
            color="dark blue" ),
  axis.text.x=element_text(size=14,face="bold"),
  axis.text.y=element_text(size=14,face="bold"),
  legend.position = "none",
  panel.background = element_rect(fill="white"),
  panel.grid.major = element_line(color="light grey")) +
coord_flip()
```

Visit HK*Propel* to see the plot of Power 5 schools with athletics expenses in millions of dollars, by conference, for the 2016 to 2018 seasons.

Visit HK*Propel* to access
the video tutorial on
map plots.

MAP PLOTS

Another fun data plotting tool is the *usmap* package. It is used in this section to first look at the distribution of Division I schools throughout the United States and then to look at the distribution of total Directors' Cup points throughout the United States. Lastly, it is used to look at the distribution of total Directors' Cup points in selected states.

United States Map Plots

Map visuals are impactful and powerful tools for describing data. As you develop these plots, certain modifications will be made to enhance their final appearance. However, to get started, you need to create a new object called s1 using the count() function, which you learned about in chapter 2, to develop totals for the number of Division I schools in each state. This can be done using the css$state factor variable. When s1 is created, change the column names to "state" and "schools" using the colnames() function.

```
# Creating the new s1 object using the count function
s1 <- count(css$state)

# Changing the s1 column names to state and schools
colnames(s1) <- c("state","schools")
```

Now that you have the new s1 object ready to go, you can create your new p11 object using the **plot_usmap()** function. The required inputs for the *usmap* package include the data= setting, which references the data to be used in the plot (s1); the values= setting, which references the measured variable to be used in the plot ("schools"); and the color= setting, which will be used to draw the outlines of the states.

```
# Creating the p11 object and checking the result
p11 <- plot_usmap(data = s1, values= "schools", color= "gray")

# Checking the result
p11
```

Already, the output should look pretty impressive considering how little effort it required. To really get this map to pop, however, you can use some of the functionality of *ggplot2* to make some aesthetic changes. The changes include

- customizing the color range,
- adding a title to the color scale legend, and
- moving the color scale legend above the map.

To customize the color range to be displayed in the states and add a title to the color scale legend, use the **scale_fill_continuous()** function. Within the function, you will set low= values and high= values to whichever colors you choose. The fill color is based on the total number of Division I schools that exist in each state. States with a small number of Division I schools will lean toward the color indicated by the low= setting. States with a large number of Division I schools will lean toward the color indicated by the high= setting. Because it is a continuous fill, the colors of the states will fluctuate accordingly between the low= and high= settings. For this example, the `low=` setting is set to "white" and the `high=` setting is set to "dark blue". This means the colors of states between low and high will be some variant of purple. Lastly, so viewers know what they are looking at, give the color scale legend a title indicating what the scale describes. This modification requires a `name=""` setting.

```
# Customizing the color range and giving the color scale legend a
title
p11 + scale_fill_continuous(low="white",high="dark blue",
            name = "Division-I Schools by State")
```

The final alteration for the plot is to move the color scale legend above the map (see figure 3.10). To do this, you can set the position of the legend using the `theme()` function along with the `legend.position=""` setting.

```
# Moving the color scale legend above the map
p11 + scale_fill_continuous(low="white",high="dark blue",
            name = "Division-I Schools by State") +
 theme(legend.position = "top")
```

To develop a map illustrating the distribution of total Directors' Cup points by state, few alterations are required. The first thing that must be accomplished, however, is to create a new object that captures the total number of points by state. Name this new object `dc`, which stands for Directors' Cup. Creating the `dc` object requires the use of the `aggregate()` function learned in chapter 2 to develop totals for the number of Directors' Cup points in each state. When `dc` is created, change the column names to "state" and "points" using the `colnames()` function.

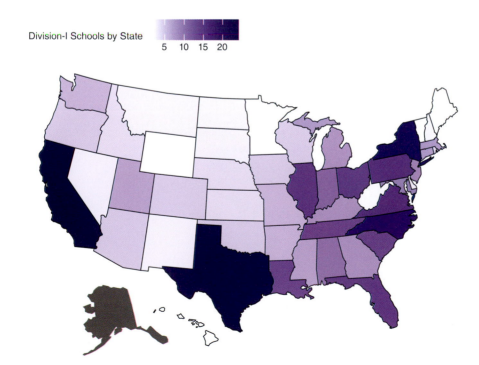

FIGURE 3.10   Distribution of Division I schools by state.

```
# Creating the new dc object using the aggregate function
dc <- aggregate(css$ntotf, by=list(css$state),sum)

# Changing the dc column names to state and points
colnames(s1) <- c("state","points")
```

Now that you have the new dc object ready to go, you can alter the p11 object and final plot coding in minor ways to achieve your goals. To give the plot distinction, the high end fill color will be changed to dark green. Additionally, the legend key will have to be widened so that the values do not overlap one another when presented horizontally above the map (see figure 3.11). This can be achieved using the legend.key.width= setting within the theme() function. These minor alterations are highlighted in red.

```
# Altering the p11 object
p11 <- plot_usmap(data = dc, values= "points", color= "gray")

# Changing the Division-I schools map to the Directors' Cup map
p11 + scale_fill_continuous(low="white",high="dark green",
          name = "Directors' Cup Points by State") +
  theme(legend.position = "top",
    legend.key.width=unit(3,"line"))
```

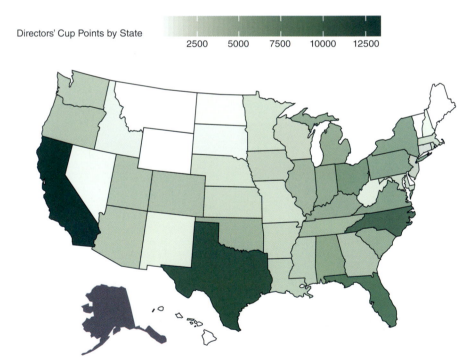

FIGURE 3.11   Distribution of Directors' Cup points in the United States (2016-2018).

Customized States Map Plots

Mapping the entire United States for each analysis is not a requirement. In fact, you can hand-select which states you would like to include. There are also presets for different regions of the country, as well as states broken down by counties. For the purposes of this example, a plot of total Directors' Cup points for the southern states of Alabama, Mississippi, South Carolina, Florida, Louisiana, and Georgia will be developed. Start by creating a subset of data named *southern* using the *css* dataset.

```
# Creating the southern subset
southern <- css[css$state=="AL" | css$state=="MS" |
          css$state=="SC" | css$state=="FL" |
          css$state=="LA" |css$state=="GA",]
```

Now that you have the *southern* subset developed, you can use the aggregate function to create an object named sp, which stands for southern points, and rename the columns "state" and "points" using the colnames() function.

```
# Creating the new sp object using the aggregate function
sp <- aggregate(southern$ntotf,by=list(southern$state),sum)

# Changing the sp column names to state and points
colnames(sp) <- c("state","points")
```

Using the same coding structure as you did for demonstrating the distribution of total Directors' Cup points throughout the United States, you can do the same for the southern states included in the analysis. To get started, create your new p12 plotting structure. To select the specific states for inclusion, use the include= setting along with the combine c() function. In this plotting structure, make the border color black. Lastly, include a labels=T statement to display the state abbreviations on this map plot.

```
# Creating the p12 plotting structure
p12 <- plot_usmap(include=c("AL","MS","SC",
          "FL","LA","GA"),
       data=sp, values="points",
       color="black", labels=T)
```

Now that the p12 plotting structure has been created, you can produce the final plot using the same code as before, when you developed the distribution map plot for total Directors' Cup points throughout the entire United States. For the purposes of this final mapping plot, change the low end color to "cornsilk" and the high end color to "cyan" to really make it stand out (see figure 3.12). The only other alteration required is to alter the name= setting (clarifying this map is for selected southern states) and drop the unit setting from 3 to 2 in the unit() function.

```
# Creating the Directors' Cup map plot for selected southern
states
p12 + scale_fill_continuous(low="cornsilk",high="cyan",
 name = "Directors' Cup Points by Selected Southern States") +
 theme(legend.position = "top",
   legend.key.width=unit(2,"line"))
```

There are a number of different mapping elements and settings that can be modified using the plot_usmap() function to tailor map plots to your needs. You are encouraged to further research this package. It is a fun and easy way to bring data to life.

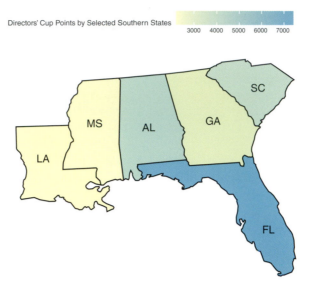

Directors' Cup Points by Selected Southern States

3000 4000 5000 6000 7000

FIGURE 3.12   Distribution of Directors' Cup points in selected southern states (2016-2018).

Interview With a Professional

Bryson Johnson, Assistant Basketball Coach, George Mason University

Analytics has become increasingly popular in managing decisions during competition or making decisions in the front office—for example, roster and personnel decisions. The most concrete example of the value of analytics in the management of sport is the financial commitment programs teams are investing in. Professional teams have an analytics department that tracks the specific data that they require to make the most informed decisions possible based on the values of their organization. Not only has analytics grown within programs, but companies have emerged and businesses have developed in an effort to monetize on this growing trend. Companies such as Synergy Sports Technology and KenPom have commonly used analytics tools in the basketball world that help programs outsource some of their analytical needs.

Maybe the biggest adjustment in sport has been the use of analytics in real time for coaches. The coaching profession requires quick decisions to be made based on observations. Analytics has been used to compliment the observations of the coach and help make quicker, more informed decisions, in real time. There have been varying levels of acceptance of analytics in the coaching profession, but I would argue every coach has become more reliant on analytics comprehension in the last 10 years than before. Long story short, analytics is extremely important in the management of sport because of the practical and competitive advantages it provides, but also because of the growth in companies that specialize in analytical data for sport-specific reasons. Just follow the money!

Brian Anweiler, Athletic Director, Wake Forest Community College

As a college athletic director, I rely on analytics in a variety of ways. From an academic perspective, we look at student-athlete performance in the classroom, including grade point average, successful course completion rates, and other academic performance indicators, to determine what measures may need to be taken within a sport program or targeted student population to promote academic success.

BONUS CODING: PLOTTING WITH AN IMAGE

I have oftentimes been asked if it is possible to create data visualizations in which a company, school, or team logo can be displayed as a data point rather than a traditional data point or name. The use of images in plots is actually easier than you may think. While it requires a little bit of setup on the front end, it is relatively easy to include images in a plot from a coding perspective. Throughout this bonus plotting sidebar, I will walk you through a plot that will achieve the following goals:

- Examine the relationship between athletics expenses and Directors' Cup points in the Sun Belt Conference for the 2016 to 2017 season.
- Use an image to represent Troy University as a data point on the plot.
- Use school names and traditional data points to represent the other Sun Belt schools on the plot.
- Customize different plot elements in *ggplot2* to make the plot aesthetically pleasing and impactful.

GETTING STARTED

1. Download the image Troy.png included in the web materials and save it somewhere on your computer.
2. Use the `install.packages()` function to install the following required packages: *ggimage*, *magick*

CODING STEPS AND EXPLANATIONS

```
# Plotting Using Images as Data Points

# Data Preparation
css <- read.csv("css.csv")
css[,1:4] <- lapply(css[,1:4], as.factor)
css$div <- factor(css$div,
         levels = c("DI","FCS","FBS","Power 5"))


# Activate the Required Packages
library(ggplot2)
library(ggrepel)
library(ggimage)
library(magick)
# Create an image object in RStudio using the image_read() function
# along with the Troy.png image that is saved on your computer
# You will need to reference your file path in the coding structure
# The name of the newly created image object will be ggtroy

ggtroy <- image_read("/Users/christopheratwater/Pictures/Troy.png")

# There are number of alterations you can make to the newly
# created image object such as removing negative space around
# the image, changing the image size, etc. An option most
# people want is to make the surrounding area of an image
# transparent so it does not cover up other data points or
# plot elements when it is placed in a data visualization.
# To achieve this, use the image_transparent() function and
# reference the image object name as well as the primary
# background color that you would like to disappear (in our case white).

# Set Transparent Background
ggtroy <- image_transparent(ggtroy,"white")
```

(continued)

BONUS CODING: PLOTTING WITH AN IMAGE (CONTINUED)

```
# Once you have altered the image,
# overwrite the current version using the image_write() function
# along with the image object name, a path= setting
# and a format= setting.

# Save Altered Image
image_write(ggtroy,
          path="/Users/christopheratwater/Pictures/ggtroy.png",
          format="png")

# Now that your image is prepared, you are ready
# to create the required subsets of data for plotting.
# One subset will include every school in the Sun Belt except for Troy
# and the other subset will include only Troy.

sun <- css[css$conf=="Sun Belt" & css$school !="Troy",]
troy <- css[css$school=="Troy",]

# Now you are ready to plot - The critical core elements are in red.
# The other elements are included to make the final product pop!
# Have Fun!

plot <- ggplot(data=sun, aes(x=expm1, y=ntot1))

plot + geom_text_repel(label=sun$school, color="firebrick4") +
 geom_point(color="black", size=2, shape=21, fill="white") +
 geom_image(data=troy,
    image="/Users/christopheratwater/Pictures/ggtroy.png",
    size=0.1) +
 ggtitle("Sun Belt Expenses & Directors' Cup Points 2016-2017") +
 xlab("Athletics Expenses in Millions") +
 ylab("Directors' Cup Points") +
 theme(panel.background=element_rect(fill="white"),
    panel.grid.major = element_line(color="gray90"))
```

RESULT

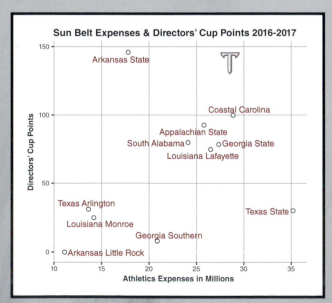

SUMMARY

You have now gained the skills necessary to create aesthetically pleasing data plots that are capable of making an impactful statement when presented to a client or end user. You have become equipped with the techniques required to work with base plotting structures in R as well as more advanced techniques using packages such as *ggplot2*, *ggrepel*, and *usmap*. Throughout this chapter, you were provided with tips and tricks for making modifications to your plotting structures and plots. The information gleaned is sufficient to take on just about any data plotting task, but there is much more out there.

As you continue to grow in terms of imagination and spend more time working with plotting in R, you will find that a great community exists in open forums and chat rooms where you can ask questions and perhaps even provide a few answers of your own. This chapter focused on some of the classic plots including scatterplots, boxplots, histograms, density plots, line plots, and violin plots. You were also introduced to using text in plots to highlight specific cases and, lastly, how to work with geographical mapping plots. Now that you understand how to work with quantitative data in R and are capable of plotting data in a visually stunning manner, it is time to take a look at analytics in action in chapter 4, Data-Driven Decision-Making.

ONLINE ACTIVITIES &HKPropel »

Visit HK*Propel* to access the video tutorials, *css* dataset, College Sports Supermodel Variables Chart, chapter art supplements, exercises, and a key terms review activity for this chapter. Your instructor may also release the assignments, assignment forms, and quiz available for this chapter through HK*Propel*. These tutorials, activities, and exercises are designed for interactive learning and to assist students as they learn the material.

REFERENCES

Analyttica Datalab. 2019. "Density Plots." Last modified June 4, 2019. https://medium.com.

Galarnyk, Michael. 2018. "Understanding Boxplots." Last modified September 12, 2018. https://towardsdatascience.com.

Lewinson, Eryk. 2019. "Violin Plots Explained." Last modified October 21, 2019. https://towardsdatascience.com.

## 4

DATA-DRIVEN DECISION-MAKING

Julio Aguilar/Getty Images

CHAPTER OBJECTIVES

After completing this chapter and the associated online exercises, you will be able to do the following:

· Understand the purpose of a *k*-means cluster analysis and how it is developed.

· Describe how and why player positions have evolved and changed over time in the Women's National Basketball Association (WNBA).

· Describe the growth and sustainability of the Call of Duty League based on three key areas: (1) star power of their professional players, (2) social media share of voice and sentiment, and (3) attendance and viewership numbers.

· Analyze the effectiveness of marketing efforts in America by European football clubs.

· Articulate the impacts of country of origin, age, viewership, and video game usage on club logo and club sponsor logo recognition.

· Create basic visualizations using historical National Football League (NFL) player evaluations.

· Given a new NFL player prospect, add their specific evaluations to the historical visualizations.

· Add the historical and new player evaluation metrics to an HTML-based dashboard.

· Comprehend and communicate the differences in prize money between male and female professional athletes.

KEY TERMS

average minute audience	factorial ANOVA	Silhouette score
draft	peak concurrent viewers	within cluster sum of squares (WSS)
drill	scout	

R FUNCTIONS

%/%	geom_density	render
%%	geom_vline	scale_color_manual
complete.cases	group_by	scale_fill_viridis_d
data.frame	gt	split
filter	head	summarise_all
flex_dashboard	lapply	tail
fviz_nbclust	melt	valueBox
kmeans	pivot_longer	viridis

Throughout chapter 4, you will be exposed to analytics applications that are practical and impactful. These analyses vary in focus and can be used to make the decision-making process easier. The examination of the evolution of player positions in the WNBA can be used to help teams draft and deploy the best players possible in modern women's professional basketball. The assessment of European football marketing and brand recognition in America demonstrates how many people are familiar with different European clubs and club sponsors in a growing market. The analysis of esports examines the growth of an emerging sport while discussing what it means for the future of this relatively new form of sport to the marketplace. The NFL player evaluation study demonstrates how different metrics can be used to evaluate talent accurately and effectively. Finally, the analysis focusing on a comparative analysis of salaries and prize money between male and female professional athletes provides perspective on a critically important disparity that exists in professional athletics. Overall, these five unique cases and applications provide a baseline for the importance of analytics in the sport business world.

MACHINE LEARNING ANALYSIS: WNBA PLAYERS' POSITIONS ANALYTICS APPLICATION

Michelle Brandao, MS; Jingting Liu, MS; and Ceyda Mumcu, PhD

Traditionally, there are five positions in basketball—point guard, shooting guard, small forward, power forward, and center—although at times, they are condensed into guard, forward, and center classifications. Basketball, in general, has evolved in recent years to become a faster game, relying on more shooting, especially from the 3-point line. These changes have been documented for the National Basketball Association (NBA) (McMahan, 2018). Similarly, the Women's National Basketball Association (WNBA) and the play style have evolved in time. We examined the player positions in women's professional basketball and analyzed if the WNBA has also become position-less like the NBA (Kalman and Bosch, 2020). We used cluster analysis, an unsupervised machine learning method, to identify player positions within the WNBA based on player performance statistics. Results of this study provide a new way to look at the player positions in the WNBA, which would be particularly important for roster management, especially during the WNBA draft, free agency, and trades. In addition, the results would be useful in managing team lineups and talent development through youth and college basketball.

Data Capturing and Preparation

For the analysis, we obtained player performance statistics for the 2019 WNBA regular season from the WNBA Advanced Stats (2019) and the Basketball Reference website for 157 players. We saved the data as a *.csv* file and named the data frame *WNBA_data*. The code below shows the columns (variables) in the dataset. Please see table 4.1 for a description of the variables used for the study.

Visit HK*Propel* to download the WNBA dataset.

```
WNBA_data <- read_csv("WNBAtrue.csv") #Upload the data
colnames(WNBA_data)

## [1] "Player"  "TEAM"    "GP"      "MIN"    "POS"     "PTG"    "3PAr"
## [8] "FTr"     "OREB%"   "DREB%"   "AST%"   "STL%"    "BLK%"   "TOV%"
## [15] "USG%"    "TS%"     "PER"     "LESS5FT" "5-9FT"  "10-14FT" "15-19FT"
## [22] "20-24FT" "25-29FT"
View(WNBA_data)
```

TABLE 4.1   WNBA Variable Descriptions

Variable	Description
Player	Player names
Team	Team names
GP	Games played; sum of the total games played
MIN	Average minutes played: the formula is **total minutes played / total games played** It measures the average minutes played in the season.
POS	Position name (G: guard; F: forward; C: center)
PTG	Average points per game: the formula is **total points / total games played** It measures the average points per game.
3PAr	3p = point attempt rate: the formula is **3P FGA / FGA** It is a measure of the percentage of field goal attempts (FGAs) made from the 3-point range.
FTr	Free throw rate: the formula is **FTA / FGA** It measures how often a player gets to the free throw line by dividing free throw attempts (FTAs) by field goal attempts (FGAs).
OREB%	Offensive rebound percentage: the formula is **100 × (ORB × (Tm MP / 5)) / (MP × (Tm ORB + Opp DRB))** Offensive rebound percentage is an estimate of the percentage of available offensive rebounds a player grabbed while she was on the floor. ORB: offensive rebound; Tm: team; MP: minutes played; Opp: opponent; DRB: defensive rebound

*For more information, see the article "Calculating PER" (www.basketball-reference.com/about/per.html).
Adapted from www.basketball-reference.com.

(continued)

TABLE 4.1　WNBA Variable Descriptions *(continued)*

Variable	Description
DREB%	Defensive rebound percentage: the formula is **100 × (DRB × (Tm MP / 5)) / (MP × (Tm DRB + Opp ORB))** Defensive rebound percentage is an estimate of the percentage of available defensive rebounds a player grabbed while she was on the floor.
AST%	Assist percentage: the formula is **100 × AST / (((MP / (Tm MP / 5)) × Tm FG) − FG)** Assist percentage is an estimate of the percentage of teammate field goals (FG) a player assisted (AST) while she was on the floor.
STL%	Steal percentage: the formula is **100 × (STL × (Tm MP / 5)) / (MP × Opp Poss)** Steal percentage is an estimate of the percentage of opponent possessions (Opp Poss) that end with a steal (STL) by the player while she was on the floor.
BLK%	Block percentage: the formula is **100 × (BLK × (Tm MP/ 5)) / (MP × (Opp FGA − Opp 3PA))** Block percentage is an estimate of the percentage of opponent 2-point field goal attempts blocked by the player (BLK) while she was on the floor. The formula specifically focuses on blocks of the opponent's 2-point field goal attempts by subtracting the opponent's 3-point attempts (3PA) from their total field goal attempts (FGAs).
TOV%	Turnover percentage: the formula is **100 × TOV / (FGA + 0.44 × FTA + TOV)** Turnover percentage is an estimate of turnovers (TOV) per 100 plays.
USG%	Usage percentage: the formula is **100 × ((FGA + 0.44 × FTA + TOV) × (Tm MP / 5)) / (MP × (Tm FGA + 0.44 × Tm FTA + Tm TOV))** Usage percentage is an estimate of the percentage of team plays used by a player while she was on the floor.
TS%	True shooting percentage: the formula is **PTS / (2 × TSA)** True shooting percentage is a measure of shooting efficiency that takes into account field goals, 3-point field goals, and free throws. PTS: points; TSA: True shooting attempt (calculated as FGA + 0.44 × FTA)
PER	Player efficiency rating is a per-minute rating developed by ESPN.com columnist John Hollinger presenting a player's contribution by adjusting her accomplishments, which includes subtracting mistakes such as missed shots, turnovers, and personal fouls.*
Less5FT	Field goal percentage of shots of less than five feet: the formula is **FGM / FGA for that area** It measures the percentage of shots made in that area.
5-9FT	Field goal percentage of shots of between five and nine feet: the formula is **FGM / FGA for that area** It measures the percentage of shots made in that area.
10-14FT	Field goal percentage of shots of between 10 and 14 feet: the formula is **FGM / FGA for that area** It measures the percentage of shots made in that area.
15-19FT	Field goal percentage of shots of between 15 and 19 feet: the formula is **FGM / FGA for that area** It measures the percentage of shots made in that area.
21-24FT	Field goal percentage of shots of between 20 and 24 feet: the formula is **FGM / FGA for that area** It measures the percentage of shots made in that area.
25-29FT	Field goal percentage of shots of between 25 and 29 feet: the formula is **FGM/FGA for that area** It measures the percentage of shots made in that area.

*For more information, see the article "Calculating PER" (www.basketball-reference.com/about/per.html).

We removed players who had limited playtime (less than 12 minutes per game) to create a robust dataset. Minutes are crucial for players to be able to show their skills. An average of 12 minutes per game, which is 30 percent of the game time in the WNBA, was set as the criterion for players to be included in the analysis. In order to remove players who averaged less than 12 minutes per game, we used the *dplyr* package and filtered the data. With the removal of players averaging less than 12 minutes per game, the final sample size has become 112 players.

```
WNBA_data <- WNBA_data %>% filter(MIN>12) ## remove all the
players that play less than 12 min a game
```

Preliminary Data Analysis

Before running the cluster analysis, we conducted several descriptive statistics to establish a better understanding of the dataset. First, we examined the number of guards, forwards, and centers in the dataset by creating a bar plot using the *ggplot2* package. The guards consist of more than half of the dataset with 62 players. The forwards (n = 36) are the second most prevalent player group in the data followed by the centers (n = 14).

```
library(gridExtra)
ggplot(WNBA_data, aes( x = POS)) +
geom_bar(fill = "lightblue") + ylab("Count") + xlab("Positions")+
theme_classic() + geom_text(stat='count', aes(label=..count..),
vjust=-.4) + labs(title = "Number of Players by Position",
caption = "Source:sports-reference.com\nwnba.com")
```

Visit HK*Propel* to view the bar plot for the number of players by position.

Second, we looked at the central tendency and dispersion of each continuous variable by player positions. We grouped the data by position via the **group_by** function from the *tidyverse* package, and then we used the function **summarise_all** to get the mean and the standard deviation of all continuous variables (see table 4.2). Finally, we used `boxplots` to present a visualization of the results by positions. We pivoted the data by using the **pivot_longer** function and then used the `ggplot` to plot all the continuous variables.

```
WNBA_data %>% select(-c(Player, TEAM, MIN, GP)) %>%
 group_by(POS) %>%
 summarise_all(funs(mean, sd)) %>%
 pivot_longer(!POS,names_to = 'key', values_to = 'value') %>%
 separate(key, into = c("Features", "stat"), sep = "_") %>%
 pivot_wider(names_from = 'stat', values_from = 'value') %>%
 mutate(mean_w_sd = paste0(round(mean, 2), " (", intToUtf8("177"),
 round(sd, 2), ")")) %>%
 select(POS, Features, mean_w_sd) %>%
 pivot_wider(names_from = 'Features',
 values_from = mean_w_sd) %>% rename(Positions = POS) %>% gt() ##
 Create the statistics summary table
```

TABLE 4.2   Summary Statistics by Positions

Variable	Center	Forward	Guard
PTG	11.62 (±4.55)	8.55 (±4.12)	8.59 (±4.03)
3PAr	0.11 (±0.14)	0.22 (±0.18)	0.4 (±0.17)
FTr	0.3 (±0.14)	0.26 (±0.11)	0.24 (±0.1)
OREB%	7.37 (±2.52)	6.83 (±2.6)	2.1 (±1.12)
DREB%	17.54 (±3.61)	16.05 (±4.53)	8.76 (±2.8)
AST%	10.9 (±5.42)	11.45 (±5.26)	19.67 (±8.33)
STL%	1.39 (±0.48)	1.87 (±0.77)	1.92 (±0.67)
BLK%	3.56 (±1.37)	2.46 (±1.57)	0.75 (±0.49)
TOV%	13.33 (±3.09)	15.49 (±4.64)	16.04 (±5.24)
USG%	21.04 (±5.14)	19.42 (±3.87)	19.63 (±4.21)
TS%	56.38 (±4.59)	51.86 (±5.83)	49.54 (±6.16)
PER	19.31 (±4.6)	15.61 (±5.45)	12.54 (±4.12)
Less5FT	61.93 (±4.73)	58.19 (±8.59)	54.13 (±9.93)
5-9FT	38.19 (±6.78)	34.29 (±12.72)	31.55 (±13.95)
10-14FT	40.87 (±12.75)	38.55 (±18.63)	36.22 (±16.15)
15-19FT	45.04 (±11.75)	35.51 (±10.52)	33.09 (±13.67)
21-24FT	28.56 (±27.6)	35.23 (±19.9)	33.05 (±8.56)
25-29FT	16.32 (±20.47)	23.15 (±21.6)	30.44 (±15.2)

WNBA variable descriptions are found in table 4.1.

Visit HK*Propel* to view the visualization of summary statistics by position and to review the video tutorial on boxplots.

```
WNBA_data %>% mutate(POS = as.factor(POS)) %>% pivot_longer(c(GP,
MIN,PTG:`25-29FT`), names_to = "stats", values_to = "values") %>%
ggplot(aes(x = as.factor(POS), y = values, fill = POS)) +
geom_boxplot(alpha = .8) + facet_wrap(vars(stats),
ncol = 3, scales = "free") +
scale_fill_discrete(name = "Positions")+ xlab("Feature")+
theme_gray() + theme_bw() + theme(legend.position = "none",
strip.text = element_text(face='bold')) ## Create the boxplot
```

The forwards reported large standard deviations in eight variables (3PAr, OREB%, DREB%, STL%, BLK%, PER, 10-14FT, 25-29FT). This indicates that the forwards in the WNBA possess varying skills in multiple aspects of the game, especially in rebounding and 3-point shooting. Some forwards are more offensive than others, and they demonstrate different strengths. In other words, forwards in the WNBA have a heterogeneous skill set.

The guards revealed large standard deviations in six variables (TOV%, TS%, AST%, Less5FT, 5-9FT, and 15-19FT), which was anticipated, especially when it comes to turnovers and assists. Guards are more ball-dominant than centers and forwards, meaning that they have the ball in their hands longer during a possession. Thus, turnover percentage and assist percentage are two performance metrics that differentiate better players from average or below-average guard players. In addition, mid-range and close-range shooting percentages reported large variance, indicating that some guard players are better at scoring closer to the basket than other guards.

Lastly, the centers disclosed large standard deviations in four variables (PTG, FTr, USG%, and 20-24FT). These variables are offensive performance statistics, indicating that some teams rely more on their center players than others, especially illustrated by the usage percentage (USG%), which is the percentage of team plays that a player is involved in while on the court. In sum, the preliminary exploratory analysis of the data revealed variations in player performance statistics within each position, indicating versatility in the skills of WNBA players. It is also supporting evidence for the WNBA players' capability to perform in more than one traditional basketball position.

K-Means Cluster Analysis of WNBA Players

We performed a *k*-means cluster analysis, an unsupervised machine learning technique, with the entire dataset (n = 112 WNBA players) to understand how similar or distinct the players are and whether the WNBA players still fit into the traditional guard, forward, and center classifications in basketball.

K-means cluster analysis identifies the *k* number of centroids and allocates each data point to the nearest cluster while keeping the centroids as small as possible (Garbade, 2018). In other words, cases similar to each other are placed into the same cluster to create a cohesive group that is distinct from the other clusters. With this analysis, we aimed to group the WNBA players into naturally forming clusters based on their performance metrics with the Euclidean distance algorithm. Before running the analysis, we removed categorical variables (Player, Team, and POS) from the dataset, as *k*-means analysis is restricted to continuous variables. In the next step, we removed GP and MIN because they are not performance metrics. Finally, we used the `sapply` function to scale and normalize the data prior to the analysis and added player names to the data frame.

```
WNBAdata_clustering <- WNBA_data %>%
select(!c(Player,TEAM,POS,GP,MIN)) #remove the variables "Player,
team, position, game played and minutes)
WNBAdata_clustering_norm <- sapply(WNBAdata_clustering,
scale)## scale the data
rownames(WNBAdata_clustering_norm) <-WNBA_data$Player ##
add the players name to the normalized data
```

To find the optimal number of clusters (*k*), **within cluster sum of squares (WSS)** and the **Silhouette score** (also known as elbow method) were used. The Silhouette score measures the quality of the clusters by determining how well each object fits in its cluster; higher Silhouette scores indicate better clustering. We used the `fviz_nbclust` function to determine and visualize the optimal number of *k* clusters.

```
fviz_nbclust(WNBAdata_clustering_norm, kmeans, method = "wss")
fviz_nbclust(WNBAdata_clustering_norm, kmeans, method =
"silhouette")
```

Visit HK*Propel* to view the charts for the number of clusters by WSS and Silhouette score.

Although the expectation was to find three to five naturally occurring player clusters representing the traditional positions in basketball (guard, forward, and center), both

WSS and the Silhouette score identified the optimal *k* to be two. This initial result indicates that in the WNBA, there are two types of players based on players' game statistics, and the players do not neatly fit into traditional positions in basketball. In other words, the WNBA has also become position-less, and women's professional basketball players have versatile skills allowing them to play more than one position. Please see figure 4.1 for the visualization of the two-cluster solution.

Once the optimal number of *k* was determined, we ran a *k*-means cluster analysis with Euclidean distance measure to identify the clusters using the kmeans function and visualized the clusters using the fviz_nbclust function.

```
set.seed(1)
km.res <- kmeans(WNBAdata_clustering_norm,2, nstart = 25)
fviz_cluster(km.res, WNBAdata_clustering_norm, ellipse = TRUE,
ellipse.alpha= 0.2,
            palette = "Set1", repel = TRUE, ggtheme = theme_
            minimal(),
            main= "WNBA Clusters", xlab= FALSE, ylab = FALSE,
            labelsize= 6,lwd=.3)
```

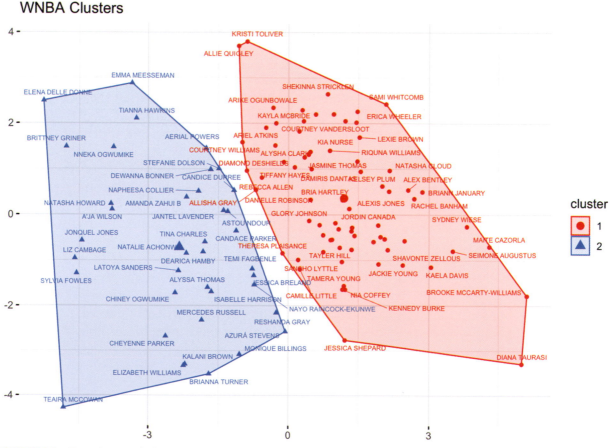

FIGURE 4.1   Two-cluster solution.

Following the *k*-means analysis, average performance metrics for each cluster were calculated by using the `aggregate` function to examine the type of players grouped in each cluster. With the *gt* package, a table presenting these statistics was then generated (see table 4.3).

```
Clusters_data<- aggregate(WNBA_data,
by=list(cluster=km.res$cluster),
mean) ## Averages of each cluster
Clusters_data <- Clusters_data %>% mutate_if(is.
numeric, round, 2)%>% select(-c(Player, TEAM,
POS, MIN, GP))
library(gt)
gt(Clusters_data)
```

Cluster 1: Post Players

Based on the average player performance statistics, the players that formed Cluster 1 possess center and forward skills; thus, this cluster is labeled as the "Post Players." They averaged 10.69 points per game and have a player efficiency rate of 18.46. Compared to the second cluster, these players are better rebounders (OREB% 7.66 and DREB% 17.28) with a higher shot block percentage (3.06 percent), a lower 3-point attempt rate (0.13), and a lower assist percentage (10.9 percent). Additionally, they are better shooters around the basket. These players have a higher shooting percentage at 5-9FT (36.9 percent), 10-14FT (38.3 percent), and 15-19FT (39 percent) than the second cluster.

TABLE 4.3   Summary Statistics of Two-Cluster Solution

Variable	Cluster 1	Cluster 2
PTG	10.69	8.07
3PAr	0.13	0.39
FTr	0.29	0.23
OREB%	7.66	2.54
DREB%	17.28	9.59
AST%	10.91	18.51
STL%	1.78	1.86
BLK%	3.06	0.93
TOV%	14.13	16.24
USG%	20.67	19.27
TS%	54.46	49.44
PER	18.46	12.28
Less5FT	60.41	54.35
5-9FT	36.89	31.39
10-14FT	38.33	37.15
15-19FT	39.03	33.47
21-24FT	33.01	33.28
25-29FT	17.63	30.80

WNBA variable descriptions are found in table 4.1.

Cluster 2: Guard Players

The second cluster is labeled as "Guard Players" because they have guard skills. They average eight points per game with an efficiency rate of 12.28. They have a higher assist percentage (18.5 percent), higher 3-point attempt rate (39 percent), and a higher steal percentage (1.86 percent). They are also better overall shooters based on their shooting percentages, especially for the long-range (for 25-29FT, 31 percent and for 20-24FT, 33 percent). They are not great offensive rebounders (OREB% 2.5) or good shot blockers (0.93 percent BLK). Please see below for a line graph of the clusters' player performance metrics and code.

```
cluster_data_plot %>%
 ggplot(aes(x = feature, y = z_value, color = cluster)) +
 geom_point(size = 2) +
 geom_line() +
 gghighlight(use_direct_label = FALSE) +
 facet_wrap(~ cluster,ncol =2) +
 labs(x = "Feature", y = "Scaled Group Means",
          title = "Visualizing the Clusters") +
 scale_x_discrete(guide = guide_axis(angle = 90)) +
 scale_color_brewer(palette = "Set1") +
 theme_bw() +
 theme(legend.position = "bottom", strip.text = element_
text(face='bold'))
```

Visit HK*Propel* to view the charts for the player performance statistics for the two clusters.

In sum, the WNBA players have become more versatile in skills in recent years, advancing beyond what traditional positions in basketball require, and they are able to perform in multiple positions. However, the WNBA teams still draft and trade players by position. Therefore, further examination of the three main positions in basketball (guard, forward, center) may identify evolving skills for each position and the value they bring to the teams.

K-Means Cluster Analyses of WNBA Players by Positions

In the second part of this case study, three separate *k*-means cluster analyses were conducted to examine guard, forward, and center positions. The original data captured from WNBA Advanced Stats (2019) and Basketball Reference (2019) provided player positions for each player on the dataset. By using each player's position as declared by the WNBA, data was filtered to create three separate data frames: *guards*, *forwards*, and *centers*. Following the same procedure from the first part of this case study, each dataset was prepared for the analysis, the optimal *k* was identified, and then a *k*-means analysis was run and visualized. The procedure was as follows:

1. Filter the data by position using the *tidyverse* package and the **filter** function.
2. Scale the data using the `sapply` function.
3. Find the optimal *k* using the `fviz_nbclust` function.
4. Cluster the data by using the `kmeans` function.
5. Visualize the cluster by using the `fviz_cluster` function.
6. Visualize a table with the mean of all variables for each cluster by using the *gt* package and **gt** function.
7. Visualize the cluster means by using the *ggplot2* package.

Analysis for the Guard Players

The code for the aforementioned procedure is provided below.

```
Guards <- WNBA_data %>% filter(POS == "Guard") #filter by position
Guard
Guards_clustering <- Guards %>% select(!c(Player,TEAM,POS,GP,
MIN)) #remove the variables "Player, team, position,
game played and minutes)
Guards_norm <- sapply(Guards_clustering, scale) # scale the data
rownames(Guards_norm) <-Guards$Player # add the players column

# Identify optimal K
fviz_nbclust(Guards_norm, kmeans, method = "wss")
fviz_nbclust(Guards_norm, kmeans, method = "silhouette")

set.seed(2)
km.res_guard <- kmeans(Guards_norm,2,
nstart = 10) ## cluster the guard position
fviz_cluster(km.res_guard, Guards_norm, ellipse = TRUE, ellipse.
alpha= 0.1,
          palette = "Set1",repel = TRUE, ggtheme = theme_
          minimal(),
          main= "Guards Cluster", xlab= FALSE, ylab = FALSE,
          labelsize= 6,lwd=2) ##visualize the cluster
```

Visit HK*Propel* to view the charts for the number of clusters by WSS and Silhouette score.

Two different types of guard players were identified with the analysis (see figure 4.2 for the visualization of the analysis). This was an unexpected result considering the three traditional guard positions in basketball: point guard, guard, and shooting guard. However, guard players in the WNBA have become extremely versatile, and they are able to play multiple positions. For instance, the two-time champion Kristi Toliver started as a point guard in her first championship game and as a shooting guard in her last championship game. Some other WNBA players who have been able to play multiple guard positions during their career are Diana Taurasi, Skylar Diggins, Jackie Young, Kelsey Plum, and Arike Ogunbowale.

```
Guards_clustering_data<- aggregate(Guards,
by=list(cluster=km.res_guard$cluster), mean)
Guards_clustering_data <- Guards_clustering_data %>% mutate_if
(is.numeric, round, 2) %>% select(-c(Player, TEAM, POS, MIN, GP))
library(gt)
gt(Guards_clustering_data) ## create a table
```

Visit HK*Propel* to view the table for the summary statistics of two guard clusters.

Further examination of performance statistics for the two guard clusters revealed one group to be more scoring oriented than the second group. Based on the performance statistics, the clusters were named "Buckets Guard" and "Role Guard."

FIGURE 4.2 Two-cluster solution for guards.

Cluster 1: Buckets Guard

"Buckets Guards" averaged 11.7 points per game and had an efficiency rate of 15.8. They are 3-point shooters and have the highest usage percentage among the guards with 21.4 percent. Their 3-point attempt rate is the highest among all WNBA players at 42 percent. They shoot 35.6 percent from the 3-point line (20-24FT) and are also good at long-range shots (37.4 percent from 25-29FT). Overall, they are good shooters and good passers. The data suggested these are the scoring guards, and some of the best players from this cluster are Diamond DeShields, Courtney Williams, Arike Ogunbowale, and Allie Quigley.

Cluster 2: Role Guard

"Role Guards" are similar to the Buckets Guards except for averaging fewer points per game (5.7 points), which is the lowest in the WNBA. Although they have a high 3-point attempt rate (0.38), they are less efficient than the Buckets Guards with a PER of 9.5 and have a low usage percentage (18 percent), suggesting that these are role players. This group includes some of the best defenders and floor-general point guards such as Briann January, Jordin Canada, Natasha Cloud, and Alana Beard. Please see figure 4.3 for a visualization of the performance metrics for the guard clusters.

```
Guards_clustering_data$cluster <- c('Cluster 1: Buckets Guard',
'Cluster 2 : Role Guard')
Guards_Cluster_plot <- Guards_clustering_data %>%
 pivot_longer(!cluster, names_to = 'feature', values_to = 'z_
 value')
 Guards_Cluster_plot %>%
 ggplot(aes(x = feature, y = z_value, color = cluster)) +
 geom_line(alpha = 2, aes(group = cluster)) +
 geom_point( size = 2) +
 gghighlight(use_direct_label = FALSE) +
 labs(x = "Feature", y = "Scaled Group Means",
         title = "Visualizing the Clusters") +
 scale_x_discrete(guide = guide_axis(angle = 90)) +
 scale_color_brewer(palette = "Set1") +
 theme_bw() +
 theme(legend.position = "bottom", strip.text = element_
 text(face='bold'))
```

Analysis for the Forward Players

The same procedure was followed and an analysis conducted for the forwards, and the results identified three groups of players among the WNBA forwards. The code for the analysis was as follows:

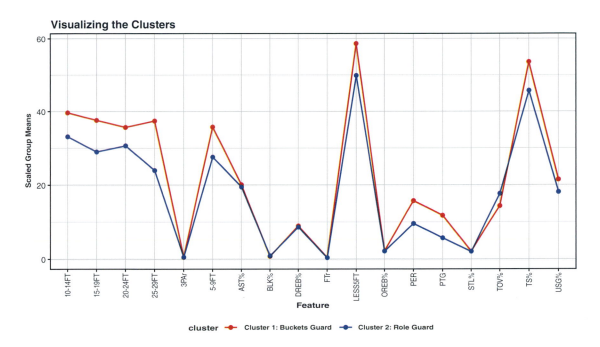

FIGURE 4.3   Guard clusters' performance metrics.

```
# Filter the data
Forwards<- WNBA_data %>% filter(POS == "Forward") # filter the
data by position (Forward)
Forwards_clustering <- Forwards %>%
select(!c(Player,TEAM,POS,GP,MIN)) # remove the variables "Player,
team, position, game played and minutes)
# Scale data
Forwards_norm <- sapply(Forwards_clustering, scale)
rownames(Forwards_norm) <-Forwards$Player # add the players name
to the normalized data
# Identify K
fviz_nbclust(Forwards_norm, kmeans, method = "wss")
fviz_nbclust(Forwards_norm, kmeans, method = "silhouette")
```

Visit HK*Propel* to view
the charts for the number
of clusters, by WSS and
Silhouette score, for
forwards.

```
# k-Means
set.seed(3)
Forwards_km_res <- kmeans(Forwards_norm,3, nstart = 10)
fviz_cluster(Forwards_km_res, Forwards_norm, ellipse = TRUE,
ellipse.alpha= 0.1,
        palette = "Set1",repel = TRUE, ggtheme = theme_
        minimal(),
        main= "Forwards Cluster", xlab= FALSE, ylab = FALSE,
```

Visit HK*Propel* to view the
three-cluster solution for
forwards.

Based on the player performance statistics, the three forward clusters were named "Driver Forward," "Future Center," and "Shooting Forward." The code for the average statistics for the three forward clusters and line plots are shown below.

Visit HK*Propel* to view the table for the summary statistics for the three forward clusters

```
# calculate the average of stats for each cluster
Forward_data <- aggregate(Forwards,
by=list(cluster=Fowards_km_res$cluster), mean)
Forward_data <- Forward_data %>% mutate_if(is.numeric,
round, 2) %>% select(-c(Player, TEAM, POS, MIN, GP))
gt(Forward_data)
```

Visit HK*Propel* to view the forward clusters' performance metrics.

```
Forward_data$cluster <- c('Cluster 1: Driver Forward',
'Cluster 2 : Future Center', 'Cluster 3 : Shooting Forward')
Forwards_plot <- Forward_data %>%
 pivot_longer(!cluster, names_to = 'feature',
 values_to = 'z_value')
Forwards_plot %>%
 ggplot(aes(x = feature, y = z_value, color = cluster)) +
 geom_line(alpha = 2, aes(group = cluster)) +
 geom_point( size = 2) +
 gghighlight(use_direct_label = FALSE) +
 labs(x = "Feature", y = "Scaled Group Means",
         title = "Visualizing the Clusters") +
 scale_x_discrete(guide = guide_axis(angle = 90)) +
 scale_color_brewer(palette = "Set1") +
 theme_bw() +
 theme(legend.position = "bottom", strip.text = element_
 text(face='bold'))
```

Cluster 1: Driver Forward

Players within the "Driver Forward" cluster averaged 6.4 points per game and had a player efficiency rate of 14. They are typical forward players who mostly perform in the perimeter. Although they can take 3-point shots, they are better drivers, as indicated by their higher field goal percentage for Less5FT (58 percent), free throw rate (0.33), and low 3-point attempt rate (0.04). They are very good rebounders, both offensively (OREB% 8.96) and defensively (DREB% 15.2), and the best shot blockers among all forwards (BLK 2.8 percent). Chiney Ogwumike, Elizabeth Williams, and Brianna Turner are the prime examples of Driver Forwards.

Cluster 2: Future Center

The "Future Center" players are forwards with guard skills. They average 13.6 points per game and have the highest player efficiency rate (PER 22.5) and usage percentage (23.5 percent) among all forwards. They have a high 3-point attempt rate, shooting at 26 percent. Future Centers can play close to the basket and also score from the 3-point line and mid-range. They are very good rebounders, both offensively (OREB% 7.5) and defensively (DREB% 18.8), and good shot blockers (BLK% 2.5). Some of these players are the centers in small lineups for their teams. For instance, Jonquel Jones starts for the Connecticut Sun as a center with Alyssa Thomas. This duo reached the WNBA finals in 2019. Similarly, Breanna Stewart, who is listed as a forward, played with Natasha Howard, who is also a forward, during their championship run in the

2018 season. The last two of the three championship teams played with two forwards instead of the traditional lineup of a small forward and a center. Another example is when Nneka Ogwumike and Candace Parker played the frontcourt in 2017 for the Los Angeles Sparks. Lastly, the WNBA champion and regular season most valuable player (MVP), the forward Elena Delle Donne, plays the center in small lineups. All the players mentioned above are in this cluster. If this trend continues, it suggests that they could be the future centers of the WNBA.

Cluster 3: Shooting Forward

Performance statistics suggest that these players are "Shooting Forwards," as they have a high 3-point attempt rate (31 percent) with a shooting percentage of 34.4 from 20-24 FT. In addition, they have a low free throw rate (0.17), which suggests that they play in the perimeter and do not drive to the basket, often receiving physical contact. They are better at defensive rebounding (DREB% 14.9) than offensive rebounding (OREB% 4.8), which is another indication that they play in the perimeter. Alysha Clark, Glory Johnson, and Candice Dupree are some of the well-known players in this cluster.

Analysis for the Center Players

The same procedure was used and analysis performed for the center players, and the results yielded five groups of players among the WNBA centers. The code for the analysis is as follows:

```
#Filter the data
Centers <- WNBA_data %>% filter(POS == "Center")
Centers_clustering <- Centers %>% select(!c(Player,
TEAM,POS,GP,MIN)) #remove the variables "Player,team, position,
game played and
#Scale the data
Centers_norm <- sapply(Centers_clustering, scale) # scale the data
rownames(Centers_norm) <-Centers$Player # add the players name to
the normalized data
#Identify k
fviz_nbclust(Centers_norm, kmeans, method = "wss")
fviz_nbclust(Centers_norm, kmeans, method = "silhouette")
```

Visit HK*Propel* to view the charts for the number of clusters, by WSS and Silhouette score, for centers.

```
#k-Means
set.seed(5)
Centers_km.res <- kmeans(Centers_norm,3, nstart = 10)
fviz_cluster(Centers_km.res , Centers_norm, ellipse = TRUE,
ellipse.alpha= 0.1,
         palette = "Set1",repel = TRUE, ggtheme = theme_
         minimal(),
         main= "Centers Cluster", xlab= FALSE, ylab = FALSE,
         labelsize= 9,lwd=3
)
```

Visit HK*Propel* to view the five-cluster solution for centers.

Based on the player performance statistics, the five center clusters were named "The Most Valuable Player," "Traditional Post Player," "Center Role Player," "Adapted Traditional Post Player," and "3-Point Shooter Center." The code for the average statistics for the five clusters and line plots are shown next.

Visit HK*Propel* to view the table for the summary statistics for the five center clusters.

```
Centers_data_post<- aggregate(Centers, by=list(cluster=Centers_
km.res$cluster), mean) # Average scores of each cluster
Centers_data_post <- Centers_data_post %>% mutate_if(is.numeric,
round, 2) %>% select(-c(Player, TEAM, POS, MIN,GP))
gt(Centers_data_post) #Create a table
```

```
Centers_data_post$cluster <- c("Cluster 1: The Most Valuable Player",
"Cluster 2: 'Traditional Post Player", "Cluster 3: 'Center Role
Player'", "Cluster 4: Adapted Traditional Post Player"
, "Cluster 5: 3-Point Shooter Center")
Centers_plot <- Centers_data_post %>%
 pivot_longer(!cluster, names_to = 'feature', values_to = 'z_
value')
Centers_plot %>%
 ggplot(aes(x = feature, y = z_value, color = cluster)) +
 geom_line(aes(group = cluster)) +
 geom_point( size = 2) +
 gghighlight(use_direct_label = FALSE) +
 labs(x = "Feature", y = "Scaled Group Means",
         title = "Visualizing the Clusters") +
 scale_x_discrete(guide = guide_axis(angle = 90)) +
 scale_color_brewer(palette = "Set1") +
 theme_bw() +
 theme(legend.position = "bottom", strip.text = element_
text(face='bold'))
```

Visit HK*Propel* to view the performance metrics for the center clusters.

Cluster 1: The Most Valuable Player

Emma Meesseman was the only player in this category. She can be described as a center with guard skills. She is referred as the new point guard of the current-day WNBA. The data shows that she is a different type of center. She averaged 13.1 points per game, and she had the highest PER (27.3) among all WNBA players. She was so valuable to her team, the Washington Mystics, during the 2019 season and earned the Finals MVP award. She is a very good shooter, a passer, and an efficient 3-point shooter. She makes good decisions and does not turn the ball over. She plays more on the perimeter yet has a high field goal percentage for shots taken closer to the basket (Less5FT 65.2 percent) as well. When compared with guards, she has a slightly higher assist percentage (21.7) and a lower turnover rate (8.4). Although Breanna Stewart did not play during the 2019 WNBA season because of an Achilles injury, we anticipate that she will be in "The Most Valuable Player" category along with Emma Meesseman.

Cluster 2: Traditional Post Player

These are the most traditional post players among all center players in the WNBA. They average approximately 10 points per game and have an efficiency rate of 20.2. Most often, these players engage in offense in areas closer to the basket. They are good scorers and the best offensive (OREB% 10.9) and defensive (DREB% 20.8) rebounders among all centers. In addition, they go to the free throw line often, which is typical for a basketball player who performs mostly in the paint or drives to the basket frequently. They have higher field goal percentages for shots taken from areas less than 5 feet to the basket, while they can shoot from up to 19 feet away from the basket. They are valuable to their teams with a usage percentage of approximately 20 percent. Sylvia Fowles and Teaira McCowan are two great examples of "Traditional Post Players."

Cluster 3: Center Role Player

These players average 8.3 points per game and have a 16.4 player efficiency rate. They are versatile players. However, they do not stand out on any performance statistics. Their usage percentage (16.7) is one of the lowest among all WNBA centers, which indicates that they are role players. They are "average" shooters who attempt shots from various distances to the basket, while their strength is shooting from close distance with a field goal of 62 percent from less than 5 feet to the basket. Jantel Lavender and Natalie Achonwa are examples of players in this cluster.

Cluster 4: Adapted Traditional Post Player

These players average 17.5 points per game. They are high scorers and shot blockers, great rebounders, and good passers. They have the second-highest player efficiency rate among all center clusters with 21.6. They are similar to the Traditional Post Players but better shooters at 10-14FT (42.1 percent) and 20-24FT (51.73 percent), and they are better passers with a 14.9 assist percentage. The data also suggests that they are adapting to the changing game by spreading the floor and shooting 3-point shots. However, their strength is still in the low post and rebounding. Tina Charles, a prime example for this cluster, attempted 17 3-point shots in her first six seasons and a combined 154 3-point shots in her last two seasons. Adapted Traditional Post Players are extremely important to their teams, with the highest usage percentage (28.2) among all WNBA players.

Cluster 5: 3-Point Shooter Center

These players average 9 points per game and have a 15.3 player efficiency rate. They take 3-point shots consistently with an attempt rate of 38 percent, the second-highest rate among all WNBA player clusters. In addition, they have a low free throw rate (the second lowest of all WNBA players), which is typical for shooters. Furthermore, they are better at defensive rebounding (DREB% 18.3) than offensive rebounding (OREB% 4.7). Collectively, having a limited number of offensive rebounds, a low free throw rate, and a high 3-point attempt rate suggests that these players often perform in the perimeter. Last, they have the lowest usage percentage of all WNBA player clusters, indicating their limited involvement in their team's possession. Stefanie Dolson and Amanda Zahui B. are two of the players from this cluster.

The results of the study reported two naturally forming player clusters among all WNBA talent, while the analyses by position identified 10 different versions of basketball positions. In other words, collectively, the talent in the WNBA has become more homogenous while individually players have become more versatile. The results also provide supporting evidence for the evolution of traditional positions in women's basketball, documenting the change in the WNBA with the game becoming faster and more offensive, mimicking the NBA. The WNBA players have evolved beyond the traditional characteristics of guard, forward, and center positions in basketball. Nowadays, they are able to perform in multiple positions, which has made the WNBA a dynamic league.

ESPORT ANALYTICS APPLICATION

Victor Arias, MBA

Mirroring the rise of the Internet, video games have grown to become a cultural connector that spans borders, generations, and languages. As global communities of players have grown, so has the potential for professional gamers, gaming tournaments, and prize money. According to a 2019 *Forbes* article, esports as a global industry already exceeds $1 billion in revenue with a viewing audience of over 443 million worldwide (Ayles, 2019).

Esports, the professional iteration of gaming, is considered one of the fastest-growing sports in terms of revenue and fandom as compared to traditional leagues like Major League Baseball (MLB) and the National Hockey League (NHL). While some traditional sports leagues struggle to reach and maintain new generations of fans, esports leagues lean into their social media savvy communities, primarily online, that skew younger and are global.

Many of today's most popular esports leagues have become household names. Fortnite holds a yearly World Cup with a total prize pool of over $30 million. League of Legends can be seen on ESPN and has held similar championship tournaments since 2011. Overwatch League follows a traditional sports model with a 20-team, city-based structure complete with a regular season and playoffs. The Call of Duty League (CDL) launched in January 2020 under a traditional sports model that includes 12 permanent city-based teams, including global presences in Canada (Toronto Ultra), the United Kingdom (London Royal Ravens), and France (Paris Legion), with live in-arena competitions, playoffs, and a championship tournament. In year one of operation, the success of the CDL banked on the appeal and popularity of the Call of Duty video game franchise to garner interest from the general public. However, the popularity of the video game itself doesn't necessarily translate to fans of the professional esport players and teams that comprise the league.

For the CDL to have a successful first year as a legitimate sports league, it would need to look at additional metrics and adjust its competitive format in light of the Covid-19 global pandemic. The CDL focused on three key areas:

Enthusiastic Call of Duty fans at a launch event in early 2020.
Hannah Foslien/Getty Images

1. Star power of its professional players
2. Social media share of voice and sentiment
3. Attendance and viewership numbers

Tapping into the existing behavior of fandom is something the CDL did well while marketing the newly formed league on social media. Esports pros in the CDL have grown up playing online since they were preteens, and many have amassed large social media followings. In addition, because these gamer pros grew up playing competitively online, they are used to engaging with their communities on platforms like Twitter and YouTube and are considered accessible to everyday fans who follow them. Unlike traditional athletes, whose highlight reels on YouTube are the closest connection a casual fan may have, esports pros routinely stream live to their followers with in-game tutorials, tips on how to improve, and even how to talk trash like a true gaming pro.

For Call of Duty League in particular, Twitter is the most popular social channel for discussing the game and the league. Pro CDL players regularly match or outshine other professional stars in terms of social following and fan engagement. A sampling from July 2021 of the most-followed athletes, with followers in the millions (M) or thousands (K), in the NHL (Alex Ovechkin, 2.5M), NASCAR (Jimmie Johnson, 2.5M), and MLB (Robinson Cano, 492.9K) showed that they had similar reach to the top CDL accounts:

- Scump (Seth Abner, @scump, OpTic Chicago) 2.2M followers
- Formal (Matthew Piper, @FormaL, OpTic Chicago) 907.4K followers
- Crimsix (Ian Porter, @Crimsix, Dallas Empire) 850.1K followers

For metric number two (social media share of voice and sentiment), earned media coverage through public relations outreach is always a baseline measure of share of voice. However, with an overall shrinking media landscape and even smaller number of outlets dedicated to gaming and esports, social media share of voice and sentiment provides a better and faster understanding of how the general public is engaging with CDL's product and content.

With Covid-19 halting the play of all other major sports leagues worldwide, the CDL was still able to continue competitive play through online tournaments. In a way, professional esports, as one of the few competitive sports being played at the time, was able to capitalize on social media share of voice in the absence of the typical sports that would otherwise dominate social discussions during this time period.

From the start of the regular season in February 2020 until the playoffs and championship tournament in August, the monitoring tool Talkwalker was used to generate reports on both traditional media coverage and social media share of voice and sentiment. As an example, below are some highlights of the social report for the month of August (the regular season ended July 31, playoffs began August 19, and Championship Weekend took place August 29-30):

Coverage Highlights (August 1 through September 2, 2020)

- Social conversation: 29.1K social media posts, with the majority of the social conversation stemming from Twitter (92.8 percent), followed by forums (6.7 percent) such as Reddit.
- Traditional media: 4.4K articles, with a cumulative reach of 11.7 billion impressions
- Media sentiment: largely neutral (75.1 percent) to positive (19.8 percent) in tone

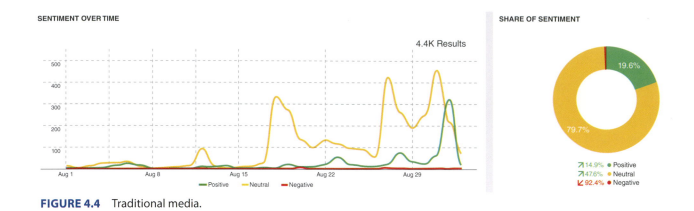

FIGURE 4.4   Traditional media.

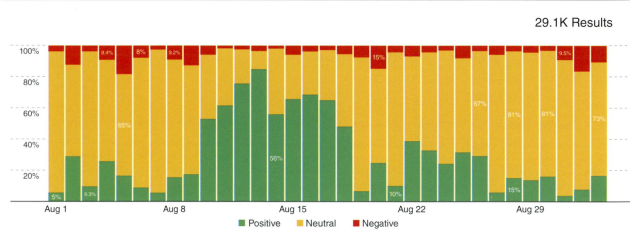

FIGURE 4.5   Social media.

As you can see, overall conversations about the CDL dropped off in early August because the regular season was coming to an end in late July. However, by mid-August, both traditional coverage (figure 4.4) and social conversation (figure 4.5) increased with the start of the playoffs and, later, Championship Weekend at the end of the month. The league did a great job of increasing visibility primarily on social media, with over 29,000 social media posts about CDL driven by Twitter, the preferred platform for many in the community to discuss video games, gamers, and esports. To top this off, positive sentiment of the social posts was nearly 20 percent. This can be considered a huge win during a crucial time period for CDL since it is widely known that Twitter can be a platform where negative sentiment runs rampant in the form of "trolls" and an overly critical community of gaming enthusiasts.

For the final metric (attendance and viewership numbers), the CDL launched with the intention of hosting live, in-person competitions at each of the 12 host cities for each team, but with Covid-19 closures, the league was only able to host two live events at the start of the regular season. Normally, attendance plus online viewership tells the full story of success for each CDL event, but for 2020, viewership alone was the measurement of success.

CDL streamed all matches on YouTube, its exclusive streaming partner, rather than compete with a more gaming endemic channel like Twitch. This decision also came with challenges, since many in the gaming community do not normally visit YouTube to watch live gaming competitions or tutorials. Communicating that You-Tube is where all CDL live matches and video-on-demand content could be found was a priority for the league. The hope was to change viewership behavior for many esports fans and bring in new fans through the widely used global platform while also serving as one of the only esports leagues on YouTube instead of the crowded gaming platform Twitch.

When looking at viewership numbers, CDL would work with Nielsen to provide final metrics and reports. There are several terms associated with the reports that are helpful to understand before explaining the results.

- **Average minute audience (AMA)**: The average amount of viewers watching the live event(s) at any given minute during the specified time span (match, week, season). AMA is the average number of people watching a broadcast at any minute during the broadcast, calculated by the total minutes watched divided by total minutes broadcast. In short, it's how many people are watching the content on average, which is exactly how Nielsen measures linear TV.

- **Peak concurrent viewers**: The total amount of viewers watching live on the CDL YouTube channel at one time.

  - YouTube data is pulled directly from YouTube Analytics for each of the CDL channels. The partnership between Activision Blizzard Esports (which owns CDL) and Google/YouTube was announced in January 2020 in a watershed moment for all esports.

  - Activision Blizzard Esports and the CDL are industry leaders in developing metrics to measure viewership and growth and have partnered with Nielsen since 2018, developing the early adoption of AMA as a standardized viewership metric.

- **Live+3**: The total number of viewers watching within three days after the original live air date.

The CDL hit a peak viewership of 162K during the playoffs when its most popular team, the Chicago Huntsmen, took on OpTic Gaming Los Angeles in an elimination match. This bested the previous high mark of 115K viewers of the New York Home Series (week 11) of the regular season during the Chicago versus Atlanta FaZe match and a previous high of 113K during the Atlanta Home Series when the Florida Mutineers took on the Huntsmen (week 3).

The playoffs had an overall Live+3 AMA of 85K and nearly 2M hours watched, the highest viewership of the season so far. The last day of elimination matches reached 97K Live+3 AMA. The series between the Chicago Huntsmen and OpTic Gaming Los Angeles for the final Championship Weekend spot received 162K Live+3 AMA.

The championship finals match had a Live+3 AMA of 297K with 1.8M unique viewers tuning in to watch the Dallas Empire win over the Atlanta FaZe. This is the most viewership ever for any Call of Duty esport event. CDL partnered with influencers such as Vikkstar123, CouRage, and NoahJ456 to co-stream the finals match, which helped increase viewership sources beyond the CDL YouTube channel alone. Championship Weekend had an overall Live+3 AMA of 236K and 1.7M hours watched. Overall, CDL had a reach of 10M total viewers in its inaugural season.

Based on these three key metrics, the CDL's inaugural season established positive building blocks for the future. The popularity of the game title along with the rise in esports as a form of entertainment has reinforced CDL's timing for launching. The star players have name cache with built-in fan bases from social media and will only continue to grow as the CDL becomes more visible through media coverage and its streaming channels and content. It remains to be seen if YouTube is the right fit for an esports property, but more year-over-year comparisons will help to make that determination. It will also be interesting to see how a full season of in-person events and attendance factors into the future of the CDL and its ability to bring in new fans.

Beyond these key metrics of success, there are some other macro factors that should also be considered when understanding how this league in particular is built for long-term success. At the professional level, many team ownership groups include influential and successful businesspeople who believe in the product. For example, Gary Vaynerchuk (@GaryVee) is part owner of the CDL's Minnesota RØKKR franchise and has expanded his media company's services to include a gaming vertical. The ownership group is also comprised of the Wilf family, owners of the NFL's Minnesota Vikings. The LA Guerrillas franchise is owned by Kroenke Sports & Entertainment, a group that also owns the NFL's LA Rams. The Seattle Surge team is owned by Canucks Sports & Entertainment, the same owners of the Vancouver NHL franchise. Actor Michael B. Jordan of "Creed" fame is a primary investor in Andbox, the ownership group of CDL's NY Subliners team. These proof points reinforce the big business of esports and, in particular, of the CDL in its aspirations of being viewed as a successful sports league among the likes of the NFL, NBA, NHL, and MLB.

Beyond the future of the league, the future of budding esports professional gamers is another positive aspect for CDL and for gaming in general. The CDL has a Challengers path-to-pro circuit that serves as the equivalent of a minor league farm system to help **scout** and replenish talent at the pro levels. The league even has a City Circuit designed to take casual competition to the next level by giving fans a chance to compete on behalf of CDL team cities.

Separate organizations like PlayVS are dedicated to making esports an official varsity sport for high schools across America while connecting students and teams with colleges that offer scholarships for playing and creating video games. One thing that PlayVS touts is the successful adoption rate of esports in high schools because it promotes collaboration and strategy, many times with teachers acting as coaches. Last, but not least, esports is truly gender-agnostic, which is something that no other sports leagues can claim. Since there is no separation of competition between men and women, like the NBA and WNBA, boys and girls in high school play together on the same teams and compete against each other outright. This differentiating factor is sure to future-proof esports as inclusive in response to calls for equal representation and pay in sports led by the U.S. Women's National Soccer Team.

Judging from the level of investment and enthusiasm for esports, it's clear that this is big business, with the opportunity for increased revenues expanding each year. Success hinges on more viewership and converting new fans to esports so that more money can be made for the teams and leagues competing for fan attention.

EUROPEAN FOOTBALL ANALYTICS APPLICATION

Christopher Atwater, PhD

In the spring of 2018, over 600 individuals in America attempted a questionnaire on European football marketing and brand recognition. Of those individuals, 567 completed the first three categorical variables (leagues followed, hours spent weekly

Logos of Real Madrid and the Chelsea FC teams are among the most recognizable of the European football clubs.
Oscar J. Barroso/Anadolu Agency via Getty Images

watching European football, and years spent watching European football) as well as the measured variables portion of the questionnaire (club logo and club sponsor logo recognition) in their entirety. These responses were used to demonstrate whole group results.

The instrument for this study was designed using the Wix website creator. Wix not only allows for the use of interactive content but also provides a backend data collector. This data collector puts all online responses in a *.csv* format that can later be exported and used in a variety of data analysis platforms, including RStudio. The instrument contained a series of 16 factor variables along with 36 club logos and 18 club sponsor logos.

Once developed, the survey was distributed on a national listserv for sport management professionals and was also hosted on social media sites. Additionally, participants were encouraged to forward the link to other potential participants. A phone and tablet version was also developed to make it easy for participants to get involved.

This study presented interesting insights into the intersection of viewership and EA Sports FIFA video game usage in relation to club logo and club sponsor logo recognition. This data is not only useful for different clubs and club sponsors but also for EA Sports and the producers of other sport-based video games, as well as those working to sell ad space within the programming of those games.

The independent categorical factor variables analyzing the impact of country of origin, age, the extent to which participants engage in the EA Sports FIFA video game, and the extent to which participants follow European football on a weekly basis were used to compare results among different groups of participants identified in the study. These results were used for descriptive and inferential statistical analysis of the impact of the selected independent categorical factor variable classifications on club logo and club sponsor logo recognition.

Following the completion of data collection for the study, the *eufs* dataset was imported into RStudio, where necessary adjustments were made to the structure of the data. The result of using the structure function `str()` indicated that the first 16 variables were being classified as character variables (nominal string variables) rather than independent categorical factor variables. Additionally, the first seven variables required a specific order rather than the traditional alphabetical order ascribed by R. In this instance, the "yes" responses were required first and the "no" responses second, since only the affirmative responses were being reported. Lastly, character variables 8-16 needed to be recoded as factor variables. The coding for the sequence described above is as follows:

```
# Importing the eufs dataset
eufs <- read.csv("eufs.csv")

# checking the structure of the eufs dataset
str(eufs)

# Changing the first seven character variables to factors
# and putting them into a custom order using lapply()
eufs[,1:7] <- lapply(eufs[,1:7],factor,levels=c("Yes","No"))

# Changing character variables 8-16 to factors using lapply()
eufs[,8:16] <- lapply(eufs[,8:16], as.factor)

# Checking the result of altering the first 16 variables
summary(eufs[,1:16])
```

Once the structure of the data was corrected, the next step was to create totals columns using the `apply()` function. In the *eufs* dataset, each row represents an individual participant. Columns 1-16 are factor variables. Columns 17-70 are numeric variables represented in the form of integers. Variables 17-52 represent the 36 different club logos represented in the study. Variables 53-70 represent the 18 different club sponsor logos represented in the study. When participants were able to correctly identify a club logo or club sponsor logo, they received a score of 1. When participants were unable to correctly identify a club logo or club sponsor logo, they received a score of 0. Thus, the range of total score per participant for club logos was 0-36 and for club sponsor logos was 0-18.

Visit HK*Propel* to access the video tutorial for the *eufs* dataset and to download the dataset.

Secondarily, it was important to understand the percentages that these totals represented in terms of club logo and club sponsor logo recognition. Therefore, four new columns of data were created to represent these figures across all participants:

- eufs$tc—total club logos recognized
- eufs$tcp—percentage of club logos recognized
- eufs$ts—total club sponsor logos recognized
- eufs$tsp—percentage of club sponsor logos recognized

To create the new columns of data, the `apply()` function was used in conjunction with a `MARGIN=1` setting to indicate the embedded `sum()` function would be working with data by rows rather than columns. Once the sum total for the `eufs$tc` and the `eufs$ts` variables were calculated, the percentages were attained by dividing the sum total of clubs result by 36 and the sum total of club sponsors result by 18. Lastly, multiplying the results by 100 to move the decimal place, and then employing the round function to minimize the decimal places included in the final result to one place, worked to create the four new columns of data critical for analyzing final results between groups based on the factor variables.

```
# Total Club Logos Recognized (eufs$tc)
eufs$tc <- apply(eufs[,17:52], MARGIN=1, FUN=sum)

# Percentage of Club Logos Recognized (eufs$tcp)
eufs$tcp <- round(100*apply(eufs[,17:52],
          MARGIN=1, FUN=sum)/36, digits=1)

# Total Club Sponsor Logos Recognized (eufs$ts)
eufs$ts <- apply(eufs[,53:70], MARGIN=1, FUN=sum)

# Percentage of Club Sponsor Logos Recognized (eufs$tsp)
eufs$tsp <- round(100*apply(eufs[,53:70],
          MARGIN=1, FUN=sum)/18, digits=1)
```

Visit HK*Propel* to access the video tutorials on the apply() function.

The Extent to Which Americans Follow European Football

The opening three questions of the study focused on the extent to which Americans follow European football. These questions offered participants an opportunity to identify which leagues they follow, how many hours per week they spend watching European football, and how many years they have been following European football. The leagues included in this portion of the study were the Big Five leagues of English Premier League, La Liga (Spain), Bundesliga (Germany), Serie A (Italy), and Ligue 1 (France) as well as the two elite European football competitions of the UEFA (Union of European Football Associations): the Champions League and the Europa League.

Because the first three questions in the study produced factor results rather than numeric results, traditional statistical measures such as means could not be employed. Therefore, the table() function was used within the sapply() function to capture **n counts** for the first seven factor variables (European football leagues). This procedure was followed by the use of operators and the round function to get results in percentages. The coding for the percentages is similar to what was done for creating new columns of data.

```
# League viewership
# n counts
sapply(eufs[,1:7],table)
# percentages
round(100*sapply(eufs[,1:7],table)/567, digits=1)

# Hours spent per week watching European football
# n counts
table(eufs$hours)
# percentages
round(100*table(eufs$hours)/567, digits=1)

# Years spent following European football
# n counts
table(eufs$years)
# percentages
round(100*table(eufs$years)/567, digits=1)
```

Table 4.4 demonstrates the extent to which Americans follow European football leagues, how many hours per week Americans spend watching European football, and how many years Americans have been following European football.

TABLE 4.4   Viewership Patterns of European Football in America

Variable	Options	n	%
Leagues Americans follow	English Premier League—England	295	52.0%
	La Liga—Spain	167	29.5%
	Bundesliga—Germany	136	24.0%
	Serie A—Italy	95	16.8%
	Ligue 1—France	69	12.2%
	UEFA—Champions League	286	50.4%
	UEFA—Europa League	124	21.9%
Hours spent per week watching European football leagues	0 hours	248	43.7%
	1-4 hours	240	42.3%
	5+ hours	79	13.9%
Years spent following European football leagues	0 years	247	43.6%
	1-2 years	34	6.0%
	3-4 years	62	10.9%
	5-6 years	55	9.7%
	More than 6 years	169	29.8%

Opinions on the Effectiveness of European Football Marketing

Before completing the club logo and club sponsor logo recognition portion of the questionnaire, participants were asked to respond to the following statement: "Overseas leagues have been effective in promoting European football in America." Of the 567 participants, 152 selected the option "I have no opinion." To properly prep the data for this result, a custom order for the factor variable was created.

```
# Creating a custom order for the factor variable `eufs$marketing`
eufs$marketing <- factor(eufs$marketing,
          levels=c("No Response",
             "Strongly Disagree",
             "Disagree",
             "Agree",
             "Strongly Agree"))
```

Next, a subset called *e* was created to eliminate participants who did not offer an opinion on the matter.

```
# Creating a subset to eliminate "No Response" results
e <- eufs[eufs$marketing!="No Response",]
```

Once the subset was created, the final n counts and percentages could be calculated using the remaining 415 participant responses.

```
# Marketing Effectiveness
# n counts
table(e$marketing)
# percentages
round(100*table(e$marketing)/415, digits=1)
```

Table 4.5, based on the 415 participants remaining who offered an opinion, demonstrates the extent to which Americans feel European football has been effectively promoted in America. Results indicate that 73.7 percent of Americans who participated in the study agree or strongly agree that European football has been effectively promoted in the United States.

TABLE 4.5   The Extent to Which Americans Feel European Football Has Been Effectively Promoted

Variable	Options	n	%
"Overseas leagues have been effective in promoting European football in America."	Strongly disagree	17	4.1%
	Disagree	92	22.2%
	Agree	234	56.4%
	Strongly agree	72	17.3%

Club Logo and Club Sponsor Logo Recognition Results

Following the introductory questions that focused on the extent to which Americans follow European football, participants were provided with a list of the European football clubs included in the study. These clubs represent a number of leagues throughout Europe and were selected for their history, current performance, and past accomplishments. The clubs included in the study were AC Milan, Ajax, Arsenal, Atletico, Barcelona, Bayern Munich, Benfica, Besiktas, Chelsea, Dortmund, Everton, Fenerbahce, Feyenoord, Galatasaray, Inter Milan, Juventus, Leicester City, Liverpool, Lyon, Manchester City, Manchester United, Marseille, Monaco, Montpellier, Napoli, Nice, Paris Saint-Germain, Porto, Real Madrid, Roma, Schalke, Sevilla, Tottenham, Valencia, Villarreal, and Wolfsburg.

For the club logo recognition portion of the study, the logos of all 36 teams were presented minus identifying characteristics such as names and locations.

This portion of the questionnaire was completed by 567 participants. They were asked to match club logos with their appropriate club names. Results for all 36 clubs were tabulated using the sum function within the sapply() function, which works along columns of data. Each of the columns (17-52) represent a club logo. To present the findings as percentages, totals were divided by 567 as well as rounded and multiplied by 100 to move the decimal place. Because the results were desired in a specific order (from most recognized to least recognized), an object named tc was created, which stands for total clubs.

```
# Creating the tc object
tc <- round(100*sapply(eufs[,17:52],sum)/567, digits=1)
```

Once the tc object was created, it was put in order by creating a new object tco (which stands for total club order) using the order function.

```
# Creating the tco object
tco <- tc[order(-tc)]
```

To get the final desired result, the **head** and **tail** functions were used along with an n= setting to produce a list of the top 10 (most recognized) club logos and bottom 5 (least recognized) club logos included in the study, as shown in table 4.6.

```
# Top-10
head(tco, n=10)

# Bottom-5
tail(tco, n=5)
```

Club Logo Recognition by Country of Origin

Of the 567 participants who completed the club logo and club sponsor logo recognition portions of the study, 503 participants identified as either being raised in a foreign country or in the United States. These participants were used to create a subset for analysis named *origin*.

```
# Creating a subset to exclude "No Response"
origin <- eufs[eufs$origin!="No Response",]
```

Results were then aggregated by country of origin to demonstrate the n counts, means, and standard deviations of club logo and club sponsor logo recognition. To develop n counts, means, and standard deviations simultaneously, a new function called f1 was created. This new function was used to aggregate data in all areas of the study.

```
# Creating the f1 function for n counts, means and sd
f1 <- function(x) c(n=length(x),
          mean=round(mean(x), digits=1),
          sd=round(sd(x), digits=1))
```

Additionally, independent sample *t*-tests were performed to examine the differences in group means to understand if a significant relationship exists between the different levels of country of origin and club logo and club sponsor logo recognition (see table 4.7).

```
# Club logo recognition by origin - n counts, means, and sd
aggregate(origin$tc, by=list(origin$origin),f1)
```

```
# Origin - CLUBS
# Boxplot
boxplot(origin$tc~origin$origin, outline=F,
    main="Club Logo Recognition by Origin",
    xlab="Origin",
    ylab="Total Club Logos Recognized",
    col=c("red","yellow"), alpha=0.6)

# Density Plot
p1 <- ggplot(data=origin, aes(x=tc,
              fill=origin))
p1 + geom_density(color="black", size=0.8,
alpha=0.8) +
 scale_fill_manual(values=c("red", "yellow")) +
 xlab("Total Clubs Recognized") +
 ylab("Density") +
 theme(axis.ticks = element_line(color=NA),
   plot.title = element_text(hjust=0.5),
   legend.box.background = element_rect(fill="white"),
   legend.title = element_blank(),
   legend.position = c(0.55,0.81),
   legend.direction = "horizontal",
   legend.background = element_rect(fill=NA,
              color="black",
              size=0.8),
   legend.key = element_rect(color="gray95"),
   panel.background = element_blank(),
   panel.grid = element_line(color="skyblue"),
   panel.grid.minor = element_blank())
```

Those who identified as being raised in a foreign country rec-ognized more club logos on average than participants raised in the United States (figure 4.6). Based on the difference in mean scores by country of origin, a *t*-test was run.

TABLE 4.6   Most and Least Recognized Club Logos

Variable	Team	%
Top 10 club logos	Barcelona	75.0
	Manchester United	63.3
	Chelsea	63.1
	Paris Saint-Germain	59.1
	Real Madrid	58.6
	Tottenham	53.1
	Liverpool	52.6
	Juventus	52.2
	Arsenal	51.5
	Dortmund	50.3
Bottom 5 club logos	Monaco	27.7
	Benfica	26.3
	Montpellier	19.9
	Nice	19.2
	Fenerbahce	19.0

TABLE 4.7   Club Logo Recognition by Origin

Origin	*n*	*M*	*SD*
Foreign country	65	23.4	12.8
United States	438	15.3	13.4

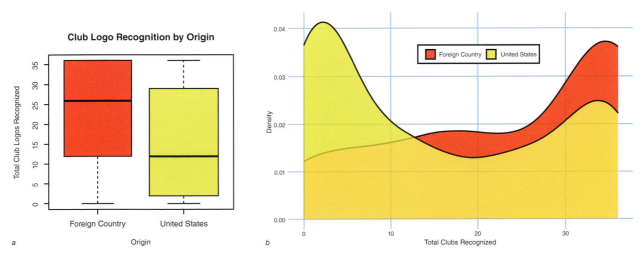

FIGURE 4.6 Club logo recognition by (*a*) origin and (*b*) distribution of data.

```
# Club logo recognition by country of origin
t.test(origin$tc~origin$origin)
```

The results of the analysis were significant when using country of origin as a factor with the recognition of club logos $t(86) = 4.73$, $p < 0.01$.

Club Logo Recognition by Age

Of the 567 participants who completed the club logo and club sponsor logo recognition portions of the study, 503 participants indicated their age. These participants were used to create a subset for analysis named *age*.

```
# Creating a subset to exclude "No Response"
age <- eufs[eufs$age!="No Response",]
```

Results were then aggregated by age to demonstrate the n counts, means, and standard deviations of club logo and club sponsor logo recognition (see table 4.8). Additionally, one-way analysis of variance (ANOVA) was performed to examine the differences in group means to understand if a significant relationship exists between the different levels of age and club logo and club sponsor logo recognition.

```
# Club logo recognition by Age - n counts, means, and sd
aggregate(age$tc, by=list(age$age),f1)

# Age - CLUBS
# Boxplot
age$age <- factor(age$age,
        levels=c("18-21","22-25","26-29",
          "30-41","42+"))
boxplot(age$tc~age$age, outline=F,
   main="Club Logo Recognition by Age",
   xlab="Age",
   ylab="Total Club Logos Recognized",
   col=c("Green","Red","Blue","Yellow","cadetblue1"))

# Density Plot
p3 <- ggplot(data=age, aes(x=tc,
            fill=age))
p3 + geom_density(color="black", size=0.8, alpha=0.75) +
  scale_fill_manual(values=c("green","red","blue",
            "yellow","cadetblue1")) +
  xlab("Total Clubs Recognized") +
  ylab("Density") +
  theme(axis.ticks = element_line(color=NA),
    plot.title = element_text(hjust=0.5),
    legend.box.background = element_rect(fill="white"),
    legend.title = element_blank(),
    legend.position = c(0.55,0.81),
    legend.direction = "horizontal",
    legend.background = element_rect(fill=NA,
```

```
                 color="black",
                 size=0.8),
  legend.key = element_rect(color="gray95"),
  panel.background = element_blank(),
  panel.grid = element_
  line(color="skyblue"),
  panel.grid.minor = element_blank())
```

TABLE 4.8   Club Logo Recognition by Age

Age	n	M	SD
18-21	136	18.3	14.9
22-25	135	18.6	14.0
26-29	52	17.5	13.5
30-41	100	13.8	12.0
42+	80	10.4	10.2

Generally speaking, as age increased, the mean score of club logos recognized by participants decreased (figure 4.7). Based on the difference in mean scores by age, a one-way ANOVA was run.

```
# Club logo recognition by age
a1 <- aov(tc~age, data=age)
anova(a1)
```

The results of the analysis were significant when using age as a factor with the recognition of club logos $F(4, 498) = 6.75$, $p < 0.01$. Following the analysis, post-hoc tests were run.

```
# Post-Hoc Tests
emmeans(a1,pairwise~age, adjust="tukey")
```

The age group that most significantly differed from others was the 42+ category, whose results were statistically significantly different from all groups at the .05 level with the exception of the 30-41 age group.

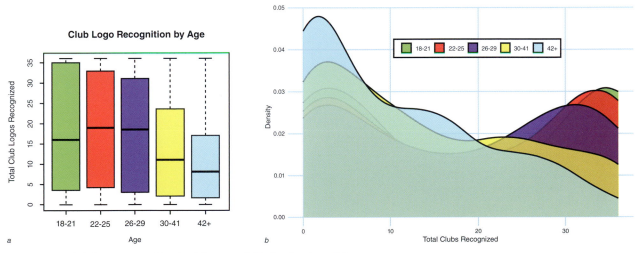

FIGURE 4.7 Club logo recognition by (*a*) age and (*b*) distribution of data.

Club Logo Recognition by EA Sports FIFA Video Game Usage

Of the 567 participants who completed the club logo and club sponsor logo recognition portions of the study, 504 participants indicated their level of engagement in the EA Sports FIFA video game. These participants were used to create a subset for analysis named *fifa*.

```
# Creating a subset to exclude "No Response"
fifa <- eufs[eufs$fifa!="No Response",]
```

Results were then aggregated by video game usage to demonstrate the n counts, means, and standard deviations of club logo and club sponsor logo recognition. Additionally, one-way ANOVAs were performed to examine the differences in group means to understand if a significant relationship exists between the different levels of EA Sports FIFA video game usage and club logo and club sponsor logo recognition. The results are given in table 4.9.

TABLE 4.9   Club Logo Recognition by Video Game Usage

EA Sports FIFA video game usage	n	M	SD
Never	222	8.7	10.2
Rarely or monthly	158	17.2	12.8
Weekly or daily	124	29.1	9.1

```
# Club logo recognition by
# video game usage - n counts, means, and sd
aggregate(fifa$tc, by=list(fifa$fifa),f1)

# Video Game Usage - CLUBS
# Boxplot
fifa$fifa <- factor(fifa$fifa,
        levels=c("Never","Rarely or Monthly",
            "Weekly or Daily"))
boxplot(fifa$tc~fifa$fifa, outline=F,
   main="Club Logo Recognition by Video Game Usage",
   xlab="Video Game Usage",
   ylab="Total Club Logos Recognized",
   col=c("darkseagreen1","skyblue1","khaki1"))

# Density Plot
p7 <- ggplot(data=fifa, aes(x=tc,
            fill=fifa))
p7 + geom_density(color="black", size=0.8, alpha=0.8) +
 scale_fill_manual(values=c("darkseagreen1","skyblue1","khaki1"))
 +
 xlab("Total Sponsors Recognized") +
 ylab("Density") +
 theme(axis.ticks = element_line(color=NA),
   plot.title = element_text(hjust=0.5),
   legend.box.background = element_rect(fill="white"),
   legend.title = element_blank(),
   legend.position = c(0.52,0.88),
   legend.direction = "horizontal",
   legend.background = element_rect(fill=NA,
               color="black",
               size=0.8),
   legend.key = element_rect(color="gray95"),
   panel.background = element_blank(),
   panel.grid = element_line(color="skyblue"),
   panel.grid.minor = element_blank())
```

Each escalating level of EA Sports FIFA video game usage resulted in a higher mean score of club logos recognized by participants (figure 4.8). Based on the difference in mean scores by EA Sports FIFA video game usage, a one-way ANOVA was run.

```
# Club logo recognition by video game usage
a3 <- aov(tc~fifa, data=fifa)
anova(a3)
```

The results of the analysis were significant when using EA Sports FIFA video game usage as a factor with the recognition of club logos $F(2, 501) = 140.8, p < 0.01$. Following the analysis, post-hoc tests were run.

```
# Post-Hoc Tests
emmeans(a3,pairwise~fifa, adjust="tukey")
```

All group comparisons for the EA Sports FIFA video game usage factor variable were statistically significant at the .05 level.

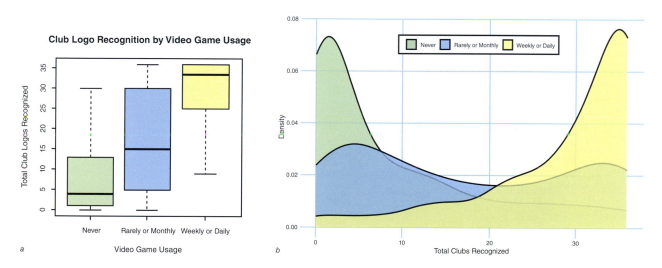

FIGURE 4.8   Club logo recognition by (*a*) video game usage and (*b*) distribution of data.

Club Logo Recognition by EA Sports FIFA Video Game Usage and Viewership

To further examine the effect of EA Sports FIFA video game usage on club logo and club sponsor logo recognition, **factorial ANOVAs** were conducted to compare the main effects and interaction effects of EA Sports FIFA video game usage and hours spent per week watching European football.

Of the 567 participants who completed the club logo and club sponsor logo recognition portions of the study, 504 participants indicated their level of engagement with the EA Sports FIFA video game as well as the hours they spent watching European football per week. These participants were used to create a subset for analysis named *fh*.

```
# Creating a subset to exclude "No Response"
fh <- eufs[eufs$fifa!="No Response" & eufs$hours!="No Response",]
```

Results were then aggregated by video game usage and hours spent per week watching European football to demonstrate the n counts, means, and standard deviations of club logo recognition (see table 4.10).

TABLE 4.10   Club Logo Recognition by Video Game Usage and Viewership

Frequency of EA Sports FIFA video game usage	Hours spent by participants watching European football weekly	*n*	*M*	*SD*
Never	0 hours	131	2.7	3.9
	1-4 hours	77	15.4	9.8
	5 or more hours	14	27.1	8.7
Rarely-Monthly	0 hours	56	6.0	7.2
	1-4 hours	80	21.2	11.0
	5 or more hours	22	31.3	6.3
Weekly-Daily	0 hours	10	20.9	14.9
	1-4 hours	75	27.7	9.1
	5 or more hours	39	33.8	3.4

```
# Club logo recognition by video game usage and viewership
# n counts, means, and sd
aggregate(fh$tc, by=list(fh$fifa,fh$hours),f1)
```

Based on the difference in means, a factorial ANOVA was conducted on the influence of two independent variables (EA Sports FIFA video game usage and hours spent watching European football by participants weekly) on club logo recognition.

```
# Factorial ANOVA
fa1 <- lm(tc~fifa*hours, data=fh)
anova(fa1)
```

All effects were statistically significant at the 0.05 significance level (see figure 4.9). The main effect for EA Sports FIFA video game usage yielded an F-ratio of $F(2,495) = 46.37$, $p < 0.01$, indicating a significant difference between the categories of no usage ($M = 8.68$, $SD = 10.24$), rarely-monthly usage ($M = 17.21$, $SD = 12.85$), and weekly-daily usage ($M = 29.1$, $SD = 9.12$). The main effect for hours spent watching European football by participants yielded an F-ratio of $F(2,495) = 114.77$, $p < 0.01$, indicating a significant difference between the categories of 0 hours ($M = 4.58$, $SD = 7.16$), 1-4 hours ($M = 21.41$, $SD = 11.16$), and 5 or more hours ($M = 31.8$, $SD = 6.04$).

The interaction effect was also significant $F(4,495) = 3.81$, $p < 0.01$.

```
# Visualizing the interactions of hours and fifa
# on total clubs recognized
emmip(fa1, fifa~hours) +
 scale_color_discrete(name = "FIFA Video Game Usage") +
 xlab("Hours Spent Watching European Football Weekly") +
 ylab("Total Club Logos Recognized") +
 ggtitle("Club Logo Recognition by EA Sports FIFA Video Game Usage
 and Viewership") +
 theme(legend.position="top",
   plot.title=element_text(size=16),
   axis.title = element_text(size=12))
```

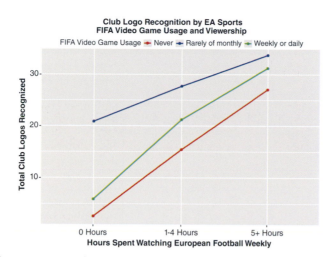

Visit HK*Propel* to view the full club sponsor logo recognition results.

FIGURE 4.9 Club logo recognition by video game usage and viewership, factorial ANOVA analysis.

NFL PLAYER EVALUATIONS ANALYTICS APPLICATION

Ted Kwartler, MBA

Each year, aspiring collegiate American football athletes are evaluated for their inclusion in the league **draft**. Before the draft, these exceptional athletes are invited to attend workout **drill** sessions, with specific drills allowing for easier player comparisons. Standardized evaluations are needed because there are over 100 collegiate football programs and each is incapable of playing every other team. As a result, scouts and team personnel must find a series of evaluations to determine the likelihood of success at the professional level. The cost of signing a rookie athlete who does not work out is high for a team. With the 2020 collective bargaining agreement in place, a player with less than a year of NFL experience earns a minimum of $510,000 (Graziano, 2020). For top draft picks, contracts are measured in the tens of millions of dollars with some guaranteed money. Thus, a scout recommending an athlete for a top contract must be as certain as possible. Therefore, evaluations that cut across all positions among all the top athletes from the entirety of the collegiate football system can be a valuable tool.

A football team is organized into various positions, each with different skill sets on both the defensive and offensive squads. For apples-to apples-comparisons, player drill outcomes must be compared within a position. That is to say, players should be evaluated against the measurables of only their position cohort, not against all others. This is because the needs at each position vary greatly. Some positions need strength, others agility, and still others rapid acceleration. Table 4.11 describes popular positions in more detail (but is not exhaustive).

In American football, plays can be a complex series of movements executed in a planned manner by the offense. The defensive squad lines up on the other side, separated by the "scrimmage line" denoted by the ball itself. The defense must disrupt the offense's intended play. When the ball is snapped moving from the center to the quarterback, the play begins, allowing offensive players to move and defensive players to react. The short-term offensive goal is to move the ball 10 yards from the scrimmage line downfield, closer to the defensive end zone. The team must accomplish this task within four successive offensive plays or the ball will change possession. Orchestrated

TABLE 4.11   Details of Popular Football Player Positions

Abbreviation	Position	Offense/Defense	Description
OLB	Outside linebacker	Defense	Tasked with blitzing the QB and the containment of middle offensive plays.
CB	Corner back	Defense	Most often covers receivers, but sometimes will blitz the quarterback.
FS	Free safety	Defense	The FS is the last line of defense against downfield passes.
OG	Offensive guard	Offense	The guard lines up between the center and tackle and defends against a defensive rush by blocking players, enabling offensive players to advance the football.
ILB	Inside linebacker	Defense	The ILB covers the middle of the field, making tackles against RBs that make it past the scrimmage.
DE	Defensive end	Defense	Lined up on the scrimmage, the DE stops running plays or rushes the QB.
SS	Strong safety	Defense	The strong safety is a hybrid of the linebacker and defensive back, covering both pass and run plays.
DT	Defensive tackle	Defense	DTs line up against offensive guards to rush the quarterback and stop running plays.
OT	Offensive tackle	Offense	The OT's job is to defend against a defensive rush by blocking players, enabling offensive players to advance the football.
RB	Running back	Offense	The RB often accepts the ball from the QB on a handoff or short pass. The RB usually lines up behind the offensive line.
TE	Tight end	Offense	The TE is a fusion between an offensive lineman and a wide receiver capable of blocking and catching.
C	Center	Offense	The C is the middle offensive lineman and "snaps" the ball between his legs to the QB.
WR	Wide receiver	Offense	The WR is known for speed and acceleration, lining up "wider" on the offensive line in order to catch the ball or provide downfield blocking.
QB	Quarterback	Offense	Typically, the QB organizes the offensive unit and is capable of throwing, running, or handing the ball off during an offensive play.
LS	Long snapper	Special teams	Used during kicks, the LS is a center that snaps the football farther than a normal center.

plays, where the ball changes possession usually in the form of a punt, are performed by the special teams unit because the skills differ from typical offensive and defensive duties. The ultimate goal is to move the ball downfield into the defensive end zone for a "touchdown." Keep in mind, the nuances of American football are numerous and well outside the scope of this analysis.

Next, the standardized evaluations of the drill weekend should be explored. Table 4.12 lists each evaluation. Since evaluations must be compared within a cohort and each position's expectations vary widely, it is worthwhile to understand which evaluation results are prioritized.

Visit HK*Propel* to view a typical formation for both offense and defensive squads in American football.

R Coding Context

This case uses "`r-markdown`" to construct a dashboard to compare a fictitious player's statistics with drafted and undrafted historical evaluation results among athletes. Markdown is a language for documentation and is authored in plain text. However, once the markdown document is parsed, the plain text can be converted to formatted and robust text including tables, visuals, mathematical formulas, and bulleted lists. Markdown documents can be exported as .pdf and .docx presentations and, as in this case, HTML. Many of the R package documentations, vignettes, and git "*readme*" files are actually authored in markdown. The *r-markdown* libraries and syntax used in this case are simply a port of typical markdown for use in the R environment. To create a markdown file in RStudio, navigate to File > New File, then select R Markdown or simply open any plain text editor and save it with the *.rmd* file extension. However, this case adds more functionality specific for dashboards by employing a template from the *flexdashboard* library.

The basics of r-markdown are straightforward. A header defines the manner in which the page should be parsed, as well as document attributes like a title, and whether or not to include the underlying code for download. Within the document, additional pages, new columns, or rows for adding analytical artifacts are declared, in addition to the actual analysis. This example merely uses `ggplot2` to demonstrate basic functionality. The markdown author has full control of the aesthetics of visuals, document themes, and tables. In fact, additional libraries like *rbokeh* and *echarts4r* enable JavaScript visualizations, allowing the audience to zoom, mouseover, and interact with visualizations like in a web browser. The following code is meant to scaffold markdown dashboard basics using static visualizations so that you can focus on markdown syntax. However, once understood, the process can be extended and improved dramatically.

A pre-signing evaluation of a player's jumping ability may produce crowd-pleasing returns.
Ronald Martinez/Getty Images

TABLE 4.12   The Typical Universal Player Evaluations for Prospective Football Players

Players evaluation	Description	Measurement	Prioritized results
Forty	Players sprint for 40 yards on level ground.	Seconds	Acceleration and speed
Vertical jump	Standing still, players jump as high as they can.	Inches	Explosive muscle potential
Bench repetitions	From a supine position, using a 225-pound barbell, players lift the barbell as many times as possible.	Integer	Strength and stamina
Broad jump	Standing still, a player jumps forward, landing on both feet and maintaining balance.	Inches	Explosive muscle potential in a different set of hip muscles than the vertical jump
Three cone	Cones are arranged in an "L" pattern. Players start at cone "A," run to "B," then back to "A," then "C," and finally return to "A."	Seconds	Lateral movement and ability to change direction, bend, and accelerate
Shuttle run	Players start in between two lines spaced 10 yards apart. An athlete runs 5 yards to his right, crouches, and touches the line, then runs 10 yards to the other line, touching the opposing line, and then sprints back to the starting midpoint.	Seconds	Player's body control in changing directions

The output of the r-markdown will be a web page with extension .HTML. All of the underlying data, JavaScript, and coding has been constructed from the plain text. Further, it is contained in the raw file rather than on a server. As a result, the dashboard can be opened without connection to the Internet. This attribute means sharing is easy because it ships with all information and functionality within the file. It is a self-contained dashboard where the information is "client-side." Thus, sharing is easy and can done through file share or email. As long as the audience has a web browser, they will be able to access the visualizations.

Building a Flexdashboard

A header is needed to begin the markdown document. Start the markdown header with three dashes followed by the `title` attribute. Be sure to declare the text within quotations. Line breaks and spacing matter to markdown, so be sure to pay careful attention to the syntax below. Next, the header needs a declared output. This code uses a layout and functions from the *flexdashboard* library, so the namespace `flex-dashboard` is called with : : followed by the function **flex_dashboard**. After a colon and line break, the orientation is defined as `rows` because the analytical artifacts will be built and organized by row. The flexdashboard documentation and website illustrates multiple other layouts including `columns` and even mobile-optimized options. Next, the `vertical_layout` is defined to allow the user to `scroll`. This option allows the user to scroll down instead of having all information resized for the screen without a scroll bar, which can cause readability issues. Lastly, another option `source_code` is declared as `embed`. This provides a link on your HTML that allows users to see the underlying code to construct the web page. Obviously, if your analysis is proprietary or sensitive, you will want to remove this declaration. Finally, close the header with three additional dashes on the final line. As a reminder, ensure the header section has colons, spacing, and options declared properly, otherwise the HTML will not parse and you may get a cryptic error. It is a best practice to copy/paste rather than write from scratch until familiarity with the syntax is established.

```
---
title: "Workout Comparisons"
output:
 flexdashboard::flex_dashboard:
   orientation: rows
   vertical_layout: scroll
   source_code: embed
---
```

Next, the r-markdown document can accept a code chunk. This starts with three backtick delimiters, ``` ``` ```. The backtick key is usually located in the upper left of a keyboard. Next, a curly bracket in the opening delimiter chunk sets up the metadata about the code chunk. In this example, the code to be executed is written in R and the chunk has a name `setup`. Next, `include=F` instructs the markdown to execute the code and retain the objects for later analysis in the document but not to include the code itself in the final document printout. An empty code chunk with only a comment is shown below for illustration. Be sure to name each code section without duplicates or the document will fail to parse. This chunk is called "*example*"; the code will execute, creating objects, but the code itself will not be saved to the dashboard based on the `include=FALSE` parameter.

```
```{r example, include=FALSE}
# Some R code to be executed
```
```

The `setup` chunk is a great place to load libraries, read data, and perform analysis. In fact, it is a best practice to construct all artifacts used throughout the rest of the dashboard in this initial code chunk. Doing so makes it easier to enact changes in a single area of the document rather than finding the correct code chunk in a subsequent section or even page of a complex dashboard. As a result, the next section of code is a lengthy one and will be explained inside the code chunk then presented holistically to ensure spacing and syntax are understood as a whole.

To begin, load the *flexdashboard*, *reshape2*, *ggplot2*, *ggthemes*, and *viridisLite* packages. Most of these packages are popular and covered elsewhere in the book. However, the *viridisLite* package is a convenience library for selecting color-blind appropriate color palettes.

Below this section of the `setup` code chunk, a small data frame is constructed for a fictitious player. The *playerDemos* data frame is a single row with a fake athlete's basic demographic information. The `Name` column is declared with a string `Justin Billey` followed by `Pos` for position as another character string `RB`. Next, height is presented in a series of nested functions. The `Ht` column utilizes `paste` to concatenate the output of two mathematical operations. The "integer division" `%/%` will divide two numbers and only return the whole number, not the remainder or decimal. Thus 76 `%/%` 12 is simply 6. This value is concatenated to "ft" representing feet and also the output of the "modulo" operator. The `%%` modulo operator will return the remainder only. These lesser-known arithmetic operators can be useful when you need one or the other instead of a typical float number like 76 / 12 resulting in 6.33. The last two columns simply declare the prospect's weight and include a placeholder for their school.

```r
```{r setup, include=FALSE}
# Libraries
library(flexdashboard)
library(reshape2)
library(ggplot2)
library(ggthemes)
library(viridisLite)


# Inputs
playerDemos <- data.frame(Name = 'Justin Billey',
                          Pos = 'RB',
                           Ht = paste(76 %/%12, 'ft',
                                76 %%12, 'in'),
                           Wt = '215',
                          Edu = 'Hard Knocks')
```

Let's continue within the setup code chunk. After declaring the fictious player's statistics, another data frame is instantiated with the results of this player's physical drills. Again, these statistics are made up, but suppose "Justin Billey" ran the 40-yard dash in 4.56 seconds, his vertical jump was 38.5 inches, and so on. This information is captured as a one-row data frame called playerEvals. Keep in mind that the goal of this dashboard is to compare these attributes to the historical values of all similar `RB` positions for both drafted and undrafted athletes. Thus, we will now move to the historical population attributes.

```r
playerEvals <- data.frame(Forty = 4.56,
                        Vertical = 38.5,
                       BenchReps = 16,
                       BroadJump = 114,
                            Cone = 6.84,
                         Shuttle = 4.20)
```

The history object is a data frame of all player skills assessments between 2010 and 2018. The player names have been obfuscated along with other identifying information. Using read.csv along with the url function allows R to download the file directly from an online source. The dataset can also be downloaded through this book's HK*Propel* site.

Visit HK*Propel* to access and download the *historical* dataset.

```r
# Read in the data
history <- read.csv(url(

'https://raw.githubusercontent.com/kwartler/NLP_SportsAnalytics/
master/football_case_data/historical.csv'))
```

Continuing within the setup chunk, let's remove rows containing NA values. One could mean impute or even a model to replace the unknown values. However, this is more complex and invites bias into the descriptive analysis the dashboard seeks. To remove incomplete rows, use the **complete.cases** function applied to the *history* data frame. This returns a Boolean vector whether or not a row has legitimate values in all columns. This output is nested to the *left* of the square brackets. Thus, the Boolean indexes the rows of the data frame. Remember that in R, functions like dim and square bracket indexing follow "rows" then "columns," so this operation must be on the left of the comma to subset the rows.
```

```
history <- history[complete.cases(history),]
```

Next, on the right side of the comma, a vector of column names is presented using the c function. This will further subset the historical data by the columns of interest.

```
evals <- history[,c('Forty', 'Vertical','BenchReps','BroadJump',
          'Cone', 'Shuttle', 'draftStatus','Pos')]
```

At this point, the *history* data frame was reduced from 5,882 rows and 12 variables to 2,753 complete records among 7 variables in a new object called evals. Table 4.13 represents the head of this reduced dataset without player demographic information.

For simplicity within the *ggplot2* visualization package, the data is manipulated to be a long format. This is a "tidy" version, but the values themselves do not change. In order to change from a wide format to long use, the **melt** function is applied to the data frame. Table 4.14 is another head call applied to the manipulated data. Notice that the data frame now has 13,765 rows but is only four columns. Now the first six rows (actually many more) store the forty variable vertically and their corresponding values in the value column.

```
evals <- melt(evals)
```

As discussed earlier, players should be evaluated within their position cohort. This information is already stored in the player demographic object entered earlier and called *playerDemos*. This is an example of robust code because rather than declaring the same information in a second location, the code refers to the original input object value. In this example, it is RB. While declaring the position explicitly would suffice, this invites errors by forcing the author to change two places in the code. Without robust code, one could change the demographic information object but neglect to

Table 4.13   The First Six Rows of the Cleaned Original Dataset

Forty	Vertical	BenchReps	BroadJump	Cone	Shuttle	draftStatus	Pos
5.56	25.0	23	94	8.48	4.98	drafted	OT
4.72	31.0	21	112	7.96	4.39	not_drafted	OLB
4.44	35.0	17	119	7.03	4.14	drafted	CB
5.34	28.0	20	96	7.72	4.73	not_drafted	OT
4.62	35.0	10	114	6.92	4.32	drafted	FS
4.44	37.5	16	116	6.81	4.04	drafted	CB

TABLE 4.14   The Molten Data Frame Is Longer Than the Original Wide Format

draftStatus	Pos	Variable	Value
drafted	OT	Forty	5.56
not_drafted	OLB	Forty	4.72
drafted	CB	Forty	4.44
not_drafted	OT	Forty	5.34
drafted	FS	Forty	4.62
drafted	CB	Forty	4.44

update this code line. Robust code is preferred to avoid errors and reduce author effort. After applying the subset function where the Pos column of the molten data frame is equal to the Pos column of the player demographic data, the plotData object has 5,882 rows with four columns.

```
plotData <- subset(evals, as.character(evals$Pos)==as.
character(playerDemos[1,2]))
```

Next, the larger data frame will be split into a list based on the football drill. Since there are six drills in the original dataset, this translated to six values in the variable column of the molten data frame. Now **split** will create a list with six elements, one per level in the variable column, which maps back to the individual drill. The split function accepts the object to be split followed by the factor that defines the grouping. While there are other packages and methods for grouping data by levels and then applying functions, this method works well using base R functions. Figure 4.10 conceptually demonstrates the results of the data frame split.

```
plotData <- split(plotData, plotData$variable)
```

The data has been massaged into a list where each element corresponds to an individual drill for a single position. The point of the dashboard is to calculate the average by group drafted versus not_drafted within each drill, then to compare each to Justin Billey, the fictitious player. Dealing with list objects can be troublesome for new R programmers, but this code is straightforward. In the latter half of the code, the function aggregate is used. The goal is to calculate the mean of the value column by the levels of the draftStatus column within a data frame called x. While the parameter order and formula may be confusing, the function accepts a data frame, divides it into drafted versus not_drafted, and then calculates the mean for each subgroup. The nuance is that it is accepting any data frame declared as x. In order to apply this generic function to each list element, the lapply method is

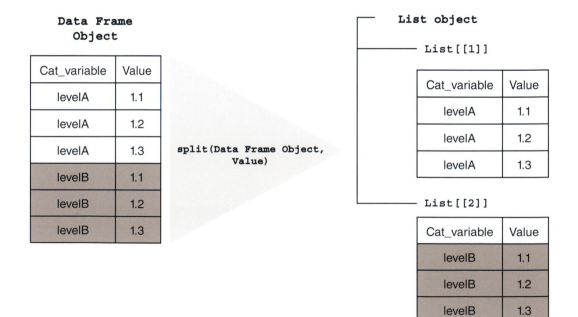

FIGURE 4.10   The concept of splitting a data frame into a list.

employed. **lapply** simply applies a function to each list element. Thus, each element represents the `x` ultimately passed to the aggregate function. The resulting muData is a list, one element per drill, with a mean value for drafted and not_drafted. For example, the muData[[1]] object corresponds to the 40-yard evaluation. Drafted running backs average 4.51 seconds while not-drafted backs average 4.61 seconds.

```
muData <- lapply(plotData,
          function(x) aggregate(value ~ draftStatus,
                  data = x,
                  FUN = mean))
```

Finally, the **viridis** function selects five color-blind appropriate hexadecimal codes for use in the dashboard. The valueBoxCols object is a vector of hexadecimal values used in color matching with a length of five. Because this is the conclusion of the setup chunk, the final line needs the three backticks ` ``` `. All data used throughout the dashboard is contained in the setup code, making any adjustment easy as it flows through the subsequent components.

```
# Color Blind ok Hex
valueBoxCols <- viridis(5)
```

Switching back to markdown, let's declare our first row so that information can be populated into the dashboard and then set up some R code chunks within the row. Row one will have large number "value boxes" with player demographic information. Each value box will need an individual R code chunk (presented below). The inputs to each value box are consistent, so understanding one translates to others.

In the first value box R section called name, the function **valueBox** is called. This function is specific to the *flexdashboard* library and requires a value to display. The value parameter accepts the first row and column of the *playerDemos* data frame. For each corresponding value box, the value declaration is changed—for example, playerDemos[1,2] for the second section. Additionally, an icon can be declared from the "Font Awesome" icon set. This icon set is widely supported and is said to be in use among 38 percent of websites. Here, the icon parameter "fa-user" corresponds to the Font Awesome user icon, a generic person-shaped icon. In other value boxes, these icons are changed to appropriate icons such as "fa-foot-ball". Lastly, the color parameter is declared using the viridis hexadecimal within valueBoxCols. Once again, this is changed for each subsequent box resulting in different color boxes.

```
Row
-----------------------------------
### Player Name
```{r name}
valueBox(value = playerDemos[1,1],
    icon = "fa-user",
    color = valueBoxCols[1])
```

Position
```{r}
valueBox(value = playerDemos[1,2],
icon = "fa-football-ball",
caption = "",
color = valueBoxCols[2])
```
```

```r
### Ht
```{r}
valueBox(value = playerDemos[1,3],
    icon = "fa-ruler-vertical",
    color = valueBoxCols[3])
```

Wt
```{r}
valueBox(value = playerDemos[1,4],
    icon = "fa-weight",
    color = valueBoxCols[4])
```

Edu
```{r}
valueBox(value = playerDemos[1,5],
    icon = "fa-school",
    color = valueBoxCols[5])
```
```

After this row, another is declared so that visuals can be constructed and added to the dashboard. This example R chunk is called "forty". The object is an integer corresponding to the list element or drill in question. The statNum value is set to 1 corresponding to the 40-yard dash evaluation. The rest of the ggplot code evaluates using statNum so that each subsequent visual in the dashboard only requires this value to change rather than changing multiple places in the visualization code.

The ggplot function accepts the data frame that is plotData[[statNum]] of the first list element corresponding to the 40-yard dash. Within the aesthetics, aes, the x-axis will correspond to the column value and be color-filled by the draftStatus. The next layer adds a **geom_density** with 0.75 opacity. This is a kernel density plot representing the distribution of the player metrics. Additionally, a vertical line is created using the function **geom_vline**, referring to Justin Billey's specific metric in playerEvals[1,statNum]. Another geom_vline is added using the average historical values for comparisons. This employs the aggregated object muData[[statNum]] with some aesthetics separate to the densities. The remaining layers adjust colors and themes and are at the discretion of the markdown author. Figure 4.11 demonstrates the resulting visualization; the rest of the dashboard will have similar visuals but refer to different metrics.

```r
Row
----------------------------------------
### Forty
```{r forty}
statNum <- 1
ggplot(plotData[[statNum]], aes(value, fill = draftStatus)) +
 geom_density(alpha = 0.75) +
 geom_vline(data=playerEvals,
 aes(xintercept=playerEvals[1,statNum]), color='black') +
 geom_vline(data = muData[[statNum]],aes(xintercept = value,color
 = draftStatus), linetype = "dashed") +
 scale_color_manual(values = c('darkgreen', 'darkred')) +
 scale_fill_viridis_d('Draft Status', option = 'C') + theme_hc() +
 theme(axis.title.y = element_blank(),
    axis.text.y = element_blank(),
    axis.ticks.y = element_blank())
```
```

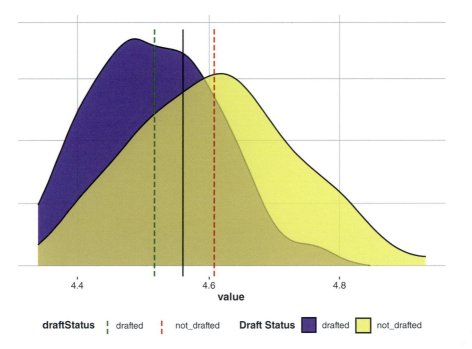

FIGURE 4.11 The resulting kernel density plot for the 40-yard dash among drafted, not drafted, and the individual player being evaluated. The average drafted value is lower than the individual player, but the not-drafted player average was well above the individual.

The next visualization on the row refers to the vertical drill. This code is exactly the same as the previous chunk except for `statNum`. The value of coding like this is that updates and maintenance are easier than having multiple expressions to change in sequence, which often invites errors that must be investigated.

```
### Vertical
```{r vert}
statNum <- 2
ggplot(plotData[[statNum]], aes(value, fill = draftStatus)) +
 geom_density(alpha = 0.75) +
 geom_vline(data=playerEvals,
 aes(xintercept=playerEvals[1,statNum]), color='black') +
 geom_vline(data = muData[[statNum]],aes(xintercept = value,color
 = draftStatus), linetype = "dashed") +
 scale_color_manual(values = c('darkgreen', 'darkred')) +
 scale_fill_viridis_d('Draft Status', option = 'C') + theme_hc() +
 theme(axis.title.y = element_blank(),
   axis.text.y = element_blank(),
   axis.ticks.y = element_blank())
```
```

After these initial visuals are added, another row is easily added along with new visuals. Adding visuals is as simple as a copy/paste as long as the `statNum` is adjusted for each list element. The final complete markdown script is shown in its entirety below. Much more can be done with dashboarding, especially when employing dynamic plots and improved layouts and themes. However, this case demonstrates how a dashboard can be quickly constructed, adjusted, and shared with football scouts for a quick evaluation of a player against others. Updating the individual player is easy as it occurs in the setup section.

```
---
title: "Workout Comparisons"
output:
 flexdashboard::flex_dashboard:
   orientation: rows
   vertical_layout: scroll
   source_code: embed
---


```{r setup, include=FALSE}

# Libraries
library(flexdashboard)
library(reshape2)
library(ggplot2)
library(ggthemes)
library(viridisLite)


# Inputs
playerDemos <- data.frame(Name = 'Justin Billey',
                          Pos = 'RB',
                           Ht = paste(76 %/%12, 'ft',
                                 76 %%12, 'in'),
                           Wt = '215',
                          Edu = 'Hard Knocks')


playerEvals <- data.frame(Forty = 4.56,
                        Vertical = 38.5,
                       BenchReps = 16,
                       BroadJump = 114,
                            Cone = 6.84,
                         Shuttle = 4.20)

# Read in the data
history <- read.csv(url(

'https://raw.githubusercontent.com/kwartler/NLP_SportsAnalytics/
master/football_case_data/historical.csv'))

# Clean, remove NAs rather than impute
history <- history[complete.cases(history),]

evals <- history[,c('Forty', 'Vertical','BenchReps','BroadJump',
        'Cone', 'Shuttle', 'draftStatus','Pos')]
evals <- melt(evals)

plotData <- subset(evals, as.character(evals$Pos)==as.
character(playerDemos[1,2]))
plotData <- split(plotData, plotData$variable)
muData <- lapply(plotData,
          function(x) aggregate(value ~ draftStatus,
                  data = x,
                  FUN = mean))
```
```

```
# Color Blind ok Hex
valueBoxCols <- viridis(5)
```

Row

Player Name
```{r name}
valueBox(value = playerDemos[1,1],
    icon = "fa-user",color = valueBoxCols[1])
    ```


Position
```{r}
valueBox(value = playerDemos[1,2],
    icon = "fa-football-ball",
    color = valueBoxCols[2])
```


Ht
```{r}
valueBox(value = playerDemos[1,3],
    icon = "fa-ruler-vertical",
    color = valueBoxCols[3])
```


Wt
```{r}
valueBox(value = playerDemos[1,4],
    icon = "fa-weight",
    color = valueBoxCols[4])
```


Edu
```{r}
valueBox(value = playerDemos[1,5],
    icon = "fa-school",
    color = valueBoxCols[5])
```

Row

Forty
```{r forty}
statNum <- 1
ggplot(plotData[[statNum]], aes(value, fill = draftStatus)) +
 geom_density(alpha = 0.75) +
 geom_vline(data=playerEvals,
 aes(xintercept=playerEvals[1,statNum]), color='black') +
 geom_vline(data = muData[[statNum]],aes(xintercept = value,color
 = draftStatus), linetype = "dashed") +
 scale_color_manual(values = c('darkgreen', 'darkred')) +
 scale_fill_viridis_d('Draft Status', option = 'C') + theme_hc() +
 theme(axis.title.y = element_blank(),
   axis.text.y = element_blank(),
   axis.ticks.y = element_blank())
```

Vertical

```{r vert}
statNum <- 2
ggplot(plotData[[statNum]], aes(value, fill = draftStatus)) +
 geom_density(alpha = 0.75) +
 geom_vline(data=playerEvals,
 aes(xintercept=playerEvals[1,statNum]), color='black') +
 geom_vline(data = muData[[statNum]],aes(xintercept = value,color
 = draftStatus), linetype = "dashed") +
 scale_color_manual(values = c('darkgreen', 'darkred')) +
 scale_fill_viridis_d('Draft Status', option = 'C') + theme_hc() +
 theme(axis.title.y = element_blank(),
   axis.text.y = element_blank(),
   axis.ticks.y = element_blank())
```

Bench Reps

```{r reps}
statNum <- 3
ggplot(plotData[[statNum]], aes(value, fill = draftStatus)) +
 geom_density(alpha = 0.75) +
 geom_vline(data=playerEvals,
 aes(xintercept=playerEvals[1,statNum]), color='black') +
 geom_vline(data = muData[[statNum]],aes(xintercept = value,color
 = draftStatus), linetype = "dashed") +
 scale_color_manual(values = c('darkgreen', 'darkred')) +
 scale_fill_viridis_d('Draft Status', option = 'C') + theme_hc() +
 theme(axis.title.y = element_blank(),
   axis.text.y = element_blank(),
   axis.ticks.y = element_blank())
```

Row

Broad Jump

```{r jump}
statNum <- 4
ggplot(plotData[[statNum]], aes(value, fill = draftStatus)) +
 geom_density(alpha = 0.75) +
 geom_vline(data=playerEvals,
 aes(xintercept=playerEvals[1,statNum]), color='black') +
 geom_vline(data = muData[[statNum]],aes(xintercept = value, color
 = draftStatus), linetype = "dashed") +
 scale_color_manual(values = c('darkgreen', 'darkred')) +
 scale_fill_viridis_d('Draft Status', option = 'C') + theme_hc() +
 theme(axis.title.y = element_blank(),
   axis.text.y = element_blank(),
   axis.ticks.y = element_blank())
```

```
### Cone
```{r cone}
statNum <- 5
ggplot(plotData[[statNum]], aes(value, fill = draftStatus)) +
 geom_density(alpha = 0.75) +
 geom_vline(data=playerEvals,
 aes(xintercept=playerEvals[1,statNum]), color='black') +
 geom_vline(data = muData[[statNum]],aes(xintercept = value,color
 = draftStatus), linetype = "dashed") +
 scale_color_manual(values = c('darkgreen', 'darkred')) +
 scale_fill_viridis_d('Draft Status', option = 'C') + theme_hc() +
 theme(axis.title.y = element_blank(),
   axis.text.y = element_blank(),
   axis.ticks.y = element_blank())
```

Shuttle
```{r shuttle}
statNum <- 6
ggplot(plotData[[statNum]], aes(value, fill = draftStatus)) +
 geom_density(alpha = 0.75) +
 geom_vline(data=playerEvals,
 aes(xintercept=playerEvals[1,statNum]), color='black') +
 geom_vline(data = muData[[statNum]],aes(xintercept = value,color
 = draftStatus), linetype = "dashed") +
 scale_color_manual(values = c('darkgreen', 'darkred')) +
 scale_fill_viridis_d('Draft Status', option = 'C') + theme_hc() +
 theme(axis.title.y = element_blank(),
   axis.text.y = element_blank(),
   axis.ticks.y = element_blank())
```
```

Once the markdown is functioning properly with an eye-pleasing theme, the markdown needs to be rendered. This is the process of turning the markdown plain text code with R chunks into a dashboard to be reviewed and shared as an HTML file. The *r-markdown* package contains a function **render** that allows programmatic parsing of the *.rmd* file. Simply pass in a path to the file path. The example below has a path to a desktop folder containing the *.rmd* file. This line of code is *not* to be within the markdown itself but instead typed in the console directly. Alternatively, within RStudio, there is a button titled "knit" at the top of the markdown file that will stitch together all components of the file.

```
rmarkdown::render('~/Desktop/NLP_SportsAnalytics/football_case_
data/example.Rmd')
```

The markdown is parsed into a simple web page for review, as shown in the online player evaluation dashboard figure. A HTML document is saved to the working directory and can be shared as a client-side, serverless web page. With more fluency in markdown, it is possible to construct dynamic dashboard plots, websites, ebooks, and even blogs. However, this case demonstrates the basic C functionality as a foundation.

Visit HK*Propel* to view the player evaluation dash-board demonstrating our sample player's impressive vertical jump compared to historical player prospects, among other drills.

COMPARATIVE ANALYSIS OF MALE AND FEMALE PRIZE MONIES AND SALARIES ANALYTICS APPLICATION

Lisa Delpy Neirotti, PhD

Women in sports have long been pushing for the right to equal play and equal pay. Major landmarks in this fight took place a half century ago with the passage of Title IX in 1972 and Billie Jean King's U.S. Open Tennis boycott to ensure equal prize money in 1973. With the heightened global attention to equality and inclusion of historically marginalized people, coupled with the increased social activism of athletes, the pressure is on more than ever to narrow the gender pay gap in sports.

To better understand how much and why female athletes earn what they do, a numerical analysis was conducted for professional basketball, soccer, tennis, golf, softball, cricket, and esports. The discussion will begin with the most equal of all sports, tennis.

There are several variables to consider when comparing male versus female athlete salaries. For individual sport athletes, these variables include the number and level of tournaments and the prize money offered. For team sports, variables include the length of the season/number of games, the number of teams, and total spots available. Also, for sports where a few star players earn much more than others, the median versus mean should be considered, as the average may be skewed.

Tennis

It isn't by chance that women's professional tennis players are the highest-paid female athletes to date. The fight for equal pay started in 1970 when nine female tennis players founded their own tour, now the Women's Tennis Association (WTA), and in 1973 Billie Jean King threatened to boycott the U.S. Open resulting in the first Grand Slam tournament to offer equal prize money to men and women. It took until 2007 for all four Grand Slams to follow suit with Wimbledon being the last. Unfortunately, tournament prize money outside of the Grand Slams is not always equal. Only four other tournaments provide equal prize money: Indian Wells, Miami, Madrid, and Beijing, with each offering $1,354,010 in prize money in 2019. Of the other Association of Tennis Professionals (ATP) and WTA tournaments, it is important to review the number and level of tournament when analyzing prize money. A *New York Times* study that looked outside the Grand Slam tournaments found the annual prize money for the top-100 earners in the WTA was roughly 80 cents to every dollar earned by the top-100 men in the ATP (Rothenberg, 2016).

Starting in 2021, WTA reorganized its tournament structure and merged the previous Premier Mandatory and Premier 5 tournaments into a single higher tier, referred to as WTA 1000 tournaments and the expected prize money is $1 million for each. The future continues to look bright, with the WTA tournament prize money worldwide doubling in 10 years from $86 million in 2009 to $179 million in 2019, the last full season played before Covid-19 (WTA Tour Press Release, 2021; WTA Tour Press Release, 2020; Reuters, 2020).

When comparing career prize money totals as of May 2021, Serena Williams, the highest-paid female, earned $94,253,246—which is 36.35 percent less than Novak Djokovic, the highest-paid male, who earned $148,092,073. Williams turned pro in 1995 at age 14 and Djokovic in 2003 at age 20 (Forbes, 2021).

Golf

When analyzing prize money in golf, like tennis, it is important to consider the number of tournaments in the men's Professional Golfers' Association (PGA) versus the Ladies Professional Golf Association (LPGA). In 2019, there were 46 men's and 33 women's tournaments, with an average prize purse of $7,469,565.22 to $2,127,273, respectively (LPGA earning 28 percent of the PGA average). Overall, PGA tournament earning potential was five times higher than that of female golfers with a total prize pool of $343,600,000 to $70,200,000. Although the LPGA total prize pool increased by $3 million in 2021, the PGA's increased by $45 million and added five tournaments.

Football (Soccer)

At the World Cup level, the Federation International Football Association (FIFA) has faced criticism for the prize pool for the 2019 Women's World Cup of $30 million compared to the 2018 Men's World Cup of $400 million. Thirty-two teams competed in the Men's World Cup, with the winning team earning $38 million. This means the 24 Women's World Cup teams that competed were all playing for less than what the one men's champion team received. The women's champion team earned $4 million. Looking at the prize pool as an average per team competing, the women averaged $1.25 million whereas the men averaged $12.5 million.

Regardless of how you analyze the numbers, the men's prize pool is more than 12 times the women's—or, conversely, the women receive 7.5 percent of what the men do. When comparing the commercial value of the women's and men's tournaments, the television viewership of 1.12 billion and 1.13 million live spectators for the 2019 Women's World Cup in France were approximately a third of the 2018 Men's World Cup 3.57 billion TV viewers and 3.03 million live spectators. If this percent was applied to the total prize pool available of $430 million for both men and women, the women's total prize pool should have been a third or $141.90 million. FIFA has doubled the women's prize pool from $15 million in 2015 to $30 million in 2019 and plans to double it again to $60 million for the 2023 tournament, but this is still not 33 percent of the men's tournament earnings, and the gap continues as the men's prize pool increased to $700 million for the 2022 World Cup, which is a 57 percent increase from 2018 and an 80 percent increase since the 2014 World Cup.

Since FIFA historically packaged the men's and women's tournaments together to sell broadcast and sponsorship rights, the association admits that the amount of revenue allocated to the Women's World Cup is arbitrary. This has changed recently, so in the future, the value of Women's World Cup will be truly measured. According to Fox Sports, the television ad revenue totaled $96 million for the 2019 Women's World Cup, a 120 percent increase from expectations. Corporate sponsors like Visa are now including contract clauses that spending should be equal between men and women and have pledged to spend equal amounts in marketing of the men's and women's tournaments.

With 13.36 million women and girls now playing organized football globally, the pressure is expected to grow (Lange, 2020; BBC News, 2019). At the national level, the Women's U.S. National Team entered a gender-discrimination lawsuit against the U.S. Soccer Federation. The case was dismissed because of differences in the collective bargaining agreement (CBA). The women's CBA guarantees a base salary of $100,000 plus incentive-based bonuses, whereas the men's CBA is entirely performance based with no guaranteed salary but higher bonuses. Considering that the minimum salary for women playing in the National Women's Soccer League (NWSL) is 26 percent of the minimum salary for men playing in Major League Soccer (MLS)—$22,000 to $84,000—the option of a guaranteed salary was appealing to women, whereas depending on the success of the season could limit their earnings.

In November 2019, Australia's women's soccer team negotiated a landmark four-year deal with Football Federation Australia that ensured the women would be paid as much as their male counterparts. It also guaranteed equitable conditions, including business-class travel for international tournaments (something the men already had) and the same coaching and operational support. England, Brazil, Australia, Norway, and New Zealand have all since committed to equal pay. The gender disparity at major tournaments continues due to the discrepancy in prize money offered by FIFA, UEFA, and other tournament organizers.

Ice Hockey

In 2017, USA national team players agreed to a four-year agreement with USA Hockey, guaranteeing about $71,000 in compensation per player, plus performance bonuses of $37,500 per Olympic or World Championship gold medal, which could push incomes over six figures. The NHL helped facilitate the deal by contributing $25,000 per player to USA Hockey. Enhanced travel and medical benefits, including maternity leave, were also added for the first time. Like the situation in soccer, USA Men's Hockey players have the chance to earn high salaries in the NHL, where the minimum contract is $775,000. The National Women's Hockey League, by comparison, is a young enterprise with the salary cap per the six teams limited to $300,000. Based on 20-player rosters, the average salary would rise to $15,000 per player with a range from $10,000 to $35,000, not including bonuses that come with the league's revenue-sharing agreement with its players (Gough, 2021; Reuters, 2021; Wyshynski, 2018).

Basketball

The WNBA is the longest-running women's professional sport league, beginning in 1996 with 12 teams. Salaries continue to grow but not at the rate of the National Basketball Association with 30 teams. The current median NBA salary is $3,500,000 while for the WNBA it is $70,040. The average NBA salary is $7,359,982 and $105,248 for the WNBA. Considering the wide range of salaries in both the NBA and WNBA, it is valuable to compare the mean and median. There are 582 NBA players on the 2021 roster, with the lowest salary at $18,458 and the highest salary at $43,006,362. There are 142 WNBA players, with the lowest salary at $11,577 and the highest salary at $221,450. The new WNBA CBA starting in 2020 increased the minimum salary by 36 percent, with an average increase per year of 2 percent.

Baseball and Softball

The professional league for softball players was the National Pro Fastpitch (NPF) until the league suspended operations in 2021. The majority of players earned between $3,000 to $6,000. Each of the six teams had a salary cap of $175,000 for 16-28 players, for an average of $7,954.55. The minimum salary was $3,000 and the highest-paid player, Monica Abbott, signed a six-year $1,000,000 deal in 2016, of which $20,000 was counted as salary, with the rest paid in other ways including bonuses. Athlete United (AU) is the current professional opportunity for female softball players and is paying $10,000 for a six-week season, with earning potential up to $25,000 more based on individual achievements (Snap Softball, 2021).

When compared to Major League Baseball's minor league farm teams and independent pro league teams, the monthly salary appears comparable to the NPF ($1,100 to $1,800). However, the minor league season is double in length, so the total earning for men is at least double. Minor league baseball players also can be called up to the big leagues and earn a significant amount more, whereas there are no advancements for NPF, now AU, players. MLB players' minimum salary in 2021 was $570,500, with a median of $1,150,000 and an average of $4,170,000. The highest-paid MLB player makes $37.1 million, with 20 MLB players earning $25 million or more. When comparing the minimum salaries of the AU to MLB, female softball players earn under 2 percent (1.75 percent) of the men.

Most of the Athlete United players are also USA National Team Softball players who earned a small stipend in the lead-up to the 2020 Olympic Games and $22,500 each for the silver medal. Softball will not be in the 2024 Olympic Games, so there will be no stipend or Olympic medal bonuses between 2021-2024.

Cricket

Cricket is estimated to be the second most popular sport in the world, with a 2.5 billion global following. Currently, the top female cricket player is Ellyse Perry from Australia, whose estimated net worth is up to $14 million. In 2020, Cricket Australia increased female player payments 7.36 times from $7.5 million to $55.2 million, resulting in Perry annually earning $128,200 for playing in the Women's Big Bash League and for participating in domestic Cricket Victoria competitions. She also

Women's championship teams and players in soccer, golf, and basketball face some of the largest financial disparities as compared to their male counterparts.
Douglas P. DeFelice/Getty Images

Victor Decolongon/Getty Images

5

NATURAL LANGUAGE PROCESSING AND TEXT MINING

CHAPTER OBJECTIVES

After completing this chapter and the associated online exercises, you will be able to accomplish the following:

· Understand the use of object classes, types, and strings to code language.

· Explore basic string manipulation functions.

· Understand the five steps of a natural language processing project.

· Execute R coding scripts to perform text analysis.

· Conduct string manipulation and organization into a document term matrix to get term frequency.

· Build visualizations such as bar charts, word clouds, and pyramid plots.

· Perform word associations and sentiment analysis.

· Explore the use of data in developing insight and recommendations.

KEY TERMS

corpus	principle of least effort	text mining
document term matrix	sentiment analysis	word associations
Lasso regularization	share of voice	Zipf's law
lexicon	stop word	
natural language processing	term document matrix	

R FUNCTIONS

analyzeSentiment	gsub	tm_map
comparison.cloud	join_all	tolower
content_transformer	ngrams	trimws
customClean	pyramid.plot	VCorpus
DataframeSource	removePunctuation	wordcloud
DocumentTermMatrix	removeSparseTerms	
findAssocs	row_sums	
grepl()	strsplit	

Natural language processing (NLP) represents the collection of analytical techniques to distill information from vast amounts of unstructured language data. Often the goal of NLP or **text mining** is information reduction to learn something about the larger body of text. An analog would be calculating the average age of a country's population to understand a characteristic of the country, such as seeing whether a population growth in young families is driving the need for increased education infrastructure. The individual ages are reduced to a single value so that you can understand the country's characteristic—say, older or younger demographics—without interviewing each person individually. Similarly, using a million tweets as your data source, you can use text mining methods to extract frequent concepts, people, places, organizations, and even attitudes without reading a single tweet. The concepts in this chapter will help you reduce noise to extract meaningful information from sports-related text.

Keep in mind that text mining is among the most challenging of data science and analytics problems to do well. This is because human expression varies and communication theory dictates that the channel, messenger, and audience may all affect the intended meaning. As a result, when you start a NLP project you should understand the channel, messenger, and audience and adjust your analytical methods accordingly. First, channel impacts the language used and will likewise impact the language analysis. For example, a sports contract will obviously use a lot of boilerplate legalistic language and clauses such as "For any contract procured by the Agent and signed by the Player…." In contrast, a social media channel consisting of fans will use slang, swear words, and emojis consistent with usage in that medium. The messenger may also affect language analysis as well. For example, in Boston, sports fans regularly scream that a home run is "wicked awesome" or that an umpire call was "wicked bad." For most English speakers, "wicked" has a negative connotation, so "wicked awesome" would make no sense. However, with Boston fans as the messengers, "wicked" has an amplifying effect. To others outside of New England, a home run for their team could be "really awesome" or a poor referee call could be described as "really bad." Finally, the intended audience will affect language significantly as well. A sportscaster describing a pivotal play in a game will use language that is dramatically different from two peers discussing the same play casually over a drink. Another example is the terms a coach would use with a player at the high school, collegiate, or professional level. At each level, the expectations, athleticism, and knowledge of the sport differ, dictating the language to be different. These factors are just some of the challenges associated with NLP projects even outside the sports world. However, these challenges are also part of the reason this analysis is satisfying.

NLP is used extensively by consumers. For example, identifying spam in an inbox is a form of document classification, using both NLP and machine learning. In terms of sports, natural language processing aptly applies to fan engagement. Sports businesses measure marketing and more specifically fan engagement to improve operations. Sports organizations would be wise to incorporate long understood aspects of traditional business marketing using NLP to their industry. While document classification, human resources reviews, ticket holder propensity modeling, and other areas may also use NLP, the examples in this chapter primarily use fan engagement and expression to demonstrate concepts.

Professional Highlights

Diana Ma, Los Angeles Lakers

Even though evidence reveals a lack of women in STEM-related positions, many of those who pursue a career in sport analytics are successful. One such success story is Diana Ma, a data analyst for the Lost Angeles Lakers. She has combined her passion for basketball and statistics in her analytics career, where she analyzes aspects of player and team performance to enhance the Lakers' success.

Perhaps instigated by Yao Ming's presence on the court, Diana joined her mother and father in watching the NBA. As Ma noted, "We all hung out and had fun watching basketball together" (Wu, 2020). Her interest in statistical analysis came later, in college. As a premed major, Ma began taking statistics. For her project, she chose to use a basketball dataset to try to predict who would win the NBA championship. She began to research advanced data modeling techniques and tried to find as much literature as possible, although she notes that "there wasn't a lot of published literature analyzing basketball statistics" (Wu, 2020). She had no idea at the time that sport analytics was even an available career. It was not until she was in graduate school that she learned that some NBA teams hired data scientists. At that time, she began interning for the Indiana Pacers, gaining valuable experience as the only female data analyst for the franchise. While the franchise was very welcoming and she enjoyed both the work and the culture, in the beginning of her career, she said, "I didn't have a role model that I could look up to.... There was no one like that for me at that time" (Wu 2020).

Following her passion at the intersection of basketball and statistics, Ma continued working for the Pacers part-time while having a full-time job in digital advertising. She then became the only female on the analytics team for the Lakers. Diana Ma's advice to aspiring female analysts: "I was that little girl who didn't do well in high school math. Don't give up. Keep pushing yourself. It's hard. Many times, you are going to feel uncomfortable. In situations like that, it's important to focus on the bigger picture.... Don't give up. Keep pushing yourself" (Wu, 2020).

LANGUAGE AS OBJECT CLASSES AND STRINGS

The R programming language operates using object classes. The most common include Boolean, factor, numeric, integer, and character. In fact, the technical name of character is "string." Refer to table 5.1 to understand the difference of an object class. As you may expect, NLP uses the character string object class most often. This differs from factor levels, which can be confusing to new R programmers. Factors have distinct, often repeatable levels, such as a roster listing the university attended by the athlete. In this roster, university names by themselves are not natural language meant to express an idea but instead to assign a piece of repeatable information to the athletes on the roster. In contrast, character strings may or may not repeat, and they are most often used to convey varying meaning. In table 5.1, unlike the other object types, the character data value example is complete compared to the original sports context value. Thus, NLP requires a good understanding of the object class string and how to manipulate, correct, and adjust it for analysis.

TABLE 5.1   Common Object Classes in R

Type	Example	Sports context
Boolean	TRUE or FALSE	Did LeBron James play for the Cavaliers? **TRUE**
Factor (with distinct "levels")	Cleveland	The teams LeBron played for are **Cleveland**, Miami, and Los Angeles. Levels: Cleveland, Miami, Los Angeles
Numeric (also called "floating point")	27.1	LeBron James averages **27.1** points per game.
Integer	23	LeBron James's jersey number is **23**.
Character	"Lebron James is building a new media company that aims to give a voice to Black creators."	"LeBron James is building a new media company that aims to give a voice to Black creators."

Additionally, each object class can be contained within an object type. You are likely familiar with object types including vectors, matrices, data frames, lists, and arrays. For simplicity, in this chapter, data will be in data frames and occasionally simple vectors. For new R programmers, think of data frames as a data worksheet like Excel and a vector as a single column in that sheet. The string manipulation functions covered in this section are not exhaustive but should give you a solid foundation to build on while emphasizing typical uses.

R has multiple basic functions for dealing with strings. In this section, we will apply basic sting functions to a single tweet before applying the functions to a larger body of text.

Consider a public tweet from Rachael Evans, a Cavs PowerHouse Dance Team member (https://twitter.com/missevans__/status/1179078078561226755), which when pulled into an R session as a character string appears as the text below.

```
@missevans__: Y'all I'm really about to dance on the Cleveland
Cavaliers court starting next week \U0001f631\U0001f631\U0001f631
```

To begin, as the data scientist you may want to remove the unrecognized Unicode characters that are actually the screaming face emojis. R does not natively understand most emojis, especially since they are updated often. Thus, if you are working in a channel that frequently employs them, it is worthwhile to remove or substitute them. In the following code chunk, the character string tweet is passed to the **gsub(search, substitute, object)** function. This stands for "global substitution" and works with regular expressions to match a character pattern and then substitute it with another. The gsub syntax accepts a pattern to search for, then the replacement substitution text, and finally the object to search within.

```
# Create a single example
tweet <- '@missevans__: Y'all I'm really about to dance on the
Cleveland Cavaliers court starting next week \U0001f631\U0001f631\
U0001f631'
tweet <- gsub('\U0001f631','',tweet)
```

As shown in the output, the function identified the Unicode text, replaced it with nothing, and performed this operation within the last parameter on the tweet object. You could replace the identified pattern with any word or characters such as "emoji screaming face" so as to keep track of the emoji expression. You can apply more substitutions for contractions such as "y'all" and "I'm," although the *qdap* package has a function for this. As with many operations in R, there are multiple libraries and functions to perform substitutions, but this code gives a basic method.

```
[1] "@missevans__: Y'all I'm really about to dance on the
Cleveland Cavaliers court starting next week "
```

You will notice now that this example tweet is a retweet and the body of text is after a ":". Often, when performing analysis, you need to remove extraneous information like this because it may hinder results. In this case, the **strsplit(object, search, parameters)** string split function is helpful. It is applied to an object, searches for a pattern, and returns a list of text that has been separated by the search parameter. In this example, you have a list of one because there was one object with two elements for text on either side of the split. The meaningful text is the second element of text and can be accessed with indexing (square brackets) as shown below.

```
tweet <- strsplit(tweet, ':', fixed = T)
```

```
[1] "@missevans__"
[2] " Y'all I'm really about to dance on the Cleveland Cavaliers
court starting next week "
```

```
tweet <- tweet[[1]][2]
```

Another good base function to know when performing text analysis is tolower(-object). Often, word frequency can be useful in learning about author intent, effort, and topics in a large number of documents. For example, if you had 100,000 tweets mentioning a sports team, you may want to aggregate terms to learn about the subjects in the tweets. (In fact, we will do this later in the chapter!) R will interpret terms with different capitalization as distinct, making aggregation difficult. The **tolower()** function solves this. Let's now clean up this tweet a bit more using tolower().

```
tweet <- tolower(tweet)
tweet
[1] " y'all i'm really about to dance on the cleveland cavaliers
court starting next week "
```

Examining the resulting tweet object, you now see that "Cleveland" has been made lowercase, among other changes. This step is used to improve word frequency analysis especially in channels where users take shortcuts and may not use proper grammar. It may be the case in the collection of 100,000 tweets that one user wrote "Cleveland cavaliers" and another typed "Cleveland Cavaliers." In that case, the `tolower()` function unifies the word tokens so that "cavaliers" is correctly counted twice.

Lastly, you should notice that we have extra spacing in our tweet because of the global substitution applied earlier. After you have performed many string manipulations like substitutions and splits, accounting for unknown characters (i.e., emojis) and dealing with contractions, it is a good idea to remove the extra space. NLP is computationally intensive, so removing extraneous bytes is a good idea. Further, an extra blank space can be considered a term in some methods, which will hinder your analysis. Using the **trimws(object)** function will trim the white space from both the left and right sides of your text as shown below.

```
tweet <- trimws(tweet, which = 'both')
tweet
[1] "y'all i'm really about to dance on the cleveland cavaliers
court starting next week"
```

Although not quite string manipulation, it is often useful to locate patterns, such as words, within a body of text. The base functions grep(pattern, object, ignore. case = T) and grepl(pattern, object, ignore.case = T) are valuable aides for locating the presence of words. Each is passed through a regular expression pattern, then the object with additional parameters. The difference between **grep** and **grepl** is that the former will tell you the location and the latter will provide a logical return if the pattern is found, hence the "L" in the function. Consider the following small collection of two tweets.

```
tweets <- c('#Cavs Collin Sexton matched a career-high with 31
points. He's now averaging more than 20 per game','#Mavericks
guard Seth Curry is now shooting .442 from three-point range in
his career, moving him into 2nd place in @NBA history')
tweets
[1] "#Cavs Collin Sexton matched a career-high with 31 points.
He's now averaging more than 20 per game"
[2] "#Mavericks guard Seth Curry is now shooting .442 from three-
point range in his career, moving him into 2nd place in @NBA
history"
```

Let's find the presence of the term "cavs" and "point" using grep. After running the code, you will see that "cavs" is in the first tweet and the function returns a 1. It was recognized because of the third parameter that ignores the case. In the second function call, the return was 1 and 2. This is because the term "point" exists in the first and second tweet. As you will soon find out, the integer returns can be used to quickly find the documents with specific terms among thousands of documents.

```
grep('cavs', tweets, ignore.case = T)
[1] 1
grep('point', tweets)
[1] 1 2
```

Contrast these functions with the code below, which does not add the third parameter. Although the term "Mavericks" is contained in the second tweet, it is not identified because "mavericks" is used as the search pattern. This is another example of why to lower can be useful.

```
grep('mavericks', tweets)
integer(0)
```

Next, let's use grepl to identify the presence of a text string. Although the input of the function is the same as grep, the additional "L" means the function will return a Boolean (TRUE or FALSE) result for every document searched. Whereas the previous commands provided a 1, 1 and 2, and a 0, respectively, the grepl will provide two outputs as shown below.

```
grepl('mavericks', tweets, ignore.case = T)
[1] FALSE TRUE
```

Many of the functions used thus far are performing a match based on "regular expressions." As you get into more complex situations, such as searching for "one term OR another" or "one term AND another," you will need to explore more in depth the usefulness of regular expressions.

Lastly, keep in mind the functions here are basic string manipulations that you will use throughout the chapter and in your own analysis. For the most part, we will make them straightforward and easily understood. However, there are more functions that may need to be applied, depending on your use case. Thus, it is a great idea to research regular expressions and the most popular packages *stringi* and *stringr* for this type of manipulation.

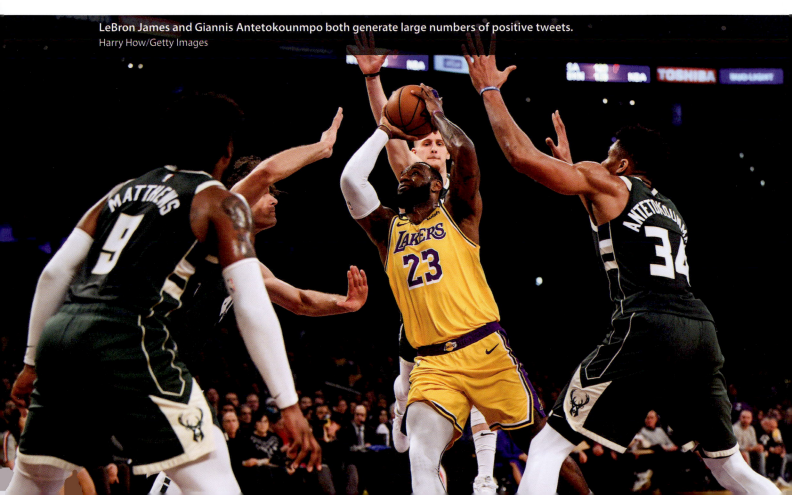

LeBron James and Giannis Antetokounmpo both generate large numbers of positive tweets.
Harry How/Getty Images

BASIC TEXT PROCESSING WORKFLOW

Now that you have a basic understanding of string manipulations, it is time to explore a basic framework for tackling a natural language processing analysis. Because of the difficulty associated with NLP stemming from the diversity of language, the first step is to clearly define the aim of the project. It may be high level, such as to explore and define methods for gauging social media fan engagement, or the aim may be something more precise, such as to analyze scouting reports alongside other athletic data to model on-field performance. Without a problem definition, you will be doing "curiosity analysis" with no direction. Given the challenges of natural language analytics, strive to be as succinct as possible and be willing to iterate and adjust along the way. Once you have a problem reasonably defined, this should lead you toward a channel and specific pieces of text for analysis. You may use online reviews, contracts, or something else, but it is rarely the entire Internet or some vast collection of unrelated and diverse documents. Next, you need to preprocess the documents, which entails organization and feature extraction. A simple example would be collecting 10,000 tweets mentioning a player. Once organized into a **corpus**, or collection of related documents, you can extract features such as **sentiment analysis** from those documents. The features or values extracted vary depending on the type of analysis you expect to perform. It could be as simple as counting the occurrence of a term or as complex as creating a modeling matrix for use in a deep neural net model to classify documents. In any case, once the appropriate features have been extracted from the documents, you then run the analysis and finally seek to address the problem definition. Once again, addressing the problem statement may be as simple as providing a visual like a word cloud or as complex as using the output of the analysis in a customer propensity machine learning model.

In review, the basic steps of an NLP project are outlined below.

1. Problem definition
2. Identifying text sources
3. Preprocessing and feature extraction
4. Analytics
5. Insight and recommendations

In this chapter, the problem we have defined as an example is fan engagement in social media for various teams in the National Basketball Association (NBA) using multiple common methods and marquee players (step 1 above). The methods can be applied to other types of documents yet are not an exhaustive set of approaches. However, the methods used in the chapter are useful and satisfying to explore.

Thus, in the NBA fan engagement example, our steps are as follows:

- Identifying text sources: We will focus on a collection of tweets amassed daily throughout the 2019-2020 NBA season.
- Preprocessing and feature extraction: Conduct string manipulation and organization into a document term matrix to get term frequency.
- Analytics: Build visualizations such as bar charts, word clouds, and pyramid plots. Perform word associations and sentiment analysis.
- Insight and recommendations: Within the provided text, identify the most discussed teams, terms, and corresponding sentiment representing the Twitter dialogue of fans and sports professionals.

IDENTIFY TEXT SOURCES, PREPROCESSING, AND FEATURE EXTRACTION

Now that we have an intended goal of understanding fan engagement in the NBA, let's load the *tm* or *text mining* library to perform more robust string manipulation and organization. In addition, data manipulation packages *slam*, *plyr*, *dplyr*, and *qdapRegex* are loaded. Lastly, *ggplot2*, *ggthemes*, *plotrix*, and *wordcloud* are loaded to create some insightful visuals from the manipulated strings. Lastly, the *SentimentAnalysis* package is loaded. This package contains various methods for measuring positive and negative word usage based on the **lexicon**.

```
library(tm)
library(slam)
library(plyr)
library(dplyr)
library(qdapRegex)
library(ggplot2)
library(ggthemes)
library(plotrix)
library(wordcloud)
library(SentimentAnalysis)
```

When performing NLP tasks, it is often a good idea to ensure strings are not considered factors. Factors are distinct levels such as "small," "medium," and "large." The levels are text but not quite in the manner of free-form natural language. The environment option code below ensures strings are not factors and turns off scientific notation.

```
options(stringsAsFactors = F, scipen = 999)
```

Let's download our data directly from an open repository. The repository https://github.com/kwartler/NLP_SportsAnalytics has multiple monthly files in this format so you can expand and change the analysis as you become more familiar with concepts throughout this chapter. The October dataset can be downloaded through this book's HK*Propel* site. In fact, as you embark on your own NLP analysis, you would need to identify your sources instead of merely downloading the curated dataset below. You could gauge fan engagement aggregated from multiple social channels or comparatively by social channel. For the sake of simplicity, the rest of the chapter uses corpora only from Twitter specifically from October during the 2019-2020 NBA season.

Visit HK*Propel* to download the *nba_oct.csv* dataset.

```
tweets <- read.csv("nba_oct.csv")
```

If your R system struggles with such a large dataset, if you are testing the code, or if your Internet connection is slow, you may declare a smaller number of rows using `tweets <- read.csv("nba_oct",nrows = 1000)` or use one of the "tiny" datasets also listed in the repository.

With the `tweet` object in your environment, you could perform normal exploratory data analysis (EDA), but since this chapter is focused on NLP principles, the code jumps into string manipulation, organization, and feature extraction as part of step 3.

Since the aim of our analysis is not to explore frequently shared links, the code below uses both `rm_url(text)` and `rm_twitter_url(text)` from the *qdapRegex* regular expression library. The code applies because Twitter sometimes uses short URLs, which means the pattern matching may change. Further, the higher level *qdap* package usually is loaded instead but doing so may be difficult because installing *qdap* on non-Windows computers is a hassle because of Java issues. However, the *qdapRegex* library should install on Ubuntu, Apple, and Windows machines with ease.

```
tweets$text <- rm_url(tweets$text)
tweets$text <- rm_twitter_url(tweets$text)
```

Next, to streamline string cleanup among multiple data files, it is often helpful to create a custom function wrapping the string manipulations you intend to perform rather than repeat code over and over. The next code chunk creates a function call **customClean**. The function accepts a corpus object, then another parameter called "stops" that is a vector of "stop words" with a default value ("SMART"). This vector of stop words will be removed from the text.

The default "SMART" **stop word** vector has 571 terms such as "the" and "why." The list was first documented in an information retrieval system created at Cornell University in the 1960s (Harman, 1993). There are multiple basic stop word lists and you should adjust them according to your analysis. In fact, adjusting the stop word list is one reason NLP is an iterative process.

Now that you understand the inputs to the function, let's move to the functions that will clean the text. The *tm* library works with a new object class called "corpus" that has functions mapped to it, hence the **tm_map(corpus)** function calls below. Further, the *tm* library has additional string manipulation functions built in, such as removeWords and removePunctuation. However, the additional use of **content_transformer** allows a function outside the *tm* library to be applied to the object class corpus. As a result, a corpus enters the function and is made lowercase using the base R function along with content_transformer before moving to *tm*'s removeWords function, which also needs the terms to remove in the stops vector. This process continues throughout the function before returning the modified corpus with all the string modified accordingly.

```
customClean <- function(corpus, stops = stopwords('SMART')){
    corpus <- tm_map(corpus, content_transformer(tolower))
    corpus <- tm_map(corpus, removePunctuation) #chk tomorrow
    corpus <- tm_map(corpus, removeWords, stops)
    corpus <- tm_map(corpus, removePunctuation)
    corpus <- tm_map(corpus, removeNumbers)
    corpus <- tm_map(corpus, content_transformer(trimws))
            return(corpus)
}
```

A common mistake among new data scientists, is not paying attention to the order of the internal functions in the customClean code. If you were to use trimws then begin to remove punctuation and numbers, more white space is created that could impact results. Within the custom function, special care must be given to the order and specific preprocessing steps depending on the type of analysis.

To apply the customClean function, the *tm* package requires the source to be defined. Depending on your analysis, documents may be in a single vector, a data frame with metadata columns like author, or a file directory. In this example the documents are in a data frame, so you must declare the `DataframeSource(data frame of text & metadata)` function. In the next code chunk, the documents are nested inside the `VCorpus(a declared source object)` function. A volatile corpus is a collection of documents held in active memory. It is volatile because if your system shuts down or you close R without saving your environment, the corpus is lost. Thus, any change you make only affects the R object, not the original documents on disk. This is the most popular method since you do not risk forever altering your original document collection by mistake. Another common mistake when using **VCorpus** with **DataframeSource** is that the first column must be named `doc_id` and the second `text`. All other columns in the data frame will be considered metadata relevant to the individual document.

```
textCorp <- VCorpus(DataframeSource(tweets))
```

Now, when you call the `textCorp` object, you no longer have a data frame. Instead, it is a corpus object class, which is actually a list of the text and metadata. Calling the object in console shows you have metadata and content.

```
> textCorp
<<VCorpus>>
Metadata: corpus specific: 0, document level (indexed): 2
Content: documents: 453875
```

Although the top-level object is vague, the data is still present. Calling `meta(a document)` on the object with a single bracket index will return the other columns now stored as meta information.

```
> meta(textCorp[1])
          created              team
1 2019-10-01 21:19:16 Atlanta Hawks
```

Similarly calling `content(a document)` with either single or double bracket indexing will provide the content information. Single brackets will return high-level information calculated by the function call, while using double brackets returns the text itself. This code examines the content of the first tweet.

```
> content(textCorp[1])
[[1]]
<<PlainTextDocument>>
Metadata: 7
Content: chars: 86
```

```
> content(textCorp[[1]])
[1] "Ole Miss: 15 Braves: 0 Falcons: 0 Hawks: 0 I enjoy suffering
with my Atlanta friends "
```

Before passing the corpus into the custom string processing function, you should always adjust your stop words to fit your analysis. In this analysis, it is likely the documents contain the team names and cities. Thus, it may be a good idea to remove them. That is done using some string manipulation and the original metadata column in `tweets$team`. The `uniqueTerms` object is made by first identifying the unique terms in the column from the original tweet *.csv* dataset. This is nested in `tolower` because the custom function makes text lowercase *then* removes stop words. Finally, this is passed to both `strsplit` and `unlist(a list object)` to get a clean vector of individual terms to be appended to the original stop words. This is because our string manipulation at this point will be working with single unique words as opposed to two or more word combinations. Additionally, words such as "game" and "basketball" are appended to the `uniqueTerms` object. Finally, in the `stops` object, the original stop words and the customized tokens are combined as shown in the `tail(R Object)` function call.

```
uniqueTerms <- tolower(unique(tweets$team))
uniqueTerms <- unlist(strsplit(uniqueTerms, ' '))
uniqueTerms <- c(uniqueTerms, 'nba', 'game', 'basketball',
'team','amp', 'preseason', 'extension', 'season')
stops <- c(stopwords('SMART'), uniqueTerms)
tail(stops, 100)
```

Now that the object is an official corpus, you pass it into the custom function to perform the string manipulations along with the newly improved stop words vector. The result of the function is still a corpus, but the text has been altered significantly. When dealing with a large amount of text, this step may take some time or even crash computers with smaller amounts of RAM. There are two remedies other than getting another computer or server with more RAM. First, you can run this code with a smaller number of documents to ensure it functions; second, you can run this code on chunks of documents, such as in sections by a single date. However, once complete it is a good idea to save this object as an RDS file to avoid having to repeat the mundane cleaning task. RDS is an optimized R file extension. The commented code below shows both how to save and read in RDS file types.

```
textCorp <- customClean(textCorp, stops)
#saveRDS(textCorp, #'~/Documents/nbaTweets/uniqueTweets/clean_A_
Oct2019.rds')
#textCorp <- readRDS( #'~/Documents/nbaTweets/uniqueTweets/
clean_A_Oct2019.rds')
```

Table 5.2 reviews the first tweet after it has been "cleaned." Overall you will see the terms "Atlanta" and "Hawks" have been removed. These were included with the stop words along with "I", "with," and "my." Do not worry if you want to perform an analysis such as sentiment while still keeping the team associated with the individual document (tweet), because the metadata has been retained. It is merely removed from the text itself. In the table, you should note the overall important information has been retained while the uninformative terms have been removed. Sometimes additional string manipulation may be needed based on the text encoding, but for this chapter's purposes, the text has been manipulated and now should be organized.

```
content(textCorp[[1]])
```

Next, the processed text will be organized into a **document term matrix** (DTM) for analysis. There are many parameters for the `DocumentTermMatrix(corpus)` function but the next code chunk accepts defaults. Once again this can be time-consuming, so saving the result is helpful.

```
textDTM <- DocumentTermMatrix(textCorp)
dim(textDTM)
#saveRDS(textDTM, #'~/Documents/nbaTweets/uniqueTweets/clean_A_
Oct2019_DTM.rds')
#textDTM <-#readRDS('~/Documents/nbaTweets/uniqueTweets/clean_A_
Oct2019_DTM.rds')
```

The result of this function is a sparse matrix. Each row is represented by a document and each column is the count of unique terms in the tweet. The matrix represents word usage among the thousands of tweets. It is usually sparse because the entirety of the matrix is the lexical diversity of the entire collection yet a single document is only a subset. For example, the first tweet is made up of seven terms after processing. However, among the 450,000+ tweets, 99,000+ unique words are used. Thus, row one will have "1" listed in seven columns and "0" in the rest of the 99,000! Some NLP examples use a **term document matrix** (TDM) instead. Rest assured, this is the same information but the transposition of the DTM created before. A TDM has rows of terms and a column for each document. Table 5.3 shows a small portion of a DTM as an example. The table is merely a small section of three tweets among thousands and three terms among thousands, and it shows the term kawhi occurred once in tweet ending in 512.

Before entering the next step, the code below will create one more DTM for analysis. The previous DTM used columns of single terms, known in NLP as "unigram tokens." This new DTM will tokenize them to "bigrams," or two-word combinations, for use later in the analysis. While bigram tokens can be more insightful than unigrams because phrases are more easily understood, the effect of increased tokenization is an ever-sparser matrix. This can make a bigram DTM harder to process computationally. While the previous example tweet was made of seven single-word tokens, the combinations of two words means the bigram version is longer. Multiply this by the many thousands of tweets and you will notice that the dimensionality grows.

To perform bigram tokenization, the following additional custom code is needed when constructing a DTM. This function accepts the text and, using the `ngrams(words to be tokenized and splitting integer)` function, will break up the columns into two-word pairs. This function is then passed to the **DocumentTermMatrix** function as an extra parameter not present previously. The resulting bigram DTM has the same number of documents but now has 536,000 two-word combinations as columns.

Table 5.2   Comparing the Effect of customClean on a Single Tweet

Original	Preprocessed
"Ole Miss: 15 Braves: 0 Falcons: 0 Hawks: 0 I enjoy suffering with my Atlanta friends "	"ole miss braves falcons enjoy suffering friends"

TABLE 5.3   A Portion of the Document Term Matrix

	kare	kawhi	kcjhoop
1179024230517805056	0	0	0
1179022022690496512	0	1	0
1179021874535243776	0	0	0

```
bigramTokens <-function(x){
 unlist(lapply(NLP::ngrams(words(x), 2), paste, collapse = " "),
   use.names = FALSE)
}
bigramDTM <- DocumentTermMatrix(textCorp,
            control=list(tokenize=bigramTokens))
dim(bigramDTM)
```

In most instances, this amount of sparse information is not needed. Unless you are doing anomaly detection, it is more likely your analysis would need to focus on the most frequent terms. The `removeSparseTerms(DTM or DTM, decimal number)` function from the *tm* package can be applied to any DTM or TDM, including the unigram version made earlier. The numeric input is a percentage of cells in the matrix that are 0, or sparse, which are to be removed. This means 0.99 entails all terms (columns) are removed if 99 percent of the cells are zero. A column is retained if 1 percent of the cells contain a nonzero number. After running the code below, the number of frequent two-word pairs is less than 1,000. The matrix is now resized to 450,000 rows by 850 columns, making analysis much easier.

```
bigramDTM  <- removeSparseTerms(bigramDTM, 0.999)
dim(bigramDTM)
```

ANALYTICS

Moving to step 4, the code transitions from these basic matrices to extract information and build visualizations. To begin, let's create a document-length matrix to help us better understand the average length of each tweet. While the output of the `DocumentTermMatrix` function is a matrix, it is actually a lightweight sparse matrix class known as a "simple triplet matrix" in which the information with zeros is not actively held in memory. The `row_sums(sparse matrix)` function is similar to the base R rowSums function but made to work on the DTM object class. The row sums are then organized alongside the document ID and team metadata from the original objects.

```
wordsPerTweet  <- row_sums(textDTM, na.rm = T)
dlm            <- data.frame(doc_id = rownames(textDTM),
                    words_per_tweet = wordsPerTweet,
                              team = tweets$team)
head(dlm)
```

With the document-length matrix made above, you can confirm the length of the first tweet is seven terms. More interestingly, you can see the average length of tweets by teams. Average tweet length can be indicative of noteworthy information, like an active roster change or news about the team, but in large corpora, the average length of a document often indicates the author's effort. An analog is an online review. The longer a review, the more likely the author of the review is passionate about the service or product. In order to get the average terms by team, the following code uses `aggregate(y ~x, data object, function)` passing in the formula "words_per_tweet" by "team" within the `dlm` object, then the `mean` function is applied. The same function can be used to get a total count of tweets by team, as shown in the second code line with different inputs. Finally, the two tables are joined by team so that each row represents a team with average words and number of tweets.

```
fanEffort <- aggregate(words_per_tweet ~team, dlm, mean)
fanCount <- aggregate(doc_id ~team, dlm, length)
fanEffort <- left_join(fanEffort, fanCount, by ="team")
```

After constructing the `fanEffort` object, the following plot is constructed with `ggplot`. The grammar of a graphics library works by giving you control of the layers within a visualization. Here the fan effort data is passed in declaring the X and Y values. Then another layer of geometric points is added to construct the scatterplot. The size aesthetic is declared based on the count of the doc_id variable calculated in the fanCount object. The last layers improve aesthetics but are optional. The resulting plot is shown in figure 5.1. Of course, this data could be normalized by the total population in the local market but is outside the scope of the chapter.

```
ggplot(fanEffort, aes(x = reorder(team, - words_per_tweet), y =
words_per_tweet)) +
  geom_point(aes(size=doc_id)) + ggtitle("Words per Tweet") +
  theme_hc() +
  theme(axis.title.x=element_blank(), axis.title.y=element_blank(),
    axis.text.x = element_text(angle = 90, vjust = 0.5, hjust=1))
```

Overall, it may be interesting to explore frequent terms among the entire corpus. In doing so, you may identify league-wide themes of interest in the October 2019 corpus. Instead of row sums, now the code uses col_sums(sparse matrix) to obtain the overall term frequency, which is organized into a word frequency matrix.

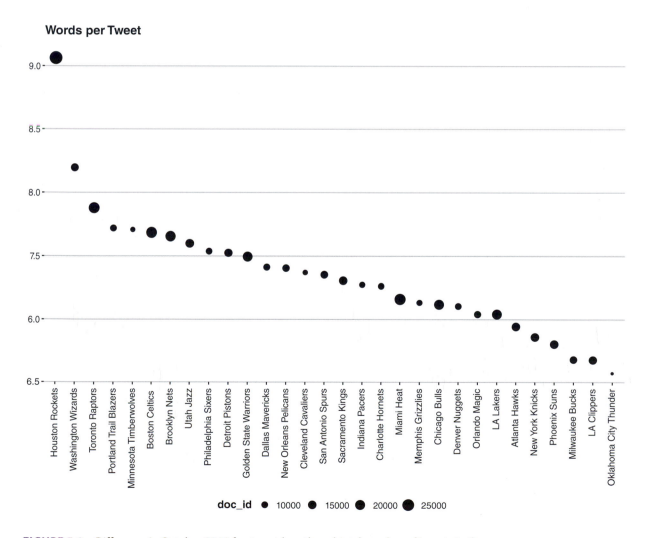

FIGURE 5.1   Difference in October 2019 fan tweet length and total number of tweets in the corpus.

Again, the information is organized into a concise data frame. After applying column sums, the result is reordered with `order(vector of numbers)` with the parameter `decreasing=T`.

```
# Word Frequency Matrix
termUseInCorpus <- col_sums(textDTM, na.rm = T)
wfm <- data.frame(term = names(termUseInCorpus),
            frequency = termUseInCorpus)
wfm <- wfm[order(wfm$frequency, decreasing = T),]
head(wfm)
```

Reviewing the top six terms using `head(R object)`, it is clear that the term "win" is important in the corpus. Interestingly, and maybe unexpectedly, the nation "China" appears frequently in the overall corpus. Alternatively, the same frequency review can be done at the team level. To do so, the previous steps would need to be repeated after "subsetting" the original tweets data frame by the team column. In essence, the steps are the same but repeated 30 times, once per team, including cleaning and working with 30 DTMs.

A popular way to visualize term frequency is with a word cloud. In this type of visual, the terms are sized according to their frequency in a corpus. The `wordcloud(terms, corresponding frequency, number of words)` accepts two vectors from the `wfm`, word frequency matrix, object. The **wordcloud** function has many parameters; most popular is the declaration of a color (shown here with "black"). The resulting word cloud is shared in the online web resource. Word clouds are often overused yet provide little insightful information. Usually the commonality and comparison clouds provide more interesting outcomes because each lets you compare and contrast two or more corpora.

Visit HK*Propel* to view the word cloud for the October NBA corpus.

```
wordcloud(wfm$term, wfm$frequency, max.words = 100,
colors="black")
```

In 2019, Hong Kong protests and LeBron James were significant topics on NBA Twitter.
ANTHONY WALLACE/AFP via Getty Images

As previously mentioned, the commonality cloud can be useful in understanding the language used in conjunction with two sections of the corpus. Outside of basketball, commonality clouds can identify terms shared between two political parties or competing product reviews. In contrast, a comparison cloud will identify the different terms used between these and more subjects.

To create a commonality cloud, the process must repeat with subsets of the original data. Given the previous scatterplot observed, there is likely a difference worth exploring among the Houston Rockets and Oklahoma City Thunder in the corpus. So, the first step is to subset the data by team. The cleaned corpus, textCorp, is in the same order as the original tweets. Therefore, a grep command used on the tweets$team column will identify the position of documents in the corpus related to the specific team. The index position is used with square brackets to reduce the entire corpus to the team in question. Next, the text content is extracted from the corpus. The textCorp object contains preprocessed text from customClean, so there is no reason to repeat this step. Instead, the team-related cleaned text is collapsed into a single document using paste(text) with the added parameter collapse. Collapsing all tweets from the Houston Rockets into a single body of text means the entirety of information is no longer 19,000+ tweets but instead is a single document with all information as a "body of knowledge related to the Houston Rockets." New data scientists often struggle with this concept of moving from individual documents to a collapsed body of information as one document. For example, one could compare an individual document like Shakespeare's *A Midsummer Night's Dream* to another, such as *The Canterbury Tales* by Chaucer. However, another way to approach a comparison is to use all of Shakespeare's works as a *single* body of text representing everything known about his writing and compare that holistically to all of Chaucer's material. This would mean the new corpus has two documents, one for all of Chaucer and another for all Shakespearian writing. The code below applies this logic to both the Houston Rockets and the Oklahoma City Thunder using paste in conjunction with collapse.

```
rockets <- grep('Houston Rockets', tweets$text)
rockets <- textCorp[rockets]
rockets <- unlist(lapply(rockets, content))
rockets <- paste(rockets, collapse = ' ')

thunder <- grep('Oklahoma City Thunder', tweets$text)
thunder <- textCorp[thunder]
thunder <- unlist(lapply(thunder, content))
thunder <- paste(thunder, collapse = ' ')
```

Once the two documents representing all tweets related to each team are constructed, they are combined. The combined large text vectors are then declared as a VectorSource(text vector) losing all metadata from before and nested in another call of VCorpus. The bothTeams corpus contains only two documents instead of the many thousands of individual tweets. Instead of a DTM, a TermDocumentMatrix(corpus) or TDM is constructed. Remember, a TDM has individual terms as rows and documents as columns. Therefore, the two-document corpus will have two columns in a TDM. Considering the bothTeams object is a smaller matrix than before, it is converted away from the "simple triplet matrix" to the normal matrix R class using as.matrix(data vectors). Lastly, one should name the two columns in the TDM in the order in which they were originally combined, so here we use "Rockets" then "Thunder."

```
bothTeams <- c(rockets, thunder)
bothTeams <- VCorpus((VectorSource(bothTeams)))
bothTeams <- as.matrix(TermDocumentMatrix(bothTeams))
colnames(bothTeams) <- c('Rockets', 'Thunder')
```

The `bothTeams` matrix can be passed to the `commanlity.cloud(TDM)` directly. The code below employs a `set.seed(number)` parameter so that the output is consistent. The visual illustrates the top 50 words by frequency that both the Houston Rockets and Oklahoma City Thunder have in common. Figure 5.2 shows that both team-related tweets mention watching live and western (conference), among other terms.

```
set.seed(1234)
commonality.cloud(bothTeams, max.words=50, random.order=FALSE)
```

Next, let's compare the two bodies of text. Using the **comparison.cloud**(TDM) function will segment terms that are nearly distinct among the two corpora. The resulting figure is not always a full disjoin of the terms because it accounts for terms that are infrequent in one document but plentiful in another. If that is the case, the terms will still be assigned to the plentiful document. The code below shows terms that overwhelmingly are in one document versus another, as captured in figure 5.3.

```
set.seed(2020)
comparison.cloud(bothTeams,max.words=50,scale=c(4,.2),
        title.size = 1,
        random.order=FALSE, colors = c('black', 'darkgrey'))
```

While word clouds are generally considered bad form in data visualization, they have merit—particularly comparison clouds. Lastly, although these examples used unigram tokens, passing in bigram and even trigram token word frequencies is accept-

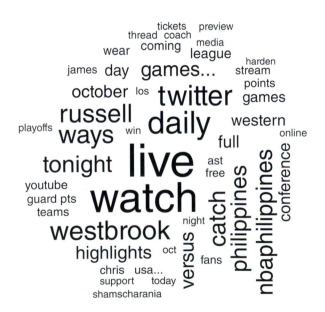

FIGURE 5.2 The top terms shared among Houston Rockets and Oklahoma City Thunder tweets.

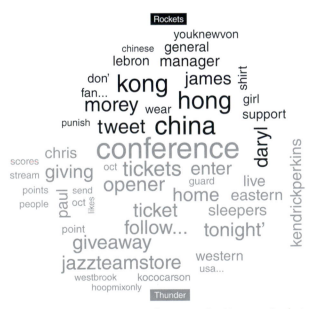

FIGURE 5.3 The comparison between the Houston Rockets and Oklahoma City Thunder shows the mentions of China for the Rockets and "home opener" more often for the Thunder.

able and often improves results because individual terms like "Lebron" and "James" or "Hong" and "Kong" are more easily associated in their proper form.

The issue with the commonality cloud is that once terms are considered inner-joined, the audience loses sight to the extent of the terms' relationship with the document or team. In the previous visuals, terms are merely shared (commonality) or not (comparison). However, a more nuanced view could be understood for terms that are shared but not in an equal manner. To visualize this, a pyramid plot is used. A pyramid plot rotates two bar charts alongside each other. In this case, bars extend in opposite directions representing each team's word frequency.

In the code below, the `bothTeams` matrix is converted to a `data.frame`, then a new column called "diff" is added and the absolute difference among the terms is calculated. Given the immense number of tokens in a corpus of this size, the data is subset to only terms that appear 10 or more times in both teams' document. Finally, the shared terms are ordered by the absolute difference and the top-N terms are selected for the pyramid plot in figure 5.4. In this code, both the subset parameter "10" and the top "35" terms are tuning parameters to improve the visualization. Depending on the corpora changing, these will improve the insightfulness of the visual.

```
bothTeamsDF <- as.data.frame(bothTeams)
bothTeamsDF$diff <- abs(bothTeams[,1] - bothTeams[,2])
top35 <- subset(bothTeamsDF, bothTeamsDF$Rockets>10 &
        bothTeamsDF$Thunder>10)
top35<- top35[order(top35$diff, decreasing=TRUE), ]

top35 <- top35[1:35, ]
```

The `pyramid.plot(data and labels)` function has multiple input parameters. First, the left-hand side of the plot needs to be declared—in this case, the Rockets column of word frequencies. Similarly, the right-side must refer to the Thunder column. In between, the terms themselves are declared by calling `row.names(data frame)` on the data frame made earlier. After the x,y coordinates are declared, the labels are assigned as a single vector with length three. Next, the gap is entered. This integer is the space between the opposing bars in the chart. It is relative to the unit shown. Lastly, the title, label for the units, and colors are added as parameters. The resulting plot is in figure 5.4.

```
pyramid.plot(lx        = top35$Rockets, #left
             rx        = top35$Thunder, #right
             labels    = row.names(top35), #terms
             top.labels = c('Rockets', 'Terms', 'Thunder'), #corpora
             gap       = 350, # space for terms to be read
             main      = 'Words in Common', # title
             unit      = 'word frequency',
             lxcol     = 'darkgrey',
             rxcol     = 'black')
```

Drilling down a level, publicists and public relations firms measure **share of voice** for brands and celebrities. This metric is tracked among others over time. The goal of "share of voice" is to understand how much of the overall dialogue in a channel is dedicated to the product, brand, or celebrity of interest. For this example, define the players of interest first.

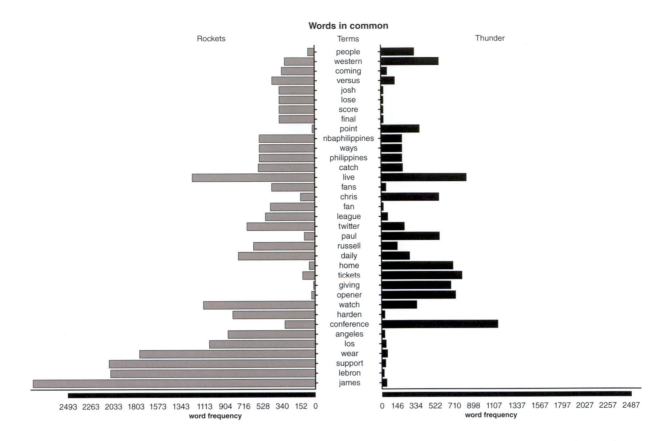

FIGURE 5.4   A pyramid plot showing the words in common and extent among the two teams. For example, "Harden" is mentioned in tweets for both teams but to a greater degree for the Rockets.

```
players <- c('kobe bryant', 'lebron james', 'giannis
antetokounmpo','kawhi leonard')
```

Don't be intimidated by the next section of code with a "for loop." A loop merely states that you will perform an action repeatedly: "for this number of times, perform these actions." In our case, the loop will perform tasks for Kobe Bryant, then LeBron James, and so on. Within the loop, the `grepl` function is searching for the pattern, a player's name, within the original text. It also reformats the date to a more legible format. To begin, the loop has a variable, i is set to 1. This means `players[1]` is represented as `players[i]`. So `grepl` will search for `player[1]`, which corresponds to "Kobe Bryant." The next time through the loop i becomes 2 and now corresponds to "Lebron James."

```
playerShare <- list()
for(i in 1:length(players)){
 print(paste('working on', players[i]))
 x <- grepl(players[i], tweets$text, ignore.case = T)
 y <- as.POSIXct(tweets$created, format = "%Y-%m-%d")
 dailyShare <- data.frame(player = players[i], doc_id =
 tweets$doc_id,
             playerMention = x, date = y)
 nam <- make.names(players[i])
 playerShare[[nam]] <- dailyShare

}
```

Examining the resulting list for Kobe Bryant is simple using the `head(R object)`. As shown in table 5.4, among the first six tweets on October 1, Kobe Bryant was not mentioned.

```
head(playerShare$kobe.bryant)
```

The result of the loop is a list with four elements, one for each of the players. The following code applies `rbind(data vectors)` within `do.call(function to construct, list)` to the list. As a result, the list elements are row-bound to unify the results into a single data frame. Once again, the data is aggregated. Specifically, the `playerMention` data is grouped by player and by date. Once grouped, the True or False values are summed. As a Boolean, R will recognize the True as 1 and False as 0. In the end, each player will have a sum of mentions for each day in the data frame, which makes a compelling visual to understand the share of voice among the four players.

```
mentionsByDate <- do.call(rbind, playerShare)
mentionsByDate <- aggregate(playerMention~player+date,
            mentionsByDate, sum)
```

The timeline results of mentions are illustrated in figure 5.5. There is a clear spike in mentions of LeBron James compared to the other players in the study. The simple ggplot call sets up the X as `date` and the Y as `playerMention` value. The `linetype` is declared by player to differentiate the lines within a colorless context. However, the lines could be changed by color and even declared using a color-blind safe palette using the *viridis* library.

```
ggplot(mentionsByDate, aes(x = date,
            y            = playerMention,
            linetype     = player)) +
 geom_line() + theme_hc()
```

Alternatively, the same data can be portrayed as a stacked bar chart. The plot layers change to declare the fill by player and add another layer to scale the colors in gray.

Table 5.4   Kobe Bryant head Results

Player	Doc_id	playerMention	Date
"kobe bryant"	1179143769574297600	FALSE	2019-10-01
"kobe bryant"	1179143120375762944	FALSE	2019-10-01
"kobe bryant"	1179142532191723520	FALSE	2019-10-01
"kobe bryant"	1179141961753792512	FALSE	2019-10-01
"kobe bryant"	1179141924218920960	FALSE	2019-10-01
"kobe bryant"	1179141590612353024	FALSE	2019-10-01

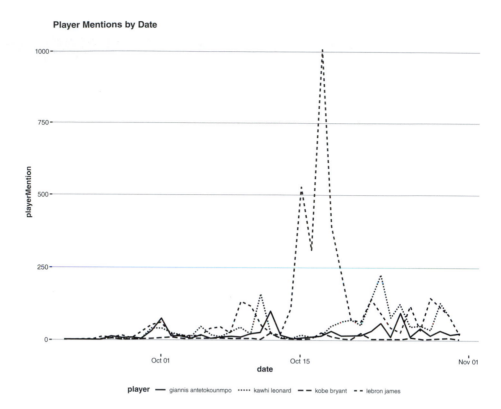

FIGURE 5.5   The number of tweets mentioning players, demonstrating changing share of voice by day.

Visit HK*Propel* to view
player mentions illustrated
as a stacked bar chart.

```
ggplot(data = mentionsByDate, aes(x = date,
              y                  = playerMention,
              fill               = player)) +
 geom_bar(position="stack", stat="identity") +
 theme_hc() + scale_fill_grey(start = 0, end = 0.75) +
 ggtitle('Player Mentions by Date')
```

In order to get a proportional bar chart, another manipulation is needed. One could use the *dplyr* package to perform the same aggregation below, but for consistency the code uses aggregate again. This time the total number of mentions among all four players is calculated for a day. This is then left-joined to the original mentions-ByDate data. As a left join, the daily values are recycled for each player. Once the join is completed, simple division will calculate the proportion of the dialogue for a player within the tweets mentioning the four players and excluding other tweets. The result of the division is captured in a new variable, mentionProportion, declared on the left side of the assignment operator. Table 5.5 demonstrates the result of this aggregation, join, and division, with a subsection of the daily proportional player mentions among tweets meeting one or more of the players. The recycling of the join is demonstrated in the repeating 175 and 48.

```
shareOfVoice <- aggregate(playerMention~date, mentionsByDate, sum)
shareOfVoice <- left_join(mentionsByDate, shareOfVoice, by
='date')
shareOfVoice$mentionProportion <- shareOfVoice[,3]/
shareOfVoice[,4]
tail(shareOfVoice)
```

TABLE 5.5   Daily Proportional Player Mentions

Player	Date	playerMention.x	playerMention.y	mentionProportion
kobe bryant	2019-10-30	5	175	0.28
lebron james	2019-10-30	77	175	0.44
giannis antetokounmpo	2019-10-31	21	48	0.43
kawhi leonard	2019-10-31	13	48	0.27
kobe bryant	2019-10-31	1	48	0.02
lebron james	2019-10-31	13	48	0.27

The following code plots this data as a proportional bar chart for a slightly different view. The code itself is basically the same, but now the Y variable refers to the proportional calculated value in `mentionProportion`.

```
ggplot(data = shareOfVoice,
    aes(x = date,
        y = mentionProportion,
        fill=player)) +
    geom_bar(position="stack", stat="identity") +
    theme_hc() + scale_fill_grey(start = 0.75, end = 0) +
    ggtitle('Proportional Player Mentions by Date')
```

Visit HK*Propel* for an illustration of the proportional share of voice within the corpus; among the four players, LeBron James dominates the dialogue.

Within text mining there is a concept of **word associations**. This is similar to correlation. When one term exists, what is the likelihood of another term being in the same document? For example, the word association between "text" and "mining" will be very high within this chapter. Not only are the terms frequent but they are also authored together. In other contexts, such as mineral mining books, "text" would likely have zero association to "mining." Word association does not incorporate frequency but merely the co-occurrence of terms; it is not scaled according to frequency of the terms. We will use the `findAssocs(DTM, terms to check and correlation cutoff)` function to identify the associated or correlated terms for our players. Notice the `players` object consists of bigram tokens—first and last name. As a result, association function will need the bigram DTM created in the previous step. The 0.01 correlation value will retain bigram terms that are associated at that value or more. Unlike mathematical correlation, this parameter cannot be negative because more words in the entire corpus are negatively correlated to the searched token. While this may seem low, the size of the corpus, lexical diversity, and the use of bigrams means many tens of thousands of bigrams have even less correlated value. As a result, the threshold is deliberately set low; however, depending on the analysis and size of the corpus, this value will need to be tuned.

```
findAssocs(bigramDTM, players, .01)
```

The returned information is a list. Within the corpus, Kobe Bryant mentions are not correlated to any particular bigram at this threshold. On the other hand, LeBron James mentions have high associated values with "Hong Kong" and "Communist

China," in addition to other basketball-related tokens. For Giannis Antetokoumpo, the most associated terms include "free agency" and "free agent." Lastly, Kawhi Leonard mostly mentions other players like "Anthony Davis" and "Paul George."

Not expecting "Hong Kong" to be associated with LeBron James, the **findAssocs** function can be explored further specifically for Hong Kong. Using the increased threshold and changing the term demonstrates the intersection of "Lebron," "Daryl Morey," and even "Donald Trump Jr." The conclusions of these results are shared in the next section.

```
findAssocs(bigramDTM, 'hong kong', .25)
```

Next, we will use the `analyzeSentiment(text vector, DTM, or corpus)` function to assess the positive or negative nature of the texts by player. This function can be applied to the entire corpus, to specific teams, or in this case when a specific player is mentioned. Often when publicists want to assess the share of voice they will look at volume, associated terms, and the sentiment. By triangulating these three components, celebrities, including athletes, teams, or brands can understand the public's perception more fully. One can understand their impact with share of voice, the associated subjects with word associations, and the positive or negative language of the public discourse with sentiment or polarity analysis. This is especially true if the analysis is run daily, weekly, or monthly for a longitudinal view. Performing these tasks over time will let the analyst understand the impact of marketing efforts, evolving online dialogue, and an athlete's role.

Interestingly, there are other methods for calculating **sentiment analysis**. Foundationally, there is polarity whether or not a statement or author's intent is positive or negative. There is also *actual* sentiment analysis trying to understand the emotional context of a statement. To understand the distinction, consider the emotional state of surprise. Surprise is an emotion that can be classified with various methods as opposed to the emotion of anger or joy. Surprise can be both positive and negative. For example, "Surprise, you just won the lottery!" is different from "Surprise, you were injured." In many contexts, both types of analysis are considered sentiment analysis but you should be clear about your intention. In this case, perform polarity analysis.

The following code demonstrates sentiment analysis, but you can use other packages that provide similar functionality. The qualitative discourse analysis package, *qdap*, has a function `polarity(text)` that robustly discovers polarity. In contrast, the *tidytext* package uses tidy data principles to join sentiment dictionaries and understand both polarity and emotion. However, both are out of context for this limited chapter.

Many of these methods rely on specialty lexicons that label words as positive or negative or, in some cases, related to a specific emotion. Table 5.6 is an example of various terms and lexicon labels from a researcher at the University of Buffalo and author of the *qdap* package, Tyler Rinker (2019), whose *sentimentr* package fine-tuned the original work of Hu and Liu (2004). The lexicon is used in both the *qdap* and *SentimentAnalysis* libraries and is referred to in the following code. The lexicon has 4,776 terms labeled as negative and 2,003 terms labeled as positive. Often, new data scientists are skeptical that a polarized or sentiment lexicon of less than 7,000 words is capable of capturing the range of human emotion expressed in text. On one hand, humans know tens of thousands of words. So, using a lexicon of only a few thousand words, one may ask how all possible emotions could be correctly labeled when people may know tens of thousands of words, each with multiple definitions and emotional contexts. In fact, the aim of this type of sentiment analysis is not complete labeling; rather, the idea is to have the majority of terms labeled correctly. For example, to express love, one may use "love," "passion," "infatuation," "obsession," and many other and more esoteric words. In reality, though, mostly "like," "love," and other common terms are used to express the "love" sentiment.

TABLE 5.6   An Excerpt of the *sentimentr* Positive and Negative Word List

Term	Value
Abnormal	"negative"
Abolish	"negative"
Yay	"positive"
Youthful	"positive"

In natural language processing, limited lexicons are useful for sentiment or polarized analysis because of **Zipf's law** accompanied with the **principle of least effort**. These two concepts mean a limited lexicon will get the majority of cases correctly labeled. First, Zipf's law states that terms are inversely proportional in word frequency. Roughly, this means that within a document, the most used term will appear twice as often as the second term. The third term will have roughly one-third the usage of the first, and so on. In this chapter, approximately 7 percent of the terms used are "the" followed by 2.5 percent "a" and 2.4 percent "of." Following Zipf's law, "a" is expected to be 3.5 percent (7 divided by 2) and "of" should be 2.3 percent (7 divided by 3). While the percentages are not exact in this body of text, the terms do follow a significant decline in usage (often being .002 or less from expected word usage). Keep in mind that this body of text uses specific terms and other channels (e.g., social media) use different terms. Zipf's law only dictates the term usage, not the terms themselves. Zipf's law holds true in many channels, although the words and corresponding frequencies will change. The shape of the steep decline (by half, one-third, one-quarter, and so on) is consistent. This is relevant because, as stated previously, someone may know tens of thousands of terms but, according to Zipf's law, there is a significant decline in actual unique terms a person uses. Thus, a lexicon does not need to list all possible terms known for all possible people and instead should focus on the frequently used terms, labeling them as positive, negative, or emotion-specific to the channel. Shakespearean words for love will differ compared to modern-day terms for love but the frequency and usage in the context of their respective channels will be similar. The other aspect of human behavior reinforcing the accuracy of a limited lexicon is the principle of least effort. This theory holds that people will exert the least amount of effort to perform a task. For expression, this means that an author will use the most commonly known words and the least amount of words necessary to express an idea. Authors will not want to take a long time to express their idea or use words needing further clarification. In turn, the audience will use the least amount of effort to comprehend an idea. If you have ever been bored in a college lecture, it is because you are likely following this principle and the professor may not be! The professor may be verbose or making a point overly complicated, essentially causing you too much work to comprehend the message. In the NLP context, this principle likely accounts for observing Zipf's law. Articulating "love" by using the word "adulation" is likely more work than the author wants, and it causes more work for the audience. As a result, most often the principle of least effort informs word choice, giving rise to a "Zipfian" word frequency.

Despite these principles, given that human sentiment is in fact varied and that the methods differ, it is a good idea to try multiple methods from *tidytext* or *qdap*, in addition to what is described below, when performing sentiment analysis. Further, adjusting the lexicon is always a good idea based on the age group and channel of the study. Adding terms like "smh," standing for "shaking my head," will make sense as a negative connotation on Twitter but not in legal briefs.

The *SentimentAnalysis* library uses a special method to adjust a sentiment lexicon for scoring. The package employs **Lasso regularization** as a statistical approach to review coefficients and select relevant terms. A Lasso regression will add bias to training data when fitting so that coefficients of terms will be 0 if there is no relationship. In this context, this means that terms are dropped if there is no relationship to positive or negative labels. For now, the chapter will accept the known lexicons without additional customization.

As before, a loop is needed to apply the **analyzeSentiment** function to each player in turn. The first time through i is equal to 1. This is used to subset the original text using `grep` to create the `idx` variable for indexing. The subset of text is then captured in the x variable. Next, the `analyzeSentiment` function is applied only to the text corresponding to the player. The returned object is a list and some additional steps are needed to organize the information. First, the total word count is selected from the corresponding list element, `sentimentX$WordCount`. Next, the floating point values are converted to binary, meaning "positive" or "negative," by applying `convertToBinaryResponse` to the appropriate list element of polarity scores. Finally, the player's name, polarity binary value, numeric polarity score, word count, and total number of tweets for that player are captured in a small data frame. This process repeats where i is 2 and so on. The loop's functionality can be changed to work on teams or other players with minimal adjustment.

```
playersSentiment <- list()
for(i in 1:length(players)){
 print(paste('working on', players[i]))
 idx <- grepl(players[i], tweets$text, ignore.case = T)
 x <- tweets$text[idx]
 sentimentX  <- analyzeSentiment(x)
 wordCount   <- sentimentX$WordCount
 polarityX   <- convertToBinaryResponse(sentimentX$SentimentQDAP)
 nam <- make.names(players[i])
 playersSentiment[[nam]] <- data.frame(player = players[i],
              polarity                 = polarityX,
              numericPolarity          = sentimentX$
              SentimentQDAP,
              wordCount   = wordCount,
              totalTweets = length(x))
}
```

The loop creates a list with length equal to the number of players, in this example four. Each player, captured as a list element, will have a data frame of polarity information for each tweet the player was mentioned in. It may be that a tweet mentioned two players; in that case, the polarity score is assigned to both. The following code row binds the information from a list to a single data frame.

```
playersSentiment    <- do.call(rbind, playersSentiment)
```

The individual tweet by player information needs to be aggregated. First, the average numeric polarity is calculated by player to create the `avgPolarity` object. Similarly, the average word count by player is aggregated in the `avgTweetLength` object.

```
avgPolarity      <- aggregate(numericPolarity~player,
                            playersSentiment, mean)
avgTweetLength     <- aggregate(wordCount~player,
                            playersSentiment, mean)
```

The next code chunk nests the tally of player and polarity information within as.data.frame.matrix(table object) using the table function. The table function counts the number of positive and negative labeled tweets by player. Nesting this inside the as.data.frame.martrix function merely allows R to interact with the table data more easily. Table 5.7 shows the tallied tweets according to their binary conversion within the loop. This is based on the numeric assessment using the *qdap* lexicon. However, unlike the original polarity function from *qdap*, this implementation from *SentimentAnalysis* does not take into account the context cluster. As such, negations like "not good" are not correctly measured, nor are amplifiers like "really good." Still, with this amount of text and applying Zipf's law, it is relatively safe to assume that most tweets do not have unrepresented amplifiers and negations. Keep in mind that entire books and degrees are devoted to correctly assessing author emotion using machine intelligence, so this example is merely a first step.

```
posNegPlayer     <- as.data.frame.matrix(
                        table(playersSentiment$player,
                            playersSentiment$polarity))
```

TABLE 5.7   Count of Tweets Labeled Positive and Negative, by Player

Player	Negative	Positive
giannis antetokounmpo	100	670
kawhi leonard	127	1,496
kobe bryant	37	97
lebron james	1,688	2,461

Finally, the row sums are calculated, and the actual row names are made into a standalone vector called player.

```
posNegPlayer$total    <- rowSums(posNegPlayer)
posNegPlayer$player   <- rownames(posNegPlayer)
```

Now that the analysis contains summarized information, a series of left-joins is needed to organize the data. The net result in plotDF is that each player will have a corresponding average numeric polarity, average tweet length, and the tallied information for "positive" and "negative" classes. Using *plyr*, the tables are joined by player name using the join_all(list of data frames) function. The additional parameters declare the joining column and the type of join.

```
plotDF <- join_all(list(avgPolarity,
            avgTweetLength,
            posNegPlayer), by='player', type='left')
plotDF
```

An interesting visualization is then constructed using the `ggplot` code below. The x-axis is declared as the numeric polarity score. The y-axis is the average word count. The bubble size is defined as the total number of tweets mentioning the specific player. Labels are then added so that the audience can keep track of the specific player. Lastly, a basic theme is applied along with a title (see figure 5.6).

```
ggplot(plotDF, aes(x        = numericPolarity,
                   y        = wordCount,
                   size     = total)) +
  geom_point(color         = 'darkgrey') +
  geom_text(aes(label      = player),
    hjust = "inward", vjust = "inward", size = 5, color = 'black')
    +
  theme_hc() + ggtitle("Oct 2019 Player Sentiment")
```

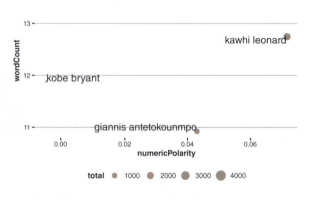

FIGURE 5.6   The longest average word count, most numerous, and relatively negative tweets refer to LeBron James.

INSIGHT AND RECOMMENDATIONS

After reviewing the visuals and outputs of functions like `findAssocs`, the following conclusions are supported with data. Possible users of these results include public relations, team marketing, and agents, among others. One caveat is that the analysis is a single month's worth of 450,000 tweets, but a more longitudinal view incorporating more robust methods is possible and may lead to other conclusions.

• The Houston Rockets have longer tweets, indicating higher author effort within the corpus or a subject germane to their team (i.e., China).

• The Oklahoma City Thunder have a small number of mentions, with a shorter average length, perhaps indicating a less active and impassioned user base.

• The October 2019 Hong Kong protests dominated the dialogue for the Houston Rockets within this single corpus.

• Among Kobe Bryant, LeBron James, Giannis Antetokounmpo, and Kawhi Leonard, LeBron has a larger share of voice on most days. On multiple days in October, LeBron captures more than 90 percent of the mentions among the four players examined.

• Terms associated with LeBron James indicate his persona has a larger cultural relevance outside of basketball, including worldwide politics (mentions of China). This contrasts with the other examined players in the corpus, indicating a willingness to weigh in on subjects other than basketball.

• Without reading a single tweet, it is clear that in October 2019, the subject of Hong Kong protesters was part of the NBA dialogue. The topic included LeBron James and Daryl Morey (general manager of the Houston Rockets). For a researcher, this type of distinct spike would necessitate a qualitative examination to improve the context. It turns out that Daryl Morey of the Houston Rockets tweeted in support of Hong Kong protesters while LeBron James stated Morey was not educated on the subject before sending the tweet. This is an example of an unexpected term in a large corpus bubbling to the top, signifying something worthy of additional research in the corpus and other sources.

- Based on volume, word association, and sentiment calculations, LeBron's interaction in October 2019 referring to the Hong Kong protests dominated the discussion and was negatively perceived in the NBA Twitter channel.

- Kobe Bryant has a small yet slightly negative mentioning in the October 2019 data. Further analysis could see how this may change over time and at the time of his death in January 2020.

- LeBron James has a large number of mentions, each of longer length and more negative than the other two active players. This may indicate that authors are impassioned and displeased with LeBron's comments regarding Hong Kong.

The 2019-2020 NBA season was remarkable. The same analysis within this chapter could be run on the month files in the repository and specific events could be captured in the analysis. For example, tracking Kobe Bryant mentions and share of voice, month to month, would surely see a significant change after his untimely death. The same can be said for nonplayer topics such as "coronavirus" or "bubble," because this season saw an unprecedented interruption and then the playoff bubble. Another perspective would be to track frequency and associations of terms related to social justice. It is likely that mentions of George Floyd are present in the data, marking an intersection of race, politics, and sports in the United States. The joy and challenge of NLP is that a rich dataset may yield many interesting quantifiable findings.

Interview With a Professional

Tom Cove, President and CEO, Sports & Fitness Industry Association (SFIA)

The question of analytics in sports highlights a great paradox. Sports are so often perceived as a "touch and feel, tradition and passion, hunch and gut decision" experience, while in reality, so many of the great innovations and steps forward in sports were driven by factual investigation and analytical assessment.

Think about our national pastime, baseball. For the sport's first 100 years, the idea of an infield shift, where three players regularly set up on one side and only one on the other, would be heresy and an invitation for the hitter to be gifted a free pass on base. Analytics, however, proved that conventional wisdom incorrect, and now shifts are a routine part of the game. The relative risk-reward of depending on three-point shots is another evolution driven by analytics that changed the game of basketball. "Going for it" on fourth down in football could be the next obvious choice, previously seen as too risky and bad coaching. Reliance on more sophisticated metrics like WAR (wins above average) in baseball now dominate not only in-game strategy but personnel decisions as well.

A different type of analytics regularly transforms the business of sport, as it relates to equipment and rates of sport participation. Consider the introduction of oversized tennis rackets and golf club heads or non-wood baseball bats. In each of these cases, products were developed with an eye on improving the experience of the user. The innovations improved overall performance in a variety of ways—power, precision, distance—but the greatest impact has been to minimize the bad hit—that is, the ball that flies wildly out of bounds. "Creating greater forgiveness" was a direct result of focused analytics looking to solve that problem. The challenge was that in each of these cases, tradition inhibited innovation. Bringing a disciplined analytics approach allowed designers to justify changes in traditional understanding of sports equipment, to the benefit of millions of athletes. The result has been effectively to create new categories of sports products, with corresponding sales and profitability benefits.

(continued)

Finally, analytics drive sports policy. Rigorous examination of budget and other allocations have been central to women's sports being able to move closer to their fair share of resources. Scientific investigation of injury rates and conditions have transformed football rules and techniques.

Simply put, the key concept is analysis. There will always be mountains of data, now more than ever in this technological age. But data by itself is just numbers. The value comes from analysis resulting in innovation.

DIVERSITY IN SPORT ANALYTICS

Reflecting the composition of many STEM (science, technology, engineering, and math) fields, the sport analytics community is overwhelmingly white and male. In fact, 70.7 percent of all sport analysts are white. Comparatively, 13.6 percent of sport analysts are of the Hispanic or Latino ethnicity and 7.5 percent are Black or African American. In 2015, at the MIT Sloan Sports Analytics Conference (SSAC), women made up a mere 14.4 percent (22 of 153) of the conference speakers (Aschwanden, 2015). While the number of women increased to 17.8 percent (24 of 135) in 2021, with 20 percent (27/135) of presenters being racial minorities, the SSAC reflects the continuing underrepresentation of women and minorities in sport analytics.

Former NBA player Jalen Rose has claimed that decision-making that is increasingly based on analytics over playing experience hinders minority players in attaining high-level management positions in basketball. While there is no doubt that minorities are obtaining front-office positions in the NBA, if algorithms supplant experiential judgment, Rose suggests that the upsurge in analytics as a determinant of advancement might serve to discourage increased diversity (Martin, 2019). A clear path forward to counter this unintended consequence of the escalation of sport analytics is to increase diversity among analysts and managers charged with the application of analytics.

As managerial positions in sport are slowly diversifying, the question remains: What can be done to improve the diversity of sport analytics? The answer is not simple, nor is it instant, but it must be constant. Promoting diversity and inclusion in sport analytics involves not only industry efforts but those in the classroom as well. Yes, industry could seek out and support aspiring sport managers with a knowledge of data analytics. Scholarships, mentorships, field placements, professional development, career fairs, and other recruitment activities can have a positive impact on diversity if properly designed and executed. In partnership with the sport enterprises, higher education has a substantive role to play in diversifying sport analytics.

Higher education has always been a key vehicle to foster social mobility, enhance diversity, and create opportunities to transform economic sectors. Given evident inequities and hampered social mobility, improving the quality of and access to specific sport analytics education has the potential to increase equality of opportunity for underrepresented populations. An appropriate college degree can be a ticket to a position as a sport analyst. And while the cost of higher education has increased over time, the actual price for many lower- and middle-income students has not (Greenstone et al., 2013). Yet students are borrowing more to garner a degree in their chosen field. However, in the end, an appropriate degree yields a high return on that investment. That is the basis for the increased number of strategic interventions designed to improve access to higher education in a manner that increases diversity to reflect the broader population.

Education plays a pivotal role in social mobility, social justice, and advancement of diversity. Academic programs provide the basis for the development of skills necessary to analyze and use data in sports and for diversifying the sport analytics landscape. University programs and courses have evolved to include sport analytics in the professional preparation of sport managers. Degrees for the preparation of analysts are often titled Data Science or Data Analytics, while programs preparing sport managers with the tools to engage in data-based decision-making fall within Sport Management or Sport Analytics degrees.

SUMMARY

Natural language processing is a powerful tool to add to your applied sport business analytics skill set. It allows for deep insights into patterns of text and for analyses that statistics cannot perform. Additionally, the application of data visualization to NLP and text mining brings the data to life. It is easy to do and can make a huge impact. The ability to harness and analyze big data to gain valuable insights into the world of sports is helpful for decision makers who deal with sports on all levels and in all applications, including marketing, player personnel, and even the players themselves and the leagues they represent, given the current tenor taking place based on current issues.

ONLINE ACTIVITIES HK*Propel* »

Visit HK*Propel* to access the *nba_oct* dataset, chapter art supplements, exercises, and a key terms review activity for this chapter. Your instructor may also release the assignments, assignment forms, and quiz available for this chapter through HK*Propel*. These tutorials, activities, and exercises are designed for interactive learning and to assist students as they learn the material.

REFERENCES

Harman, D.K., ed. 1993. *First Text Retrieval Conference (Trec-1): Proceedings, NIST Special Publication 500-207* (Gaithersburg, MD: U.S. Department of Commerce, National Institute of Standards and Technology). https://nvlpubs.nist.gov/nistpubs/Legacy/SP/nistspecialpublication500-207.pdf.

Hu, Minqing, and Bing Liu. 2004. "Mining and Summarizing Customer Reviews." In *Proceedings of ACM SIGKDD International Conference on Knowledge Discovery and Data Mining* (KDD-2004) (Seattle, WA: ACM Press), 168-177.

Rinker, Tyler. 2019. "sentimentr: Calculated Text Polarity Sentiment." Version 2.8.0. Last modified September 4, 2020. http://github.com/trinker/sentimentr.

GLOSSARY

alpha level—Also referred to as the significance level. It is used to determine the threshold for statistical significance in relationship testing at which point the null hypothesis is rejected.

average minute audience—Average amount of viewers watching the live event at any given minute during the specified time span (match, week, season).

bivariate correlation—Can be used to examine the extent to which two dependent measured variables are related. If there is a relationship between the two variables, it can be positive or negative.

boxplot—Used to demonstrate the distribution of values within a whole sample or in different groups based on factor variables for comparison. Core elements of the boxplot are minimum value, maximum value, first quartile, third quartile, median, and outliers.

categorical variable—Also referred to as a factor variable. Categorical factor variables help analysts compare data across populations or samples that vary in their makeup. Common categorical variables include age, educational attainment, income, and many more.

character—One of four common variable types used in RStudio. Character variables are generally nominal in nature and are denoted by the abbreviation "chr."

College Sports Supermodel—Dataset created to track National Collegiate Athletic Association (NCAA) Division I college athletics across a series of variables over time.

corpus—A collection of related documents to be analyzed. Multiple collections are called a corpora.

correlation—Method used to examine the strength of the relationship between two measured variables.

data analysis—The process of examining, cleansing, transforming, and modeling data for practical purposes, such as informing operational decisions.

data mining—The analysis of data from various sources using statistical modeling for predictive rather than purely descriptive purposes.

data-driven decision-making—Process wherein precise data is needed to make a decision, yielding an exact answer to a specific question.

data-informed decision-making—Process wherein data analyses are employed along with experiential and other factors in the decision process to inform strategies.

data-inspired decision-making—Process wherein predictive inference and trendspotting is derived from multiple data sources to inspire new ideas.

degrees of freedom—Estimate of the mean and variability of the mean. Degrees of freedom are tied to the distribution of data within a sample.

density plot—A plotting method that demonstrates the distribution of data throughout a data frame in a way that indicates whether the data is distributed in a normal, negatively or positively skewed, bimodal, or random manner. A density plot is like a histogram; however, the primary difference is that density plots are not constrained by bin settings and therefore create a smooth distribution curve.

descriptive statistics—Common descriptive statistics include frequencies (n counts), percentages, sum totals, means, standard deviations, and quartiles.

document term matrix—A number table that describes the frequency of terms in a collection, with terms in columns and documents in rows.

draft—The annual team selection of amateur athletes for inclusion in the professional league. Not all players are drafted, or selected, as some are still signed at a later date. However, the draft is the most common selection method for teams to choose amateur athletes.

drill—A standardized physical performance measurement collected from an athlete.

factorial ANOVA—A test used when exploring the relationship between two or more independent (factor) variables and a dependent (measured) variable.

factors—One of four common variable types used in RStudio. Factors are usually grouping variables.

filtered data—Data that has been subjected to conditions that exclude some cases based on the filter parameters.

formative evaluation—An assessment process focused on development at a specific time within a process of continual improvement.

frequencies (n counts)—The number of cases that represent the results in a statistical analysis.

ggplot2—A data visualization package used by analysts for plotting data in RStudio.

global environment—The top right quadrant in RStudio where the elements that are imported or created while working in RStudio appear.

histogram—A plotting method that is effective in demonstrating the distribution patterns of data within a given data frame. Histograms are capable of demonstrating whether data reflects a normal distribution, negatively or positively skewed distribution, bimodal distribution, or random distribution.

independent samples t-test—A test used when exploring the relationship between an independent (factor) variable comprised of two levels and a dependent (measured) variable.

inferential statistics—Statistical tests used to examine relationships between data. The four most commonly used tests are the t-test, analysis of variance (ANOVA), correlation, and regression.

integers—One of four common variable types used in RStudio. Integers are numeric and represent whole numbers that do not include fractional data.

key performance indicator (KPI)—An identified, mission-driven goal and desired outcome.

Lasso regularization—A type of linear regression that uses shrinkage. Shrinkage is where data values are shrunk toward a central point, like the mean.

learning organizations—Systems comprised of inputs, throughputs, outputs, and feedback loops; they are organized to disclose organizational effectiveness by employing evidentiary assessments to pursue continuous improvement.

levels—The number of different category groupings that are encompassed within a factor variable.

lexicon—A word list for a specific natural language processing task. An example would be a list of positive or negative words to understand the "polarity" positive or negative language of the author.

Live+3—The total number of viewers watching within three days after the original live air date.

line plot—A plotting method used to link data points together to demonstrate the relationship between two variables. As x-axis values change for one variable, it is possible to see the result the x-axis changes have on the y-axis variable.

mean—The average of a measured variable across the sample.

measured variable—Also referred to as a dependent variable. The measured variable is numeric in nature and can be represented as whole numbers (integers) or as numbers that include fractional data.

median—The middle number of a measured variable across the sample.

natural language processing—The use of artificial intelligence to understand and interpret language.

numeric—One of four common variable types used in RStudio.

observations—In RStudio, this term refers to the number of cases included in a dataset.

one-way analysis of variance (ANOVA)—A test used when exploring the relationship between an independent (factor) variable comprised of three or more levels and a dependent (measured) variable.

operators—Symbols used to perform certain functions in RStudio, such as addition, subtraction, multiplication, and division. The are 12 common operators in RStudio.

packages—Sets of functions and data that are replete with well-defined code to be used in RStudio.

peak concurrent viewers—Total amount of viewers watching live on the Call of Duty League (CDL) YouTube channel at one time.

Pearson method—A method used in correlation analysis when working with continuous scale variables.

percentages—The breakdown of representation in a sample or results. A percentage is derived by dividing the n count by the total number of cases within a sample.

post-hoc tests—Used when an ANOVA has produced a statistically significant result so that one can see which groups differ significantly based on factor variables and the measured variables.

predictive analytics—The process of forecasting by using data analysis.

principle of least effort—Any action or communication requiring the least amount of effort to complete the task.

program evaluation—The repetitive, systematic, organized approach to gathering and analyzing information to identify factors that influence a program and its decisions, actions, and outcomes.

p-value—The probability value that is linked to the alpha level. P-values that are less than the alpha level indicate a statistically significant relationship.

quartiles—Used to understand the distribution of data for an entire sample by splicing it into four groups. Oftentimes, quartiles are represented as a bell curve visually.

regression analysis—A predictive test used to examine the relationship between two or more variables and the extent to which a measured variable's outcome can be predicted by other measured variables.

regression line—Used to visualize the general trend of the data in a plot that includes changes in the x-axis and y-axis variables.

Sabermetrics—The process of objectively examining baseball through the application of statistical analyses.

scatterplot—A plotting method that is used to examine the relationship between two measured variables. Scatterplots are effective in visualizing results of correlation analyses.

scout—A team-employed professional who is responsible for identifying amateur players with potential to succeed professionally.

scripts—Lines of coding created in RStudio.

sentiment analysis—A technique to identify positive, negative, and neutral information from data.

share of voice—Measurable brand awareness in a specific market.

Silhouette score—Also known as the elbow method, the Silhouette score measures the quality of the clusters by determining how well each object fits in its cluster. Higher Silhouette scores indicate better clustering.

SMART goals—Goals whose intended outcomes are Specific; Measurable; Achievable, Action-oriented, Agreed-upon; Realistic, Relevant, Result-oriented; and Time-based, Tangible, Trackable.

Spearman method—A method used in correlation analysis when working with rank-order data.

sport analytics—The application of data analytics in a sport setting.

standard deviation—The extent to which results wander from the mean. Low standard deviation implies less variation in a sample whereas high standard deviation implies more variation.

stop words—A vector of terms that are frequent yet provide little to no information. Examples are "and," "the," and "is." Stop words are customized according to the channel and messenger.

strategic planning—The process used to identify goals, strategies, and evaluation systems that are directed toward the organizational mission and intended outcomes.

subsetted data—A dataset that is a customized form of the original larger dataset to minimize the number of cases and variables that an analyst is working with.

summative evaluation—An assessment process focused on the final outcome.

systems thinking—The framework defining links between the program resources (or inputs), the program strategies or treatments (or throughputs), the immediate results of program activities (or outputs), and the desired program accomplishments (or goal-related outcomes).

t-statistic—Examines the difference in means between the null hypothesis and sample data. If the t-statistic is zero, the null hypothesis is supported. The greater the difference in means between the null hypothesis and the sample data, the larger the t-value becomes.

term document matrix—A number table that describes the frequency of terms in a collection, with documents in columns and terms in rows.

text mining—The process of applying statistical analyses and related techniques to extract and codify information from words.

type I error—Incorrectly rejecting a correct null hypothesis in favor of an alternative hypothesis.

violin plot—A plotting method used to demonstrate the distribution of values within a whole sample or in different groups based on factor variables for comparison. It is like the boxplot; however, a violin plot also indicates, through curving, where more or less of the distribution of data lies based on how wide or thin the violin is at any point in the plot.

within cluster sum of squares (WSS)—A measure of the variability of observations in each cluster. WSS is the sum of the squares of the distances of each data point (observation) to the cluster centroid.

word associations—When one term exists, the likelihood of another term being in the same document.

Zipf's law—Within a large sample of words, the frequency of a word will be inversely proportional to its rank, with the most common word appearing twice as often as the second most frequently used word.

INDEX

Note: The italicized *f* and *t* following page numbers refer to figures and tables, respectively.

ABOUT THE AUTHORS

Photo courtesy of Beatrice Atwater.

Christopher Atwater is an assistant professor of sport management in the School of Hospitality, Sport, and Tourism Management at Troy University. He teaches analytics courses at the graduate and undergraduate levels.

Photo courtesy of Dr. Pam Baker.

Robert Baker is a professor and the director of the Center for Sport Management at George Mason University. He is a former president of the North American Society for Sport Management (NASSM), a founding board member of the World Association for Sport Management (WASM), and a founding commissioner of the Commission on Sport Management Accreditation (COSMA). He has conducted numerous presentations and produced articles on sport analytics.

Photo courtesy of Symoni Johnson.

Ted Kwartler earned his MBA from Notre Dame. He is an instructor at Harvard University. He has conducted many presentations and written articles on sport analytics. He also authored a popular book entitled *Text Mining*.